Bunyoro,
Tropical Paradox

Bunyoro, Tropical Paradox

Walter Bazley

The Pentland Press Limited
Edinburgh · Cambridge · Durham

First published in 1993 by
The Pentland Press Ltd.
1 Hutton Close
South Church
Bishop Auckland
Durham

ISBN 1 85821 065 8

Typeset by Elite Typesetting Techniques, Southampton.
Printed and bound by Antony Rowe Ltd., Chippenham.

Contents

Foreword

Individuals, like nations, are said to begin their lives with poetry and end it with prose. The first District to which an officer is appointed in an overseas territory possesses for him almost poetic overtones. There is an emotional attachment springing from his first contact with the country and its people; he is more sensitive in the early stages and his feelings are closer to the surface.

Bunyoro was my first District in the west of Uganda, an ancient kingdom ruled by a tribal chief called the Mukama. To the north lay the river Nile, to the east the Kafu river and to the west the long, sausage-shaped Lake Albert, called Mutanzige. To the south were the forests and banana gardens of Bugunda, the enemies and archrivals of Bunyoro. In this wedge of green, rain-soaked land were scattered a hundred and fifty thousand of the Banyoro people.

Bunyoro was regarded as a difficult, unlovable District but I threw myself into it heart and soul and developed an affection for the place which was not matched in all my subsequent service in Uganda. Its problems seemed insoluble, its people a race of political gasbags, its administrative structure creaking and backward-looking. Law and order was so poorly administered by the chiefs that they could not even catch a murderer who paraded himself openly. By the standards of Uganda as a whole Bunyoro was a small District but it possessed all the administrative elements of the larger ones and all of their problems. Looking back, it is hard to believe that so much experience could have been crowded into that first year of service.

Anyway, this is my story.

1

Getting There

During the late nineteen-forties, the provost of Trinity College at the University of Toronto was Professor R.S.K. Seely, who was also the British Colonial Office's recruiting representative for Eastern Canada. Provost Seely urged me to apply for the Colonial Service when I graduated and then convened an interview board whose questions I answered as best I could. He must have put in a good word because I passed and was admitted to the Devonshire course in London. This was a year of post-graduate study designed specifically to prepare candidates for Britain's overseas territories.

I had chosen to go to Uganda in East Africa at the headwaters of the Nile. The British Empire was said to have been acquired in a fit of absence of mind, but in the case of Uganda the British had at least been invited to enter the country at the turn of the century to suppress the slave trade. Hence there did seem to be a moral justification for our presence, and the name of the country itself bears this out. It was called the Uganda Protectorate. As the need for protection had diminished the emphasis of our administration changed to economic and social development and the preparation of the country for self-determination.

There were eighty-four candidates who began the Devonshire course that year, fully half of them being destined for West Africa, while East Africa claimed twenty-five and other countries such as Borneo, Hong Kong, Guyana and Fiji the remainder. I soon met the others who were going to Uganda: Bob Swainson, Roy Hiller, Doug Brown, Bazil Wheeler, Tim Hill-Lewis, Peter Lane and Arthur

Watson. In addition to other studies we received an hour's instruction a day in the Luganda language.

I must explain that in Luganda, as in other East African languages, particularly those clustered around Lake Victoria, the name of the country or tribal area begins *Bu*, hence Buganda, Bunyoro, Busoga. The language of the tribe has the prefix *Lu*, so that it becomes Luganda, Lunyoro, or Lusoga. An individual member of the tribe, whether man or woman, begins *Mu* so that a person of the Bunyoro tribe is a *Mu*nyoro. In the plural they are the *Ba*nyoro. Thus *muntu* is a person and *bantu* are people. As another example, *muserikale* is a policeman, *baserikale* more than one. A few imported words break the rule such as *gavana*, the governor, although it would be perfectly correct to call him *mugavana*. Other imported words have accommodated themselves to the language such as *mukanika*, a mechanic; *mupulida*, a lawyer or one who pleads a case. *Mudisi* was used in Bunyoro, meaning the DC or District Commissioner, and even an outrageous word *bamista*, meaning misters or gentlemen.

I will have more to say about the language as my story progresses, but at this moment it will be enough if my reader can remember *Bu*nyoro, the place; *Ba*nyoro, the people and *Lu*nyoro the language.

Luganda, the language of the Baganda tribe, was taught to us on the course because the Baganda were the most populous and influential group, occupying the land round Kampala, the commercial centre of the country. Their language was difficult but it was reasoned that once it had been learned the other languages which were linguistically related would be easier to master. This was a doubtful line of reasoning because two languages that are vaguely similar, like Italian and Spanish, have to be learned separately and understanding one does not lead automatically to an understanding of the other. Worse still was the fact that in the north of the country, Acholi, Lango, West Nile, Teso and Karamoja, the tribal languages were totally different so the decision to teach us Luganda cannot have been arrived at easily. When I reached Bunyoro, the Banyoro being the traditional enemies of the Baganda, I found Luganda to be suspect because it reminded the Banyoro of past wrongs and injustices.

The alternative to Luganda would have been Swahili. The Swahili tribe occupy a strip of coast on the Indian ocean round about the seaport of Mombasa in Kenya. At the end of the last century and the first few years of the present century, before the Uganda railway was built, the explorers, missionaries, traders and others arrived by sea at Mombasa and recruited their porters and servants from the Swahili tribe. They marched inland and learned some rudimentary Swahili but the damage inflicted on the language by people who only wished to communicate in the most basic way and cared nothing for its purity or correctness led to its becoming a sort of 'pidgin'. It became known as 'kitchen' or 'up-country' Swahili, and came into widespread use. A real Swahili would scarcely understand it, just as an Englishman cannot at first make out Pidgin English. It did, however, possess the advantage of being easy to learn. Grammar is almost non-existent and, like English, the language accommodated many imported words. *Mesa*, as an example, a table, sounds as though it came from Portuguese. *Safari*, a trip of any sort, obviously derives from the Hindustani *shikar*. *Karani*, a clerk, one who could read the Koran, comes from Arabic. The list is long and the languages from which the words sprang were many.

On the island of Zanzibar and in Tanganyika Swahili was one of the two official languages of government but in Uganda it never acquired official status. Indians in the bazaar could always speak it, as could police and army. Most chiefs could get along and the vast majority of African servants, waiters and salesmen knew enough to make themselves understood. The Baganda, however, called it the language of slavery and refused to use it so the choice fell on Luganda, a perplexing language that was difficult to learn. We were told that Mandarin Chinese was more difficult while Russian was a good deal easier.

There is one Swahili word that cannot be avoided when writing about East Africa and that is the word *askari*. It means an African soldier or policeman or any man in uniform. The word comes originally from Turkish but is so commonly used that it would hardly sound right to use the English word.

The Devonshire course was held in London using the facilities provided by the London School of Economics. My wife Jean found a small apartment on Sloane Street at the Knightsbridge end, over a grocer's shop. We had two floors, the third and fourth, and were very comfortable for the year we were there. The work kept me occupied but not excessively busy and I enjoyed it on the whole. Jean joined in the language lessons.

Our lecturers were nothing if not celebrated. Professor Arnold J. Toynbee lectured briefly on colonial history although he was a disappointing speaker. I had read his great work, *The Study of History*, and expected a towering figure and a booming personality. Instead he was the very model of scholarly modesty with a willingness to give all the credit to others. Many people regarded him as the world's greatest living historian yet we had to strain to hear him and he created the impression that he was one of us, questioning and groping but not knowing the answers.

Margaret Mead, the anthropologist, was an excellent lecturer with a penchant for the well-stated point and the memorable phrase. She spoke movingly of the uncertainties of life in a developing country, the fears that were so pervasive in the minds of indigenous people as they were jostled out of their familiar garden of Eden and thrust into an incomprehensible world.

Arnold J. Toynbee and Margaret Mead between them established one point very clearly. The historian said that the movement toward what we call civilization had been thwarted in Africa by the overwhelming challenges of nature, and just remaining alive in so hostile a world was almost unimaginably difficult. With an overwhelming challenge the response was bound to be muted. Margaret Mead picked up the lesson at that point and said that Africans lacked nothing of the intelligence of other races. Given the same education: a chance, in other words, to start at the same starting line with people of other races, they had proved themselves the equals of any on earth.

Mr Devlin, teaching criminal law, also made a deep impression. For reasons that I can only guess at I found legal studies interesting and not difficult and when the final exams came round was gratified to be placed second out of eighty candidates. The only person who beat me already had a degree in law. Mr Devlin was a clear, lucid speaker and he subsequently became Lord Chief Justice of England.

When the time came to be posted overseas I felt that the Devonshire course had fulfilled its purpose. Most important, we had made a good start in a local language and could communicate in some fashion; indeed, most of us passed our government language examinations very soon after arrival in Uganda. On the whole it had prepared us well and with only a few omissions had covered the ground. One of those omissions was that nothing had been said about how an up-country office was run; another was that health matters had not been adequately covered.

It is easy to reply that not everything could be dealt with in a year's course and that the medical people themselves were still in the dark about many of the tropical diseases that plagued us in those days. Still, I thought that more could have been done if they had been willing to make the effort and that medical instruction, tropical diseases and their avoidance should have had a higher priority. A few hours on 'office routines' would also have been helpful.

When compared against the training given by many other organizations and governments the Devonshire course was excellent. Later on in Uganda I was constantly amazed at the fact that so many white men and women arrived in the country well-intentioned but ill-equipped mentally and physically. On one occasion in the West Nile District a couple of young Peace Corps volunteers showed up at the District headquarters one morning with a long complaint about the inhospitality of the people at a village a few miles down the road. They said that it had come on to rain so they turned their motorbikes off the road and found an empty hut where they could shelter for the night. Various people came and tried to get rid of them but they refused to move and thought the locals were being unfriendly. No one could speak English and they, of course, could not speak a word of any African language. I had to tell them that they had spent the night in a leprosy settlement. There was a notice by the road which they had failed to see.

In the neighbouring territory the Belgian *administrateur de territoire* said he had been faced by an even more distressing problem. A couple of young women, determined to help the Africans, had entered the District without informing him and had naively entered into some tribal ceremony the purpose of which they had not understood. Subsequently, having been raped, they were given separate mud huts to sleep in, a hoe to cultivate the ground and informed that they were now the wives of the chief and would be beaten for disobedience. These were white girls from middle class North American families. Their rented car was taken and their shoes removed, which left them helpless. The *administrateur* heard about it and drove there immediately with the police. The marriage was not legal and he brought the two of them back to his headquarters. They had belonged to some crack-pot organization and had received two weeks 'indoctrination' before going to Africa.

As the course ended my wife presented me with a son, Frederick, named after his maternal grandfather. It happened that when he was born I was at a cocktail party at the Savoy Hotel given by His Highness Frederick Mutesa, the Kabaka of Buganda, so there were two reasons for naming him Frederick. Jean's labour pains began at a very sensible hour in the afternoon and having duly taken her to the hospital I was told by the doctor that first babies tended to take their time and that I might as well get out of the way. A cocktail party seemed as good a place as any at such a moment, in fact better than most, so there I went and phoned the hospital to give them the hotel phone number. Half an hour later as I was starting my second drink I was called to the telephone by a uniformed footman and the doctor told me the glad news. I had the presence of mind to finish my drink before returning to the hospital.

Jean was awake and seemed very happy. A few weeks later she flew to Canada with Frederick to show him off to the family while I took a ship for East Africa from the port of London. The arrangement was that I would get settled into our house, wherever that would be, and she and Frederick would join me later. The rule in those days was that officers on first appointment travelled by sea because they could be accompanied by their heavy luggage. Most officers, even bachelors, possessed several boxes of personal effects: clothes, books, safari equipment, kitchen and dining room requirements. The government of Uganda, and indeed most other overseas territories, provided housing for its officers and the houses themselves were equipped with basic and very simple furniture such as beds, chairs, tables and a cooking stove. In most up-country stations there was no electricity so officers had to provide themselves with kerosene lamps, a kerosene refrigerator and a charcoal iron.

Jean and my newborn son flew to Canada while I embarked in SS *Llanstephan Castle*, an ancient three-funnelled vessel which had been a troopship during the war. From the jetty its many decks, like an opulent wedding cake, rose white and reassuring to the boat deck from which arose tall mauve funnels. It was a floating palace compared to the sleek gray destroyer in which I had served for two and a half years during the war and the nondescript little minesweepers following the war. I settled into a double cabin which I shared with Arthur Watson, who had also served in the Royal Navy.

Roy Hiller had a good story to tell when he arrived on board. He had been to a farewell party and had been introduced to an Australian girl, 'Jo-someone-or-other who was engaged to be married'. A very short time thereafter it was he who was engaged to her and they married just before the ship sailed. Unfortunately the Colonial Office was not able to make arrangements for Jo-someone-or-other's accommodation on board and she had to follow Roy by air a few weeks later. Roy had not struck any of us in the role of speedy suitor, rather the reverse, and we were surprised and pleased on his behalf.

Also taking passage aboard the *Llanstephan Castle* to Capetown was a certain Lieutenant-Commander Caldwell, RN, who had been one of my instructors at the officer training school, HMS *King Alfred*, in 1942. I told him that the three-month course which was supposed to transform us from seamen to midshipmen could have been better and that anti-submarine warfare, for instance, had been omitted altogether. He said that the course's shortcomings were well known but the war situation had been so desperate that they had considered offering no course at all and sending us to sea as midshipmen in the hope that we would learn as we went along.

The passage to East Africa was made at a leisurely pace. We put in at the Cape Verde Islands, Saint Helena and the Cape of Good Hope. After that it was a slow progress northwards with calls at Port Elizabeth, East London, Durban, Lorenço Marques, Beira, Dar-es-Salaam and finally Mombasa. Off Cape Agulhas we met with some boisterous weather which would have been unpleasant in a minesweeper but was of small concern to a 20,000-ton steamer. Arthur and I went down to dinner but found the dining room sparsely occupied. The steward who looked after us said we might as well have a roast duck each because there was no one else to eat them and that is just what we did, aided and abetted by a bottle or two of Burgundy. There followed a rather lavish English trifle and cognac thereafter, and if our steps had become unsteady it scarcely showed with the rolling of the ship. After dinner we made a tactical error by going to our friends' cabins, waking them up and telling them in some detail what an excellent dinner they had missed. Penance had to be done and at Port Elizabeth all of us had a memorable meal of Mossel Bay oysters and local Chablis. Arthur and I paid the bill. Never have I tasted oysters like those from Mossel Bay and they were as large as saucers. The restaurant was near a lighthouse with the sea almost at our feet and was the ideal place for such a meal.

In East London Arthur and I decided on a change of scene so we took the train to Durban to see something of the country. We made a side trip to Pietermaritzburg and fell in with some South African government people who were kind enough to show us round. At that time, in 1951, South Africa had not attracted the opprobrium that has built up in recent years and I must be honest and say that we saw little with which to find fault. The African housing projects were clean and well ordered and our guide for the day, a Zulu, showed us his own house with evident pride. Much was being done for the Africans and there seemed to be goodwill on both sides.

In retrospect I suppose we were slow to recognize the full extent of South Africa's apartheid and came away thinking that the Boers, as we called them, were simply addressing their own problems in their own way. I could never quite like the white South Africans whom I met; they seemed to have uniformly expressionless faces and an unflattering accent. They resented interference but craved understanding and claimed that their problem and their solution to it was unique. A government officer had shaken his finger at us as we said goodbye. 'Wait till you find out what the African is really like. Then you'll understand.'

The ship put in briefly at Dar-es-Salaam, The Haven of Peace, and the ten or twelve officers destined for Tanganyika disembarked. After that it was Mombasa where we entered at five o'clock in the morning and berthed an hour later. An official called the Government Coast Agent came on board and asked for the Uganda and Kenya contingents. Arthur and I were the only ones on deck and we told him the others were still in bed. We gave our own names and he informed Arthur that he was posted to the Secretariat in Entebbe which is the seat of government, while for me it was Bunyoro in Uganda's Western Province. He handed us our train tickets and other papers.

'And now,' he said, 'have the kindness to rouse the rest of those useless, lazy gentlemen and tell them they have arrived. I expected them to be crowding the rail in their enthusiasm, but no, you say they are still in bed.' He turned away and we went about our errand.

We spent a couple of days in Mombasa waiting for the train to take us up-country. Having just missed one train and departures being twice-weekly events, the Coast Agent arranged for our lodging in a hotel which can best be described as occupying a niche somewhere between third and fourth class. The place possessed an entomological abundance which made me glad that Jean was in Canada.

We left Mombasa in the evening. It was hot and the carriages were survivors of that leisurely era that preceded World War I. I had read Colonel Patterson's book about the Uganda railway, he having been responsible for its construction. It was an overblown *Boy's Own* kind of story featuring man-eating lions, 'native coolies', hostile tribesmen and much else. It figures in almost every account of East Africa and it is strange that a hard-bitten, much travelled military man would possess so gushing a vocabulary. I suspect that it was heavily edited by someone else, probably his wife.

During the first night the train crossed the flat lowlands of the coast, stopped at Voi at about two in the morning, then continued on to Tsavo, the scene of Colonel Patterson's adventures with man-eating lions. At one point a pair of them created such havoc that construction had to be halted. Our train thereafter climbed to higher ground at a speed that was slower on the average than that of a wartime destroyer. Doug Brown got off at one of its frequent stops and when it pulled away without him he quite easily overtook it on foot. We saw great quantities of game animals exactly as the tourist brochures had predicted.

Nairobi had begun its life as a depot on the railway line but by the 1950s had become a modern city combining European and Indian characteristics. It was cooler at that altitude and we slept better as we rumbled onwards across the Kenya highlands and into Uganda. Two of our number left us at Jinja in Uganda's Eastern Province where the Nile surges out of Lake Victoria and begins its 4,000-mile journey northwards to the Mediterranean.

Arrived in Kampala, three days and seven hundred miles from Mombasa, we were ready to quit the *gaare y'omuka*, 'vehicle of smoke', which is the Luganda for train. We were met by an officer from the Secretariat who snarled at us and asked why the journey had taken so long; just over two months since leaving London. Arthur pointed out that we had not chosen to sail round the Cape of Good Hope and he personally had urged the captain of *Llanstephan Castle* to go faster. Arthur had a caustic sense of humour and was rarely lost for a reply, which must have been why they chose him for the Secretariat.

It has always surprised me that the individual sent to meet a bunch of new recruits must needs put them in their place, assert his authority and be generally obnoxious. It was no exception in this case and just what one would have expected from an officious non-commissioned officer in wartime. New recruits and recent arrivals seem to bring out the worst in people.

Uganda was just as I had expected it to be, a land of extremes. I had read everything that the library contained during the previous year, studied photographs and maps, ploughed through annual reports and such exotica as the Nile Waters Agreement and filled my mind with information, most of it useless or out-of-date. Kampala was crowded, busy and cheerful; Africans and their bicycles being the predominant impression.

I tried out my Luganda on the hotel waiters and they replied in English or Swahili. At least they understood, which was a step in the right direction. I made the acquaintance of Drapers store on the main street which reminded me of Ahmeds in Port Said. It was a sort of mini-Harrods on the equator which sold more or less everything. I bought some lamps and a kerosene refrigerator. At Hunt's Motors I introduced myself because they would be servicing our station wagon when it arrived from Canada. I also opened a bank account with

Barclays DCO (Dominion, Colonial and Overseas) because I was told there was no bank in Bunyoro. Finally I was put in touch with an Indian merchant who carried me and my possessions to Hoima in Bunyoro on a three-ton motor lorry. It all seemed remarkably easy.

2

The Mukama

Bunyoro was one of Uganda's smallest Districts with a population of only 150,000 but it possessed the special status of having a paramount chief, His Highness the Mukama. Only three other Districts in Uganda: Toro and Ankole in the Western Province and the Province of Buganda, shared this distinction. The best known of the four native rulers was Frederick Mutesa, the Kabaka of Buganda, at whose cocktail party I had been when our son Freddie was born. The English press called him King Freddie and made much of him and his popularity soared when, a year or two later, the governor of Uganda exiled him from his kingdom for misbehaviour.

The Mukama of Bunyoro, known also as Bunyoro-Kitara, attracted less attention in the outside world. He was an older man, in his fifties, ruling over a kingdom that was poor and insignificant. His full title was Rurakabasaija Agutamba the Mukama of Bunyoro-Kitara, which translates roughly as the Greatest of Men, the Superior Milkman. The noun Mukama derives from the verb *kukama*, to milk, implying that he was chief milkman of his tribe, the shepherd of his flock. In Lunyoro correspondence he was addressed as RA the Mukama; in English he was His Highness. Over the dinner table, with no servants present, my wife and I called him the Mook, but this was not meant to detract from the respect in which he was held by his people or the fact that we liked him and always enjoyed his company.

My first official duty in Bunyoro, having arrived only the day before, was to accompany the District Commissioner, Mr Amory, to the palace and be introduced. We straightened our ties, took our jackets from the backs of our chairs and accompanied by Stephen Kutaga, the head interpreter, drove through Hoima to the royal compound which was half a mile beyond the town. The predominant impression was that it consisted of a large number of small buildings constructed in the native style but with more than usual elaboration. The mud and wattle daubing had been carefully applied and whitewashed on the outside, the grass roofs were tied with fibres, the entrances made in the form of an arch with intricate patterns worked into the layered grass. Each of the huts was dedicated to some specific function such as the musician's hut or the hut of the Official Sister. I learned later that they remained cool inside in consequence of the thatch roof which captured the night air and did not heat up to any extent during the day.

The opposite effect was felt in the Mukama's meeting hall where we were ushered. A thatch roof would have made a meeting hall too dark and limited its size so it was built with a corrugated iron roof and no ceiling beneath. In spite of the large open vents along the walls which should have allowed the air to circulate, the room was hot and smelled of the animal skins which covered the floor. At one end was the Mukama's throne, an ornate high-backed chair that must have been made by Arab craftsmen many years before. Beneath it was an assortment of leopard skins, badly cured. There were no other chairs or tables.

The Mukama approached through the palace grounds at a slow pace accompanied by his musicians. The music grew louder and the musicians entered the hall with the Mukama behind them and a number of other people following. There were two drums, some stringed instruments, a flute with two notes and a wooden percussion instrument. As the Mukama passed us we nodded our heads and he climbed the dais and sat down heavily on his throne. The musicians trailed off into silence and arranged themselves on the cowskins to one side; those who were more notable in his entourage sat down on the dais itself. It struck me that sitting on the floor does not appear too foolish if one is wearing a white gown or *kanzu* but does not look right in western clothes.

The Mukama himself was a mild and rather innocent looking man who bore the features of his Hamitic ancestors. His skin was copper-coloured, he was of medium height and was casually dressed in western clothes. He cleared his throat and began to speak.

'I believe a new officer has been appointed to this kingdom, Mr Amory, and you wish to introduce him.'

'Yes, your Highness, I am pleased to say that His Excellency the Governor requests you to accept this officer as my assistant.'

Stephen translated and when he had finished Mr Amory began again.

'King George has confidence in him because he was an officer in the naval service in the recent war.'

Stephen seemed to be having difficulty with 'naval service' and the Mukama asked for clarification. Finally he turned to me and said in hesitant English, 'So you went upon the waters. Then you must teach ship-building to our fishermen.'

Mr Amory wasn't going to get side-tracked.

'He will devote himself wholeheartedly to the welfare of your people.'

There followed a question and answer period: why did I go upon the waters? would I learn to speak the Lunyoro language? did I have a son? would I strive for the return of the lost territories?

At the mention of the lost territories Amory sprang to my defence.

'His Excellency the Governor knows very well that you claim certain territories that are ruled by Buganda. My assistant will follow the policies and directions of the Governor, as I do. Please let that be perfectly clear.'

I was surprised at Amory's abruptness but the Mukama seemed to take it in stride and within a few minutes the meeting was at an end. He welcomed me into the District, gave me his authority to work for the good of his people and wished me luck. Finally he gave me a sly look and said he hoped I played tennis.

Back in the office Amory told me to sit down.

'Well, there you are, the Mukama and his court. My job,' he said, 'is to act as his adviser and develop a native government based on what you just saw.' He paused.

'Let's talk about the Mukama first. A rather fascinating person who tries sincerely to make improvements but doesn't always go about it the right way. You notice how he raised the question of the lost territories? He never fails to mention it but there's really nothing that we can do because the Secretary of State in Whitehall, the Governor in Entebbe and the Provincial Commissioner in Fort Portal are all emphatic that there will be no change in Bunyoro's boundaries. The Banyoro have an historic claim on two or three counties lying to the east but the official position is that they won't get them back.

'By the way, did you notice how I mentioned the King of England and the Governor of Uganda? The Mukama is impressed by individuals, not by principles or systems. The King of England embodies the heart and soul of the English people, which is something he can relate to because he does the same for the Banyoro. Kings are all much the same whether they rule over a few hundred square miles of jungle, like this one, or a vast empire. Here in Bunyoro the King of England is your best ally because the mystique of kingship is understood. The Governor of Uganda is thought of as the king's personal representative.

'I want to say a word or two about the native government,' he went on. 'In the old days the sons of chiefs were sent to the palace as pages and messengers. To an extent they were hostages in the Mukama's hands and if their fathers caused him any displeasure the boys would be killed. As they grew up, if they grew up, they were given duties in the household and appropriate titles. "The Handkerchief" *Katambala*, was responsible for wiping the royal nose, "The Swatter of Flies" must have been kept fairly busy on a hot day and the "Chief Accepter of Bribes" even more so. Some of them retained these titles and became chiefs themselves. Others received ministerial portfolios at court and continued to be called by their nicknames. My job, as you will see, is not to sweep aside this organization but to transform it to serve the needs of a modern District. The Chief Accepter of Bribes has become the Treasurer of the District Native Council, the Swatter of Flies looks after Public Works. The Guardian of the Royal Tombs continues to be responsible for the maintenance of the various tombs but it's not a full-time job so the individual concerned has a portfolio which includes native custom, the history of the Banyoro and the protocol surrounding the Mukama. A change made by my predecessor was to turn the Royal Strangler into a District sports and recreation officer, which is better than having him strangle people when the Mukama gets fed up with them. I have plans for the *Katambala*, the Handkerchief, whom I would like to see take over as District Education Officer. It may be quite a long way off because the present holder of the title didn't go to school himself. Another of my plans concerns the Guardian of the Salt Mines which in days gone by was a very lucrative business. I want him to be responsible for the Trade and Commerce portfolio and administer native markets, beer brewing and fish marketing.'

'What does the Native Council do?' I asked.

'Well, they are empowered to enact by-laws binding on Africans within the District. So far they have passed ten or eleven. The Health and Sanitation by-law, for instance, requires every household to have a deep-drop privy in the garden away from the house. Once drafted, a by-law goes to Uganda's attorney general who has the last word. He checks to see if it conflicts with other legislation, or violates human rights, or is just plain silly; and of course it can't be put into effect until he gives the go-ahead. Getting a by-law through the Council is hard work and they'll discuss it for days. The objection to the Health By-Law was that it created a danger for small children who might fall in. We were prepared for this, or thought we were, by having the Community Development department manufacture concrete slabs, two inches thick, with a hole in the centre of a size that a child couldn't get through. These are being sold at a shilling each throughout the District and of course they are fitted over the top of the privy. The truth is they work rather well. I know; I've tried.

'We also have a by-law on beer-brewing, which requires that a householder get a two-shilling permit from the chief before he brews beer, but it doesn't limit the amount he brews. Then there is the Prevention of Soil Erosion by-law, which the Agricultural Officer got them to accept last year. The basic idea is to protect the soil against the heavy rain, particularly on hill slopes, by digging bunds along the contour of the hill. But the absolutely basic by-law is the one that has to do with famine reserves. Every household is required to possess a store of food in case the rain fails. I don't believe it has failed in the past fifty years but that is not quite the point. Famines can't be discounted and while it might be possible to organize relief supplies it would take time and money to get going and meanwhile people could be suffering. The bedrock of our policy is to get people to grow enough food for themselves so that they can't possibly starve. Cash crops come second.'

'What sort of crops are used as a famine reserve?' I asked.

'You'll see all this to-morrow,' Amory said. 'We're going to Buhimba just south of here. I was touring and had only one more day when the bus accident occurred and twenty-three people were killed, so I had to get back. We'll work there tomorrow and I'll show you the ropes.'

As I left Mr Amory's office I felt more than ever grateful for that year of study in London which had prepared me for the kind of things that he had been talking about.

First, the bus accident. I found Inspector Frisby of the Uganda Police and asked him about it. He said that the bus had been designed for thirty-four passengers but was carrying more than seventy. On the roof were the usual bunches of green bananas which were heavy and caused the bus to go over on its side when the driver took a turn too fast. The only door was downwards, the emergency door at the back having been welded shut to prevent people getting on without paying. Worse still, the battery had not been secured and when the accident happened it broke free and ignited the fuel tank. It was the fire that killed people, Frisby explained; there would have been some injuries but no deaths if the emergency door had been open and there had been no fire. The fact that about fifty people were able to break the windows and get out was a miracle but practically all of them had injuries of one sort or another.

Frisby yawned and said that he had been up all night on another case.

'Would you believe it?' he asked, 'welding shut the emergency exit? Of course I'm taking the bus company to court but it seems the same thing was done to all their buses because they'd be out of business if they didn't.'

'And what about the Traffic Safety Branch,' I asked. 'They must have something like that in Kampala.'

He yawned again.

'It's a political thing. If we applied the law rigorously half the African buses and cars would be off the road. We can't clamp down at this stage of Uganda's development.'

The Mukama, the Native Government, By-laws and the bus accident; it all seemed too much for one morning; however, I got a copy of the Native Government by-laws from Stephen and read them during lunch. All were simple and to the point and left the impression that if they were properly enforced the District would be in good shape. And why, I wondered, did they not have a set of By-laws (these ones would have done admirably), for study and discussion back in London?

The first order of business that day had been to meet the Mukama. I am not sure what I had expected but I had not been prepared for the faded pageantry, the rather pathetic spectacle provided by a king with no tie and a hole in his sock. In the months that lay ahead, however, I learned to do what Amory had done, which was to ignore the surroundings and concentrate on what he represented in the minds of his subjects. It was the mystical quality that was important, not the smelly cowskins and tuneless music. This man was Bunyoro's link with the past and hope for the future; he was the object of these people's absolute allegiance which Walter Bagehot, the authority on such matters, said was the essential heart of a true monarchy. No legislature, he wrote, could manufacture such sentiments.

A few weeks later the annual ceremonies were held to celebrate the Mukama's succession to the throne and to venerate his ancestors. They made sense to an outsider, like myself, only so far as one could see through the eyes of the Mukama's subjects, a god-king who was above ordinary mortality and able, on state occasions, to transport himself to another level of consciousness. At one point in the ceremony he would go into a trance and commune with the spirits of his forefathers. No one else in the Kingdom could do this; it was his alone to converse with the dead and be guided by their counsel. As Homer put it, 'Not to everyone do the gods appear.'

3

First Safari

My introduction to the work of safari, that is to say of touring the countryside, was a brisk, one-day affair in the *gombolola* or administrative area of Buhimba, a few miles south of Hoima. It was to include a *baraza*, a meeting of all the men of taxpaying age. Amory would use it to sum up the impressions that he had gained on his earlier tour which had been cut short by the bus accident.

We set out from Hoima in Amory's car with Henry Berunga, the Agricultural Officer, Stephen and myself and arrived at Buhimba shortly before eight. We were greeted by the *saza* chief, the *gombolola* chief with his two policemen and all the *muruka* or village chiefs. I was struck by the numbers of people who had gathered.

The plan was for Amory and Stephen to work during the morning at the *gombolola* headquarters auditing the court records, checking tax returns and ensuring, in company with the *saza* chief, that the *gombolola* was being run in an honest and efficient manner. This *gombolola* was about twenty miles across and had a population of just under five thousand of whom fifteen hundred were taxpayers, that is to say men between the ages of eighteen and forty-five.

In Bunyoro as a whole the *gombolola* was the true unit of administration at the African level and governed almost every aspect of native life. Taxes, by-laws, beer brewing tickets, court cases – all were dealt with by the *gombolola* chief and his staff. The *saza* chief, a dignified and serious man in his late fifties, had five *gombololas* under his direction and his position was essentially supervisory. The difference can be summarized by noting that the *saza* chief drove a small car and spent a proportion of his time in Hoima sitting on the Native Council and its various committees while the *gombolola* chief rode a bicycle and was fully occupied with the day-to-day administration of his *gombolola*.

Meanwhile Henry Berunga and I were to tour on foot in one of the *murukas*. The name of the place was Musaijjamukulu, which means 'Old Man', and referred to a low hill in the centre of the area. Henry said he had been there about six months earlier but had been disappointed with the agricultural effort and wanted to see if any improvements had been made in consequence of his advice.

It speaks well of Amory's perception that he sent me with Henry Berunga and didn't keep me at the *gombolola* headquarters. Checking books and counting cash was a perfunctory task that could be picked up any time, but a tour through the villages with Henry, a Munyoro himself and an acknowledged expert on African agriculture, was an opportunity not to be missed. We set off into the villages, banana gardens and cotton fields and I was conscious that I had taken my first step into the African countryside. It was an exciting moment.

The overwhelming impression of that first morning was that the Banyoro people were better off than they realized. They possessed an abundance of fertile land which was theirs for the asking, a soil so rich and rainfall so plentiful that it seemed that almost anything would grow. The land belonged in theory to the Mukama, which meant that it was held in trust for the tribe as a whole. In practical terms, if a householder wanted land he had only to ask his chief to allocate it to him at absolutely no cost. Even a few miles from Hoima only one acre out of every four or five was under cultivation, the remainder 'resting' by being allowed to revert to bush and elephant grass. Further out toward the District boundary there were thousands of acres lying unused.

It was often said that for an indication of the fertility of the soil one had only to measure the height of the elephant grass. Near Hoima it was fifteen or sixteen feet, which showed that the soil was of excellent quality. In other parts of the world and in other parts of Africa such an abundance of good land was an unimaginable luxury.

An ordinary Munyoro cultivator and his family, at the time of which I write, might be expected to cultivate about three acres. The man would live in a circular hut made of mud and wattle measuring some fifteen feet across with its main supporting pole in the middle like a bell tent. The roof would be a thick thatch of grass, not just any grass but a flat-bladed variety which shed the rain and was supposed not to blow off in the wind. To build such a house would take a man a week, perhaps less if he had the assistance of an older son. If he had more than one wife, which was common, each wife was entitled to her own hut. Elderly parents or other relatives would also have theirs. In all probability a smaller hut would be set aside as a kitchen and perhaps another to accommodate the goats at night. In addition there would be an outdoor privy and several grain stores where the famine reserves would be kept. These were not unlike small huts themselves, but raised from the ground as a protection against ants and capable of holding anywhere from two hundred pounds to a ton of grain or dried cassava roots. The village, therefore, was a collection of round huts with thatched roofs surrounded by cultivated land. Ten or more people might live in such a village; the man, his wife or wives, children, elderly relatives and perhaps some sort of servant or hanger-on. Square-built houses of brick with corrugated iron roofs were rare in those days. It follows that if corrugated iron was used as a roofing material the house would have to be built square or oblong because the sheets of corrugated iron could not be fitted to a circular house. Also rare were family groupings of only two. Indeed, a family of two was almost inconceivable except immediately following marriage because it was not a satisfactory social or economic unit.

One heard a good deal of discussion at that time about the African propensity for circles rather than straight lines. It was claimed that patients in the hospital would feel more comfortable and be more inclined to a recovery if the hospital walls were curved rather than straight. I doubt the validity of this and question whether westerners for their part suffer any discomfort by being in a circular room. It feels different certainly, and takes a slight amount of adjustment but I don't think much importance can be attached to it.

Where their fields are concerned, however, the Bunyoro propensity for curved lines was a problem because nothing could be measured accurately and no acreages known for sure. No Munyoro would think of using pegs and a length of rope to produce a straight line so the resulting cultivation was haphazard and appeared disorganized to the western eye. If, in the future, the Banyoro decided to put up wire fences along their boundaries to restrain domestic animals or demarcate their property the job would be impossible because a wire fence cannot be stretched in circles.

Incidentally, it was also very easy to become lost when there were no straight boundaries. With the sun overhead or hidden by cloud and no conspicuous hills the westerner would soon lose his sense of direction when walking through cultivated land. The pathways would circle and meander leaving him disoriented. On my return to Canada I was more struck by the orderly geometrical fences of southern Ontario than by almost anything else. Indeed, I sat in the car and looked at them with fascination all the way from Toronto airport to my wife's family home, and I have to admit that they affected me as nothing else did in the first week of my leave because my mind had become so attuned to the circular and random boundaries of Bunyoro.

The division of labour in a Bunyoro family was well defined as between men and women. A man would build houses, brew beer, attend discussions and raise the cash crops: cotton or coffee. His wife was responsible for the food crops, cooking, maintaining the fire, fetching water and such sewing as she was capable of doing. The children were taught to help their parents from an early age and were often given the task of looking after sheep or goats. This meant tying them on a twenty-foot halter so they would not wander off. Making the ropes from sisal plants was undertaken by the women, who also made the mats on which they slept at night.

Every man kept a spear in his hut, also a *panga*, or long slashing knife. The cultivation was done by hoe, in Scotland called a mattock, a heavy iron blade set at right angles to the wooden shaft. The operating motion was to raise the blade over one's head and strike downwards into the soil then pull slightly towards you so that a chunk of soil or sod was loosened. In the western world we would do the same work with a garden spade or fork, but our implements were not popular in Africa because the cultivators did not wear shoes and could not have used their foot to press downwards into the ground. The soles of their feet were quite hard but could not have taken such abuse, any more than we could do it wearing bedroom slippers.

A question needs to be answered at this point: why have not tractors been introduced? Hand cultivation is hard physical work and an insult to the intelligence of modern man, and tractors might seem to be a godsend.

The quick answer is that in those areas where tractors have been used successfully the effect has been devastating on the people. They are deprived of their land and many of them make their way to the cities to find work. They nearly always end up at a level far below that which they enjoyed as small landholders, a classic instance of being displaced by machines. A single tractor operated with reasonable efficiency can work a hundred acres and might take over land formerly cultivated by ten or a dozen families. It may be argued that these families were inefficient as producers of food and should make room for more modern and productive methods. The reply that most administrators would offer is that inefficient cultivators live a relatively good life, keep a few animals, goats, sheep and chickens and will have cattle when the battle against the tsetse fly has been won. They have food from their own fields, many kinds of vegetables and fruits and such luxuries as wild honey, white ants, fish caught in the swamps, and mushrooms. With an acre or two of cotton or coffee the household will have money to spend on clothes, tools, cooking pots and a bicycle so that with hard work and good husbandry they are raised to relative affluence.

One of the problems of the tribal system of land ownership is that ordinary cultivators do not have clear title to the land which they occupy. It is nowhere legally demarcated or described and the man with a tractor is usually able to buy, bribe or threaten to the point where he takes over control. He levels the ant-hills, burns the trees and so there begins a deterioration which brings endless problems in its train. The heavy tropical rain with its large, ferocious raindrops tears at the unprotected earth and soil erosion starts. As long as the larger trees were left to stand the raindrops would shatter as they struck the leaves and the resulting damage to the soil was minimal. Added to this, the hand cultivator had been taught to make 'bunds' or banks of earth so that rainwater was trapped and didn't flow down the slope. This not only kept the soil in place but also replenished the underground water table.

The tractor driver is not so careful. Sitting atop his machine he asks nothing more than a long, straight run without curves or obstacles. He becomes converted to the Canadian type of field rather than the African one with its bumps and curves. From his high perch he does not see the soil erosion and his machine not only joins him to his land but also separates him from it so that the soil is being exploited rather than cherished. Instead of using manure from his animals to fertilize it, or banana leaves as mulch, he spreads it with artificial fertilizer and then adds pesticides and herbicides with all their attendant evils. His final act of folly is to plant maize, that most pernicious of crops, which takes everything from the soil and gives nothing back. True it is a food crop; true it produces a high rate of return, as much as five hundred grains for every one planted, but it is sudden death to the soil which thereupon requires huge quantities of fertilizer to restore it to its original productivity.

While the tractor is wrecking havoc on their land, how are the owners faring? Quite possibly they have settled in an overcrowded, disease-ridden shanty-town on the outskirts of one of the larger cities. If he is very lucky the man will find a factory job which pays the minimum wage; after all he has no qualifications, no skills and can speak only his tribal language. The only food the family can now afford is maize flour. Gone are the days of fresh vegetables such as beans which are so nourishing and restore so much to the soil. Gone are the potatoes, tomatoes, onions, peanuts and half a dozen varieties of banana. Gone is the goat's milk, honey, eggs and fish, also the fat edible rats the size of ground-hogs. He and his family are now at the starvation level and there is nothing he can do but take to a life of crime to improve his lot. Socially and morally he was not ready to leave his tribal area and without the discipline of tribal life he is vulnerable. All his life the Mukama, the chief milkman, has occupied the leopard throne and served as his god and his king. All his life the chiefs have maintained order, restrained the headstrong and told the foolish what they should do and how they should behave. Now, in the shantytown, the rules and customs of the tribe are swept aside and his education has given him no standards by which he can govern himself. He is not unteachable or even a very difficult person, rather his release from tribal discipline and lack of education leave him exposed to every temptation. Up to that time his life was lived within a framework not unlike a combination of military and monastic duty. It was what he knew, understood and respected and he had learned to fit into it. In the shanty-town all that was left to him was his tribal language and a few tribal dances, although there cannot have been many occasions for rejoicing.

The extent to which the ordinary Munyoro cultivator was adjusted to his environment is remarkable. His house could be constructed entirely of local materials for which he did not have to pay a single cent: tree branches, mud and grass held together by strips of bark which were used to tie it all together. How different from the shanty-town where nothing is free. Much of his food was gathered wild: honey, which they called 'the juice of the bee'; mushrooms; grasshoppers; and a kind of wild spinach called *dodo*. Cooking was often accomplished without pots and pans, the food being wrapped in layers of banana leaf and cooked over a low fire for an hour or more. Many other types of food were simply barbecued at the end of a stick. Clothes and blankets were fashioned from the bark of the *mutuba* tree which was stripped off and hammered out with a wooden mallet and when done properly did not harm the tree. Drinking vessels and water jars came from the various gourds which were seen growing near every house. He could even brew his own banana beer without the use of modern equipment.

In his own village, therefore, he was an artisan of survival, master of a hundred minor competencies which, added together, fitted him neatly into his little world. In the shanty-town every one of them is useless. More than this, he was sociable in his village and probably knew by name a hundred of his neighbours together with their problems, stories and family circumstances. He also knew tribal customs such as those surrounding marriage, or bringing a case before the chief, or the payment of taxes. His language, although he did not realize it, was one of rare beauty and subtlety and enabled him to be involved with the surrounding community. He was never lonely or at a loss for friendship. A few taps on his drum and the entire community would know that he had brewed banana beer and was informing his friends that they might join him. It was a little like the England of two hundred years ago when a gentleman would hold a ball but would not think of sending out specific invitations because he knew that the news would travel and his friends would do him the honour of attending. Like the Banyoro those English gentry were ethnically tied, spoke the same language and acknowledged the same sovereign. There was no diversity and few cross-currents so that all felt themselves to be related members of the community.

It is not difficult to realize why this man, this typical Munyoro, should prize two possessions beyond all else: his land and his personal dignity. Where land is concerned he seems almost paranoid because without it he becomes nothing. A Munyoro cannot leave his land and turn to something else; it constitutes a form of death and with this in mind it is not hard to appreciate how administrators in Africa have formulated their policies with regard to mechanical cultivation. Stated briefly, if individual farmers buy tractors and are able to maintain them then the greatest caution must be exercised by the authorities to ensure that they do not appropriate the land or displace traditional cultivators. Examples from elsewhere such as Mexico City, Rio de Janeiro and Buenos Aires were always quoted: millions of people removed from the land who then crowd round the cities to their own unspeakable detriment.

Henry Berunga told a story that showed that even the experts in London were vague in their minds about African farming. With a group of junior officers from Uganda he had been sent to the Canadian Prairies to see examples of extensive agriculture; huge tractors ploughing miles of flat, featureless land. They were treated to long dissertations about fertilizers, herbicides and pesticides that were applied to the land by aerial spraying. After that the storage and transportation problems of crops were discussed. To round it off a meteorologist gave them details of the harsh prairie winters.

'Can you conceive in your mind,' Henry asked, 'a more useless and unsuitable tour for people whose working life would be spent in Africa?'

On the return flight the group landed in Lisbon and managed to get a couple of days in the Portuguese countryside, which is where they should have been in the first place. They saw small farms, sometimes only three or four acres, many of them on hillsides. Each was well integrated with horse, cow, sheep, goats, a pig or two, chickens and a great variety of food crops. Their cash crops, corresponding with Uganda's cotton, were an acre or two of grape vines or olive trees, and their self-sufficiency was exactly what was being striven for in Uganda. Even the fish bones, after the cat had licked them clean, were dug into the soil near the grape vines. The point was not lost on the young agricultural officers that with a very small acreage it was possible to have a high standard of living, a comfortable house, good food on the table, wine to drink and well-educated children.

'If they can do it in Portugal, we can do it here,' was Henry's comment.

He had summed it up perfectly: a small parcel of fertile land, lovingly cared for and growing both food and cash crops. It was possible and achievable, not a pipe-dream, because the land was fertile and the people were attached to their land.

It is sobering to think what could happen in the rice-growing lands of Asia if tractors should ever succeed in taking over from people. Happily they have not done so to any extent because the fields are too small, those on the hillsides often being the size of a living room. Tractors simply cannot operate in the precariously balanced rice paddies that climb like steps up the hillsides, making manual work essential. If the teeming millions who bend their backs to grow rice were to be displaced by tractors the problems created would be insoluble.

In Uganda the cotton crop possessed one characteristic shared by rice cultivation in that it was labour intensive and could not, at that time, be performed mechanically. Cotton, therefore, the biggest moneymaker of Uganda, had a twofold value because it was also an ideal family crop and kept people on the land. The land had first to be prepared as it would be for any other crop, and planting the seed presented no great problem. Harvesting was the critical time and took all the care and attention that the family could bestow on it. The white, fluffy seed hairs had to be picked without being crushed and placed in clean sacks, not forcibly but loosely so that the hairs were not damaged. The sacks were then conveyed by bicycle or head load to the nearest cotton-buying store which was operated under the eye of the Agricultural Department at every crossroads and under almost every shady tree. The cotton would be weighed and paid for on the spot, a junior chief in attendance to see fair play. Two or three times a day a motor lorry would pick up the cotton that had been purchased and carry it to the ginnery which was a small factory where the seed was removed from the cotton fibre. Uganda cotton had a high reputation for cleanliness and length of staple and attracted the highest prices as long as it was clean and well handled. At the time of the harvest there was no school, no court cases, no meetings; whole families from young children to the aged and infirm were out picking and transporting cotton.

Cotton, of course, is an annual crop which has the advantage that increasingly disease-resistant and high-yielding strains can be developed year after year by the plant geneticists. Theoretically, therefore, improvement is an annual affair although it does not work so simply in practice. With coffee, on the other hand, the trees, once planted, last a lifetime and have the effect of anchoring the family to their land. Improvement comes with the mulching and care of the coffee trees which are also labour intensive, particularly at harvest.

Cotton and coffee and, to a much lesser extent, tobacco, were the cash crops of Bunyoro. They grew supremely well and with no land shortage it was difficult to see why the average cultivator could not make a good living for himself. Some did, and would earn thousands of shillings a year, but others were slow to adopt cash crops and continued to be land-rich and cash-poor.

Bunyoro had no agricultural experimental farm, not even a 'demonstration' farm where people could see in detail what it was that the Native Government was trying to get them to do. The government policy, however, through the chiefs, the agricultural department and the District Commissioner was abundantly clear. Every cultivator, representing something like ninety per cent of the population, was encouraged to grow a good balance of food crops and cash crops. A man could leave the land if he chose, he could follow any avocation or none, but if he remained on the land the full force of government persuasion urged him to work hard, retain his traditional skills, raise his family on an abundance of good food and make money on his cash crops. The District Council By-laws were all directed to the same end, to improve his health and standard of living, although they were not rigorously applied to young men who were just starting out. The chiefs were urged to give the young time to establish a famine reserve, dig a privy away from the house, clear the land and plant cotton. It was not that the By-laws were to be disregarded but that time was to be allowed for compliance.

The Banyoro, however, possessed no tradition of hard work or sustained effort but rather a deep-rooted distrust of moving too far ahead of their neighbours. It was not a question of keeping up with the Joneses but of keeping down with them. A Munyoro was not an individualist or a pioneer, he was stamped indelibly as one of the crowd. He had an aversion to standing out from his fellows or being different; his refuge was anonymity. Many, had they put their minds to it, could have worked harder and cultivated a larger acreage thereby making themselves better off by worldly standards, but they had a distrust of wealth that held back even the strongest. Progress was something that everyone tried to achieve equally and there were few exemplars or exceptional individuals. Riches, in Banyoro, were measured more in terms of numbers of family plus a crowd of retainers than by material possessions. A rich man was surrounded by people, not things, and became the centre of a community rather than the owner of anything he did not possess before.

The Banyoro, having once been cattle-owning aristocrats but having lost their herds to the invading tsetse fly, had a second disadvantage in addition to their mistrust of worldly success. It was the faded gentility and demoralization of those who are reduced to an inferior station in life. Their day-to-day manners and conversation illustrated this: leisurely, punctilious and elegant but not much to the point. These people were not go-getters or doers, rather the performers of some mannerly but antiquated dance which continues long after the music has fallen silent. They had not come to terms with their reduced station in life and could not accept that they were now cultivators of the soil bent over the hoe, their eyes cast downwards, not herdsmen who stand upright with spear in hand and observe distant horizons.

Henry Berunga and I returned to the *gombolola* headquarters by early afternoon for the *baraza*. People crowded into the chief's meeting hall and sat on the floor while the chiefs occupied chairs in the front row. Bicycles were left outside and the *gombolola* policeman kept an eye on them. Most men were dressed in shorts and shirt and some wore a *kanzu* or ankle-length white garment. There were no women present. The *saza* chief rose first and introduced me with a gracious little speech. Stephen translated it into English and I was struck, as I was again and again in Bunyoro, at their simple eloquence and ability to make a well-mannered, unhurried speech. He did not falter or trip over the words, and the language contains no clichés or jargon so there is a refreshing directness about it. Next it was the turn of the *gombolola* chief who introduced his eight *muruka* chiefs and then added a few words about the problems he was facing. He was nothing if not candid and I took down his remarks:

'I have been in this *gombolola* for six months before which I was chief clerk in the Native Government office in Hoima. The people here are lazy and they drink too much. Their energy goes into dancing and beer parties, not into their work. I advise them about good cultivation and better house building but when my back is turned they fall into bad ways.'

Finally they all said, '*Nyanze, nyanze*,' which is an expression of welcome.

It was then Amory's turn and he stood up with Stephen. Formality was required so he addressed the *saza* chief by his ancient and high sounding title, 'Mukwenda of Bugahya county' which translates as the One-who-is-Sent, ambassador. Next the *gombolola* chief, the Musaale or 'Arrow' of Buhimba, and lastly the *muruka* chiefs.

'I am pleased to return to this *gombolola* to finish the work that I began a few days ago.'

He paused and Stephen said it in Lunyoro.

'I was recalled to Hoima suddenly because of the tragic bus accident that killed so many of our people and injured others.'

Again a pause.

'Now I want to speak to you about the things I have seen in your *gombolola* which affect the lives of all of you.'

He spoke from his notebook about health, housing and about sending their children to school. He was a good speaker and kept it simple and to the point. I watched the four hundred faces and realized that they were taking it in although whether they would follow his advice was another thing. He also went out of his way to support the Native Government and chiefs, bolstering their authority and their efforts. It was a positive talk and one that must have left the chiefs with the feeling that they had his support and confidence.

I was beginning to realize what power the spoken word possessed in this country. These people were not readers but speakers and listeners, they did not understand pictures so all depended on that ancient Homeric ability to pass ideas directly by word of mouth. Amory was doing it not by lecturing them but by making it as bright and interesting as he knew how. If he had achieved it by way of story or parable it would have been perfect.

Two or three times he used the expression 'to make progress' and Stephen translated 'go in front'. How different, I thought, from the village near which I had lived as a child. All the talk there had been about preserving its character and antiquity, keeping out the telegraph poles, advertising signs and filling stations, of not going in front but rather staying behind. Thatched roofs, so commonplace in Bunyoro, would attract the tourists, their cameras and their money; low doorways, oak beams and antiquated windows were more prized than airy modern buildings.

When question time came a man stood up, folded his arms and asked about the return of the lost counties.

'We have suffered too much,' he said, 'it is time that justice was done and our rightful lands returned. The spirits of the dead Bakama [kings] will roam about and ask why we do not make war against our traditional enemies to recover what has been stolen from us.'

He paused to see what effect his words were having. Henry whispered, 'He puts on a good show, doesn't he?'

It was the standard question clothed in the standard rhetoric, vaguely reminiscent of Saint Bernard urging people to set off on the crusades. Amory must have answered it many times before.

'The government is well aware that the Kingdom of Bunyoro makes claim to lands that are now within the boundaries and under the rule of Buganda. I cannot give you any guarantees that they will ever be returned but I want you to understand that the more progress which you make the better your chances of being heard in the matter of these disputed territories. A prosperous kingdom, well governed and law-abiding, will be taken more seriously than one in which authority is not respected and all is wild and impoverished.

'You speak of what you have lost, your territories and your cattle, but you do not speak of what you possess, plenty of good empty land, valuable forests and lakes and rivers that are full of fish. In all of East Africa it would be hard to find another District so blessed with natural resources and yet I know that weeds are growing among your cotton plants, children are not in school and the health by-law is not being followed. If the spirits of the dead Bakama are offended it may be nothing to do with the lost territories but because famine reserves have not been maintained nor the advice of the chiefs followed as closely as it should have been.

'I hear from the *gombolola* chief that every sack of cotton from this *gombolola* had to be emptied out and inspected before being bought because some people had hidden rocks inside the sacks so as to cheat the buyer. Because of this, hundreds of people were kept waiting in line when they should have been in their fields picking more cotton. The spirits of the dead Bakama that were roaming about saw it and were angry with those who were dishonest.'

This produced a laugh, as intended, and a round of applause from the chiefs. The questioner sat down but others took his place and raised subjects as far apart as the high price of buying a wife to why bicycles should keep to the side of the road. Finally, in late afternoon, it was over and we took our leave.

'*Yeebare munno waitu*,' the chiefs said as they gathered round and shook hands. 'Thank you very much,' and they obviously meant it. Amory's presence was not resented; he was not seen in the light of a French inspector general, or even of an English auditor; he was not there to scourge but to offer help, advice and a fresh perspective. Whatever he might have said to the *gombolola* chief in private he was squarely behind him in public and the people who had come to listen would have been confronted by a solid team representing the government and its policies.

On the way home we visited the tomb of one of the Bakama, a reputedly savage individual who had ruled Bunyoro in the middle of the previous century. His contemporary, Queen Victoria, had she known about him, would not have been amused. His resting place was beneath a traditionally built hut of grass. The thatch was neatly finished and reached down to ground level. It was orderly and quiet except for the call of a solitary nightjar. This was the Westminster Abbey complex of Bunyoro, the cool, quiet place where the former glories of the nation were recollected by reference to its most memorable sons. And this one, no more nor less than the others, was a cruel, savage and ungracious creature, a tyrant who killed or maimed his own people with the same disregard that he made war on others. Here was African kingship at its worst, leaving a thousand skeletons in its wake, the depravity of power. It was not hard to imagine his spirit roaming in sorrow at the memory of his deeds and calling out with the agonized cry of the nightjar.

4

The Congo

My first real safari, which I started within a couple of weeks of arriving in Hoima, was to a place called Bugungu at the north-eastern tip of Lake Albert. Bugungu was no more than a single *gombolola*, but its remoteness and the fact that it could only be reached by water during much of the year meant that the District Commissioner or his assistant would visit infrequently. It was the one *gombolola* in Bunyoro that was not accessible by road at all seasons. Amory told me to spend a full week there, tour it thoroughly and clear up the outstanding problems. Normally a *gombolola* would occupy two days, not a week, but Bugungu was in a class by itself. For one thing it was the only place in the District where there was no sleeping sickness and cattle could be kept. It was there that the Mukama had his royal herd of pure white cows whose milk was carried to him in wooden milk pots, although it must have been sour and undrinkable by the time it reached his table.

Bugungu had a thriving fishing industry. It was impractical to market the fish in Uganda, so a buyer from the Belgian Congo bought the catch and transported it across Lake Albert to Mahagi Port whence it was conveyed to the mines and formed an important part of the miners' diet.

I was to be accompanied by Stephen who came to my office the day before with a letter file which he called the 'Safari File'. On it he had placed copies of all letters and messages that had to do with Bugungu and required action when the next touring officer was there. Also on the file were copies of the touring reports of previous District Commissioners going back many years. This gave continuity to the process of touring and with only an hour's reading one could get a feel for the place and its history. One of the letters on file was from the newly-formed Uganda National Parks organization asking whether any cultivators were living within the proposed Park. Amory had attached a note: 'You are to walk the entire boundary and see for yourself.'

Getting ready for safari was a little like preparing a ship for sea. There was the same bustle and activity, the same excitement with everybody trying to be helpful. I drew a collapsible table and chair from the store, also a camp bed, mattress and mosquito net. Stephen had said that there was a small camp at Bugungu, but I decided to take a tent with me in case it was needed. The evening before we left I packed cooking utensils, food, lamps and other requirements in four or five cardboard boxes and left them overnight in the living room. When Stephen added his bedroll and Kazimir his, the amount of baggage to be fitted into the Landrover was considerable. Amory had said, 'Take what you reasonably need. Any fool can be uncomfortable on safari. You are not an African and no one expects you to live as though you were.'

In subsequent months packing a safari became almost second nature. I always did it myself and never allowed the servants, however well-intentioned, to get involved. They could stand there, help or make suggestions, but I was the one who actually did it. The secret, I discovered, was to have safari equipment that was separate from other household possessions so there was no need to borrow pans from the kitchen, a blanket from the bed, articles of cutlery from the dining room and so on. The safari equipment was kept solely for safari and when my wife Jean joined me a few days later I asked her to make sure that anything that might be taken temporarily from the store found its way back.

Two items of safari equipment, however, had to await my first home leave. One was a five-gallon milk can for heating water. Most people used kettles and saucepans for this purpose, which was never satisfactory when heating the amount of water needed for the canvas bath or for washing dishes and clothes. Another was an iron contraption with four short legs and a grille top. It was placed over the camp fire so that the pans, water container, even toast or barbecued meat were squarely over the fire and could not spill. I had it hand-made by a village blacksmith and kept it for many years. Of course it became black and dirty from the fire but we found that it could be attached with wire to the outside of the Landrover, rather than being put inside with bedrolls and other things. It was far better than the standard three rocks for holding a cooking pot, especially in areas where there were no rocks to be found and chunks of ant-hill had to be used. These refinements might sound luxurious to the man who goes camping for a week or two every year but we were on safari for twenty weeks in an average twelve-month period.

My navy training served me well. One of the things I learned at sea was that small things have to be done correctly and no detail is too insignificant. Many people seem incapable of applying their minds to trivia so that they forget to take matches, lose the keys of the car and never have a sharp knife. One of my friends in another District, who might charitably be described as a careless individual, returned from safari, poured himself a stiff drink of gin and gulped it down. His servant, unhappily, had used the gin bottle to carry kerosene without washing off the label. My friend came to no great harm although he burped for a week. A more sensible arrangement would have been to search for a one-gallon metal can with a screw top and then sew a canvas jacket on it with needle and thread. In those days motor oils were often supplied in screw-top containers so this is scarcely asking too much.

Another item of equipment which I must have taken on every safari that I ever went on, and still possess, is an army-surplus ammunition box. I had it fitted with a hasp and staple so that it could be padlocked. It was used for carrying files and papers, tax tickets, government money and, in fact, everything 'official' that one has to take in the bush. The fact that it is still in use as a tool box, thirty-five years and half a dozen coats of paint later, speaks for itself.

Loading the safari kit in the Landrover was something which, again, I always did myself. The spare tire would have to be accessible, heavy articles placed low down, and my rifle in its canvas case lodged behind the seats. Bedding would go on top and the very last thing to go in was a freshly baked loaf of bread. We left Aberi, my head boy, standing on the front steps, his function being to look after the house in my absence. I started the car and took the red, corrugated road northwards out of Hoima.

The first few miles of our journey took us through the rolling hills and lush vegetation which lay between Hoima and the top of the escarpment. It was mid-November 1951, the weather was clear and warm and the rains tapering off. The country looked exceedingly green with banana gardens alternating with dense elephant grass. There were occasional flame trees in the jungle which appeared at a distance like blood that had fallen from the sky. Villages with mud walls and grass roofs huddled among the banana gardens but the efforts of mankind seemed insignificant in this land of remorseless nature.

At a small place called Biiso we turned west and took the road down the escarpment. Below, in its trough between the mountains, was Lake Albert, probably the last great lake in the world to be discovered by western man. Its steely surface reflected the muted colours of the mountains of the Belgian Congo and although they were forty miles distant the air was so clear that we could make out individual trees on the skyline. I drove slowly down the twisting road to the sandy floor of the valley where the road collected itself and ran straight towards the lake. The forests on the higher ground had given way to a more sparse vegetation of short grass and scattered trees. There were pools of water after the recent rains which were fed by streams cascading down the escarpment.

The little port of Butiaba was a sorry collection of huts, two or three Indian shops, an iron warehouse and not much else. The Nile paddle steamer was not in harbour but the government motor launch lay alongside so I pulled up beside it. The coxswain appeared with his assistant and in a few minutes we had the car unpacked. I assumed that the coxswain would know how to stow our safari gear so I left them and went to park the car under a tree near one of the Indian shops. Having introduced myself to the shopkeeper I asked him to keep an eye on it for a few days, after which I walked back to the jetty. I stood and stared at the launch for fully half a minute. Our safari gear had been tied to the launch's upperworks which was no more than a flimsy plywood canopy. I made them take everything off and return it to the jetty after which they passed it down to me item by item and I stowed it securely in the bottom of the boat.

'Stephen,' I said, as we pulled away, 'I am worried about this incident because what the coxswain just did was unbelievably foolish. With all that baggage on top the boat would have capsized when we got out on the lake. As you can see, the place for heavy things is at the bottom where they make it steady. If it had been someone who did not know anything about boats they would probably have been drowned.'

Stephen looked embarrassed and explained that the launch was operated by the Department of Public Works and that the crews were frequently changed. This crew, he discovered, had until recently operated a flat-bottomed ferry across the Nile.

'They put the luggage on top because they are accustomed to carrying loads on their heads. You should write a strong letter,' he said, 'to the director of the Department.'

This became the first entry in my notebook for the Bugungu safari. 'Write letter to Director of Public Works about ignorance of boat's crew and need for training.'

The government launch on Lake Albert was, like a good deal else in Uganda, antiquated and in need of replacement. I wondered how many wartime motor launches, air-sea rescue vessels and harbour craft that were no longer needed were now gathering barnacles round the coasts of Britain; if only there were some way of getting them to Butiaba and places like it.

We chugged sedately into the calm water of the lake and turned northwards toward Bugungu about twenty miles distant. The line of the escarpment faded from view to the east and at about midday the wind came to life and the waves mounted. Such a change in the weather seemed strange, a transformation from calm to moderate storm in no more than a few minutes. The waves were only about four or five feet from trough to crest, but steep and close together, giving the creaking boat an uncomfortable motion. Spray came over so we covered the safari gear as best we could and I urged the coxswain to keep the bows into the waves and reduce speed.

Nothing is easier to bear with fortitude than the misfortunes of others, and within a few minutes I found myself at the wheel of the launch with the two crew members, also Stephen and Kazimir, suffering the extremities of seasickness. The boat pitched a good deal but my main consideration was not to let it get into a beam sea since its bottom was rounded and it seemed inclined to roll. This continued for an hour; slow speed on the engine with the bows into the breaking waves and a slight corkscrew motion.

The spell was broken when it began to rain. Raindrops the size of grapes plunged from the sky and had the effect of flattening the water. Within minutes we were back on course for Bugungu and a watery sun returned to the lake. There was a foot of water sloshing about in the bottom of the boat, but after a few words of encouragement from me and groans from the crew some buckets appeared and they began to bail by hand. An hour later we reached the small jetty at Bugungu.

I mention this rather minor incident for two reasons. First, I had been in the country for only a few days and was very unsure of myself. Amory had treated me to just one day of instruction in the work of safari, which he had been careful to point out was the most important thing I would be doing during my first tour of service, and he had then sent me out on my own. True, we had done a year's course of instruction in London but it had been more theoretical than practical and had not covered everything. Now here I was thrust into a situation in which I felt completely confident, having handled cutters and motor boats in more arduous conditions when I had been a midshipman. Second, and perhaps more important, it gave me some appreciation of the African fishermen and the conditions they faced. No dugout canoe could have lasted a minute in that water with its steep, short waves, one hard upon the other. Shallow inland lakes have a vile reputation; Lake Erie, Lake Galilee and Lake Albert being among the worst.

We were welcomed at Bugungu like minor royalty. The *gombolola* chief, whose title was Sabairu (Sa-buy-roo), was at the head of more than a hundred of his men and one could not help taking an instant liking to him. He gave the impression of being a quiet authoritarian, much respected by his people. He seemed to be about fifty years of age and while he could speak no English his Lunyoro was clear and Stephen translated his words with the eloquence of the original. He greeted us, inquired as to our passage on the lake and deplored the bad weather. At this point Stephen excused himself and went to lie down on the sand in company with Kazimir and the two Public Works Department sailors so the chief and I were left to understand each other as best we could. His men unloaded the launch and set off with our safari gear on their heads.

The chief's headquarters and the rest camp were about a mile inland. The buildings were made of ant-hill and cow dung mixed together, capped by a thatched roof of swamp grass. We entered the rest house and with some help from two or three of the chief's men soon had the place organized and a pot of tea on the table. A fire had already been lit in the kitchen which stood a few yards behind. In future years I would not have been surprised or concerned that a couple of African fishermen whom I had never seen before pounced on the safari gear and began to unpack it under the chief's direction, but at that time it was something new and I was touched by their courtesy and desire to help.

I quickly discovered from Sabairu that something had gone amiss with the fish buying arrangements. Either because of the weather or because of the breakdown of his boat the buyer had not visited for two days and the fishermen, on his orders, would not be going out that night. Tons of fish had been used to fertilize their gardens. He asked me if we could use the launch and cross over to Mahagi Port at first light in the morning when the lake would be calm. It occurred to me that this would also give me a chance to hire a vehicle and pay a call on the Belgian *administrateur* at Mahagi town which was some fifteen miles inland. I had heard Amory saying that he wanted a policy of 'Hands-Across-the-Border' but he had not been able to get there himself. It had made me smile because I knew that his French was worse than mine.

By the time Stephen and Kazimir came trudging up the sandy pathway toward the rest camp, the sun was behind the Congo mountains and Sabairu and I were chatting like old friends. He understood my halting Luganda quite well but I was glad to have Stephen confirm the arrangements. Again, I had shown that I was not completely helpless. I offered Stephen a small glass of inexpensive brandy after which his morale appeared much improved.

Next morning I got up while it was still dark and roused Kazimir who was sleeping in the kitchen by the cold ashes of the previous night's fire. By seven I had breakfasted and dressed in a clean uniform at which point Sabairu and Stephen appeared and we walked down to the lake together. It was a beautiful morning, with the water like a sheet of glass, and the snorting of a hippo could be heard for miles.

At Mahagi Port we found the fish buyer, Vanden Bosche, working on his boat. He apologized for his greasy hands and pointed to the engine parts that were spread around. He explained that he had built the boat from local timber but during the war he had not been able to get a suitable engine. A diesel truck, however, had gone out of control on the mountain road and rolled a thousand feet down, killing the driver and everyone else. He had bought the wreck at a giveaway price and set about salvaging the engine and anything else which might be of use. He hired fifty men to get the heavy engine up to the road where he could load it on his truck.

'I have a new engine on order,' he said, 'and as soon as I am ready to resume buying I'll let you know by the usual method.'

'What method?' I asked. I couldn't visualize a postal service operating across the lake.

'*Engoma* (drums). We can communicate by drum when the lake is calm. I have one suspended in the tree outside my house and chief Sabairu the same. Both of us have drummers but the trouble starts when one of them is taken sick or goes to a beer party. Bad weather or strong winds also prevent messages from being sent.'

I made a mental note to find out more about this exotic means of communication and turned to the matter of getting to Mahagi to see the *administrateur*. I was convinced that Vanden Bosche was doing all he could to repair his boat so I changed the subject and asked him where I could hire a car. After some delay Stephen and I eventually found ourselves in a small pick-up van on the way up the mountain. The road was quite good, as good as our own road between Hoima and Butiaba, but I was driving on the right side which, in spite of having driven in the United States and Canada, was always a little alien to me.

My first impressions of the Congo were gained before I had any clear idea of what Uganda was like but I was able to discern some of the more obvious differences between the two countries. The countryside through which we passed was much like Uganda but on arrival in Mahagi I seemed to have entered a small Belgian town, not a District headquarters. The shops and houses were packed together and there were few gardens to be seen. I thought it strange that in so vast and empty a country there would be this rather inward-looking configuration which gave no impression of reaching out and embracing the land. The most surprising thing, however, was the number of Belgians to be seen at the office of the *administrateur*. I wondered if there was a meeting taking place.

The head clerk was also a Belgian who wrote my name on a slip of paper, surname first, then Christian name, and said he would enquire whether the *administrateur* was free. '*Je me demande . . .*' he began. 'I wonder whether you have some form of identification, or better still, a letter of introduction?' He said it with a blend of boredom and officiousness.

'No?' He turned to Stephen and dispensed with any attempt at manners. 'Who is this *garçon*?'

'This is Mr Stephen Kutaga,' I replied. 'He is a senior clerk in the office of the District Commissioner. He is not a *garçon*.'

'*Est-il évolué*?'

'He is an educated man,' I replied, 'and occupies a position of responsibility.'

'He may wait over there,' came the reply.

I turned to Stephen and spoke in English. 'He doesn't seem altogether friendly. Perhaps you would like to walk round the bazaar and I'll meet you later at the car.'

The *administrateur* saw me immediately and pushed a couple of shorts-wearing, paper-carrying individuals out of his office. I was struck by the shortness of their shorts.

'Monsieur Ba-zu-ley,' he said. 'This is indeed an honour. And what brings you to Mahagi?'

I explained that the fish-buying arrangements had broken down, a fact which I had discovered only the day before. I had crossed the lake early to see Mr Vanden Bosche and took the opportunity to present myself at the *administrateur's* headquarters and offer Mr Amory's compliments. Mr Amory regretted that he had not had the pleasure of meeting the *administrateur* but hoped to remedy the defect at an early date. I apologized for not having been able to notify him of my visit but felt sure he would understand.

The *administrateur* was in his forties, a rather short man and, I judged, a stickler for details. He smiled benignly at my preliminary remarks which I had been rehearsing on the road. He obviously enjoyed the pomposity which I injected into my short speech. His English was excellent and we spoke for almost an hour during which time I gained real admiration for the man. His constant theme was the slow progress that was being made in the Congo and the frustrations of his work.

'Let me tell you a little story,' he said. 'Your West Nile District has a border with my territory and of course I know the West Nile District Commissioner at Arua and his Assistant who is responsible for the southern Counties. It was evident to this young man that the people were moving backwards and forwards over the international boundary every week to attend a flourishing market at Zeu. I have seen the market and have nothing but praise for it: cattle, sheep and goats being bought and sold; food crops; fish from the lake; native handicrafts. To make it easier for the people the officer on your side ordered his chief to build a road from Zeu as far as the border and this was done within a few weeks. He also wrote to me explaining the action he had taken and asked if I would extend the road on our side to link up, you understand. He pointed to the advantages and said that he assumed there would be no difficulty.

'Difficulty! I am not permitted by regulation to order the building of a new road, even such a short stretch as this and I would have to account in detail for the funds expended. I sent the matter to the Commissioner at Djugu and from there it went to the governor of the Eastern Province who sent it to the Governor General in Brazzaville. But this was an *International* road so it was sent to the minister in Brussels who was to have placed it before the Belgian cabinet. And I have not mentioned the explanations, justifications, maps, even photographs which I had to supply to support my request. Difficulty! I will probably never get an answer and it worries me that things are done rapidly and efficiently on your side and so much the reverse on ours. It is not as though there were any reason for not having a road instead of letting people walk across the open fields. You see, we have a totally centralized system of government.'

The *administrateur* leaned forward in his chair. 'Did you know,' he said, 'our education system is such that boys from my territory cross the border and attend your schools? Some even go to live in Uganda with relatives so they can get some schooling. Language is no obstacle because there are Jonam, Okollo, Lendu and Lugbara tribes on both sides of the border.'

The conversation drifted into other areas and I suggested that he seemed well staffed with expatriate officers.

He shook his head. 'You in Uganda place Africans in responsible positions, your chief at Bugungu, for example. Good men rise high and learn by experience. We, on the other hand, have a policy that only a white man can be trusted so we have too many of them doing work that should be done by locals. I would prefer a smaller staff but more power to train Africans and delegate work to them.

'Do you realize,' he asked, 'that we have no Native Councils that compare with yours and there are no plans to introduce them. You are fifty years ahead of us.'

Before I left, the *administrateur* said one more thing that struck me. 'Your administration is conducted with vigour and confidence but we have been defeated in two world wars and our policy is painfully defensive.'

One final incident found its way into my notebook in connection with this visit. The *administrateur* walked with me to my borrowed car where we found a Congolese policeman speaking with Stephen. I had parked in the wrong place, and was due to pay a fine but the *administrateur* intervened and said that the matter would be overlooked. I thanked him and we said goodbye.

'Can you imagine,' Stephen said as we drove away, 'wasting time on car parking regulations. The car was off the road, as I explained to the policeman, but he said that parking there was an offence.'

Before returning to Mahagi port we paid a brief but costly visit to the shop of a certain Madame de Baetz who accepted my East African currency without demur. Her prices were steep but I bought a few cans of cheese and bacon and half a dozen bottles of wine. It seemed wrong to pass up such an opportunity and, in the event, most of it accompanied me back to Hoima to celebrate my wife's arrival from Canada.

On the return journey to Bugungu I talked with Sabairu and learned something of his background. Years earlier he had attended the first school ever established in the area, a single classroom with an unpaid teacher. Four years of schooling were all he had received but somehow he learned to read and write his own language. He had then spent twenty years working his way up the ladder via the native police, a *muruka* chieftainship and now *gombolola* chief over five thousand people. For much of the year, while the rain fell and the overland track to Butiaba was impassable, he was virtually isolated from the remainder of the District. He ruled his little kingdom of fishermen, farmers and herdsmen in splendid isolation, facing problems as they arose, dispensing justice and trying, insofar as he knew how, to improve the condition of his charges. He bore the cares and problems of five thousand people, life and death problems, yet he had no money, no facilities and no modern expertise. How many westerners, I wondered, could do what he was doing and do it as well.

Suddenly I felt excited at the prospect of my first real safari. Bugungu was ahead of me and I was going to devote a full week to this remote place. During our training we had heard about getting out into the country, coming to know the people and seeing it all for ourselves. 'Once you experience Africa,' they had said, 'you cannot be unaffected. Your life will never be quite the same.' Well, here I was, a novice who was ready to be initiated into the mysteries that would become so much a part of my life. And who better to lead me there than Stephen, the knowledgeable head interpreter, and Sabairu, the respected chief of five thousand people. What better place to start than Bugungu, isolated and magnificent on the shores of Lake Albert.

5

Bugungu

We spent the following morning at Sabairu's headquarters. Stephen and I sat at a table in the courtroom or what they called the '*gombol-ola* hall' which was a large, open building with a raised platform at one end. There was a low wall and overhanging roof round the remainder of the room where onlookers and bystanders had collected, even at this early hour. On the wall was a framed copy of the court warrant which showed that Sabairu was empowered to impose a fine of up to six head of cattle or the equivalent in sheep or goats. He could also pass sentences of imprisonment up to six months and inflict corporal punishment. His court was constituted when he himself and any two of his *muruka* chiefs were sitting, there being eight *muruka* chiefs in all. I called for the court record which was a large book maintained by one of Sabairu's two clerks in elegant handwriting. It was opened at the page where Mr Amory had signed his name on his last visit a few months before. There had been over a hundred cases in the meantime.

Stephen began to read, translating into English as he went. 'A man called Mukasha allowed his animals to stray into his neighbour's garden where they ate the vegetables and did other damage. The *muruka* chief assessed the damage at fifteen shillings and identified the footprints in the earth. The money was paid to the man who lodged the complaint.'

'What is that ink smudge?' I asked. There were similar marks elsewhere on the page.

'That is the complainant's thumb mark,' Stephen explained. 'He is illiterate and cannot sign his name as having received the money so the clerk requires him to place his thumb on the ink pad and then press it to the paper. Sometimes the clerk will write 'R.T.M.' beside it, meaning Right Thumb Mark. Much extra responsibility falls on the clerks when people are illiterate because they have to be witness to these transactions and use the man's thumb print as a receipt.'

My mind went back to the war when I had written letters for sailors who had never learned to write. I would sit down with a navy letter form in front of me and ask the sailor what he wanted to say. Sometimes he didn't know and I offered suggestions, at other times he would say things that were painfully personal and embarrassing. I had been very young then, in my teens; yes, I knew what Stephen meant when he said that there were added responsibilities when people were illiterate.

'That seems all right to me', I said. 'They took trouble and used common sense. Let's look at the next one.'

'This man made an alarm signal without any reason and was fined one goat for rousing the whole neighbourhood and causing mischief.'

Stephen paused and looked around the hall. 'The *muruka* chief is there', he said, 'Perhaps we should ask him to explain.'

A man rose to his feet when asked by Stephen if he could recall the incident.

'It is an offence in native custom to make an alarm unless it is genuine, such as a thief or wild animals or a burning house. All able-bodied men, when they hear an alarm, are required to take their spears and go to the place. Women are expected to take up the alarm because a woman's voice is high-pitched and carries a great distance.'

'Just a moment,' I said. 'I don't understand how the alarm is made.'

The *muruka* chief gave a subdued demonstration. It was a continuous cry or howl and at the same time he rapidly closed his hand to and from his mouth so that an undulating sound was produced. The similarity with a wartime air-raid siren was very obvious. It was, in fact, the old hue-and-cry of the middle ages.

'In this instance almost two hundred people appeared, myself included, only to find that the man was drunk and there was nothing wrong. Next day I accused him in front of the *gombolola* court with causing mischief.'

'Thank you,' I said. 'I have another question; this time about communicating by drums. We heard yesterday that drummers can pass messages across the lake. Will someone explain.'

Sabairu spoke up. 'On a still night we can easily hear drumming across the lake in the Congo at a distance of twenty miles or more. We know who is beating the drum because the beat is distinctive, in the same way that you can distinguish between the handwriting of one clerk and another.'

'Yes,' I said, 'I understand that a person would have certain characteristics to his drumming that would identify him but I don't see how he could send a specific message.'

'It is easier than you might think,' Sabairu replied. 'They beat the drum to a certain cadence. A gentle drumming indicates that all is well while an agitated beat means that something is wrong. You will understand it when you hear it; an alarm does not sound the same as dance music.'

'So they don't spell it out in dots and dashes,' I suggested.

'Not at all,' Stephen broke in, 'because they can't spell. It is more like playing a tune which represents certain meanings or emotions.'

The drum, I began to realize, expresses the idea, such as danger, and is independent of the language of both the sender and the hearer. It possesses more in common with music than speech.

At this point a *muruka* chief spoke up. 'I am the *muruka* chief at Ndandamire, a few miles north of here. About two months ago I was awakened by a drumbeat in the early morning, two hours before daylight. It was agitated so I went outside. I knew whose drum it was and the drumbeat he played was the one used when fishermen are seen returning to shore. It tells people to come and help pull up the canoes. But then he also beat a tune to indicate the presence of wild animals. Putting these together I concluded he was reporting a canoe being attacked by a hippopotamus. We ran down to the lake and four or five canoes were launched. We found a canoe had been bitten by a hippo. One man had drowned but the other was still clinging to the wreckage.'

We returned to the court book and continued reviewing the cases. Mr Amory had told me that one of our prime responsibilities was to ensure that justice was being administered in the native courts and this meant reading every case and asking for explanations if the record was not clear. Beyond everything, he had told me not to be technical or legalistic but rather look for substantial justice. Often, he had said, the court would reach the right decision for the wrong reasons and these could be pointed out and discussed without upsetting the case.

The power in the hands of the District Commissioner or his assistant was wide, having been established many years before when the quality of justice was more haphazard. We could overturn a decision and either rehear the case in our own court or order that it be heard in a more senior native court. Or we could wipe out a case altogether and with a brief written explanation order the fine or prison sentence remitted. Yet we almost never made use of these powers, finding better ways of calling attention to a defect or to a point on which they might have gone astray.

A case which caught my eye concerned our young doctor from Hoima. During the dry season he had attempted to drive his small car overland from Butiaba to the medical dispensary at Bugungu. Even when the rivers were dry he would have done better to use the government motor launch and in the event he got in difficulties while trying to cross the Weiga river. Hearing drums and native music nearby he went in search of assistance and found a beer party in progress. He explained who he was and asked for half a dozen men to come and push his car through, a few minutes work at most. He knew that native custom required people to lend a helping hand and that it was an offence to stand idly by. These people, however, were drunk and argumentative and being a teetotaller himself he was appalled at their manners and attitude. Finally he agreed to pay them a sum of money and they pushed his car across.

The local *muruka* chief came to hear of the incident and the men were arrested and charged with an offence under native custom. The court found them all guilty and ordered that they receive corporal punishment, do a month's work to repair the road and return the money.

My first reaction was that this was an excessive punishment although I realized there was little I could do because the corporal punishment had been administered and the month's work performed.

I also noted that the *muruka* chiefs, seven out of eight of them, had sat on the court that day. Only two were needed to constitute the court although there was no reason why more should not sit. The chief in whose area the offence had occurred acted as prosecutor and the case had attracted considerable interest. I turned to Sabairu.

'Why was this punishment inflicted?'

Sabairu stood up and spoke slowly. 'The facts of this case were not in doubt. The accused persons were drunk and argumentative when the doctor asked for help and they bargained with him to be paid money for a few minutes work. This is an offence against native custom. Native custom, however, does not say how severe our punishment will be. Let me ask you to look at the case from the viewpoint of myself and my chiefs.

'The doctor comes to us, not merely from Hoima, but from a far country, as you yourself have done. We have heard about Bulaya [Europe] and we know it is more advanced and that customs are different. We have also heard that the doctor has studied medicine for many years and that he might have chosen to cure people in a great hospital where he would be surrounded by comforts and conveniences. But he decided to come here and work for the Mukama's people and on that day to drive to our medical dispensary to make sure the medical assistant was doing his work and had the drugs he needed. We know that the doctor never charges one cent for his services, nor for medicines and bandages; we have heard that he will rouse himself at any hour to attend a sick person, or a woman in labour; yet he comes here to this *gombolola* and we cannot even push his car. Imagine how I and my chiefs felt that it should happen here, that we will gain a reputation for being thieves and drunks. How can we expect the doctor to come back and help us? How can we stand up in his presence? The whole court thought this a just punishment and all raised their hands in favour of it.'

I looked at their serious faces and realized how strongly they felt about the case. I knew that the native custom which governed it was not capricious or ill-founded because, as Stephen explained, there were many occasions in native life when a man or woman would be at a loss without the helping hand of family or neighbours. When a woman went to draw water from the spring, for instance, she would take her gourd or clay pot which might hold four or five gallons. Having filled it and set a grass ring on her head as a cushion she was then helpless to lift the gourd. The gourd is heavy and slippery, and nature gave it no handles so she is faced with an impossibility if she is by herself. Likewise when she reaches her village, unless there were others to help her, she could not remove it from her head and set it down without dropping it, some sixty pounds in weight, in which case it would certainly break.

There were some loads, like bundles of firewood, which were not fragile and could be thrown to the ground, but liquids such as water or beer carried in round, slippery gourds were the most difficult and even the strongest man could not lift a full beer gourd on or off his own head. Indeed it took two other people to handle it on behalf of the carrier.

'Imagine,' Stephen said, 'how it would be if people could not be relied on to help each other, how intolerable life would become. This customary law is not based on some theoretical consideration but on everyday situations.'

I thanked them and placed my initials against the entry. What more was to be said? This was native custom in its purest form and although it had been harsh I could not say that justice had not been done. Much later in my life I read the words of Alexander Solzhenitsyn who said that in the western world we try to solve conflicts by the letter of the law which we consider just and proper because it is the same for all. But the letter of the law is too cold and formal to have a beneficial influence. When the tissue of life is woven of legalistic relations it degenerates into moral mediocrity. It is time, he wrote, to replace human rights with human obligations.

How perfectly did the African chiefs meet the Russian sage's objections, and how precisely did they heed his advice!

Within a short time of that first safari I began to read and understand the cases myself. The good handwriting of the clerks plus the fact that many entries were similar was a help, and certain words were often repeated. *Ngaisi*, for instance, compensation for a wrong, appeared on every page. More than that, I acquired what many other officers have claimed, namely a sixth sense in identifying difficult cases. One could run through ten, twenty or thirty cases without stopping but then come across one that seemed somehow controversial or misguided. At that point I would start asking questions.

The fact that a *gombolola* chief and his *muruka* chiefs were present during the two or three hours that the court records were being examined made it a classroom, not because they were being lectured, but rather because they were being questioned. It was just as valuable to ask why they had reached a certain verdict or taken a certain decision as it would have been to lecture them. Abstract ideas of law meant little but they had a good sense of natural justice which did not often lead them astray. As that first morning ended I signed my name in the court register and returned the book to the clerk.

Next I asked Sabairu to introduce his *muruka* chiefs and the other native government staff. I wanted to grasp in my own mind the structure of a *gombolola* which was the basic unit of government at the African level. In this *gombolola* there were eight *muruka* chiefs, each one with six hundred or more people in his area. At his headquarters Sabairu had two clerks, one a court clerk and the other to handle correspondence; also three Native Government *askaris* (police). Not under his direct control but under the Fisheries Officer was a Fish Guard, a sort of Fisheries inspector. A Medical Assistant under the doctor in Hoima was in charge of the medical dispensary.

At this point Stephen and I stood up to indicate that the morning's work was over but the chiefs seemed to expect more.

'Stephen,' I began, 'I want you to tell Sabairu and his chiefs how I look forward to this safari. I am a new officer and have much to learn. You must show me this *gombolola* in detail and spare me nothing whether it be good or bad. I have left it to Sabairu to decide the details of what we will do. He knows that I must walk along the game reserve boundary and hold formal *barazas* where people can hear what I have to say. I have also told Sabairu that I want to go out in a fishing canoe and I want to see the Murchison Falls. When I get back to Hoima in a few days I shall no longer be a beginner and you will have been my teachers.'

Their eyes had been travelling from Stephen to myself as we spoke but as we finished they broke into smiles, thanked me and gathered round. As we shook hands I remembered what Mr Amory had said a few days before. These chiefs, nearly three hundred of them in the District, despite whatever they lacked in education, were superbly good judges of character. They would sum up an officer in minutes and were rarely mistaken. They would give me a nickname, if they hadn't already, which would stay with me so long as I was in the District.

'There's one type of person they detest,' Amory had said. 'The dry-as-dust civil servant who never gets angry, never laughs, never raises his voice, never takes a risk nor gets personally involved. He's not here because he loves the life and sees some point to what he is doing; no, Africa is here to advance his career; a stepping stone to somewhere else. The chiefs will see through him immediately and they will always despise him.

'Let's say you find a chief who has been criminally negligent and his people are dying of some disease which he hasn't reported. It doesn't matter how angry you get; it doesn't matter if you lose your temper and shout at him; it doesn't even matter if you throw the man in his own prison. They will forgive you and admire you because you are passionate. They'll tolerate eccentricity and they'll swallow the occasional injustice. Even cowardice, although contemptible, is not the worst sin. The very worst is detachment, aloofness, non-involvement. The officer who is clever, cold or calculating and doesn't really care, he's the absolute rock bottom in their eyes.'

On returning to the Rest House Stephen asked me if, in future, I would accept luncheon invitations from the chiefs. Some officers had tried native food but could never accustom themselves to it, a fact that was understood and not resented. However, if I were to accept one invitation it would be better to accept them all.

'You don't have to eat everything on the table,' he said. 'There is usually chicken or fish, potatoes and *matooke* [cooked bananas]. Mr Amory always accepts invitations.'

I thought back to the sort of food served at an English boarding school and subsequently in the wartime navy and decided to accept all invitations. It turned out that I never became ill from eating their food, which I attribute to the rather less than hygienic conditions of my youth.

My lunch, on that day, was a quiet meal at the Rest House. Kazimir had everything looking clean and tidy with water for washing and a tablecloth on the table. He had opened a can of corned beef and had cooked potatoes brought from Hoima. He asked for money, calling it *rupeeya*, Indian rupees, for buying vegetables, fish and eggs, and said he would keep an account of what he spent. This all seemed very reasonable so I gave him five shillings which lasted him the full safari. I sat down in the camp chair and began writing in my notebook, a habit which was continued for many years.

One entry was: '*Mutanzige*, the local name for Lake Albert. With respect to the early explorers and their desire to honour Queen Victoria's German-born consort, I like Mutanzige (Moo-tan-zee-gay) better. It suits the place.'

Another entry: 'Asked Stephen if he were a Christian or a Moslem – he often wears a red fez but crosses himself before meals. He said he was a Christian while drinking beer but a Moslem when it came to keeping more than one wife.'

A third entry: 'One of the *muruka* chiefs told Stephen that the local troublemaker will try to embarrass me with a question about the vapour trails left by aircraft flying the Nile route. He is going to say that the white man is dropping poisonous smoke that will kill the Africans so that we can steal their land. I spoke to Stephen about it and he says that a scientific explanation about water vapour freezing at high altitude and forming ice crystals cannot be translated into Lunyoro and would sound ridiculous. There are no words for water vapour, ice or freezing. Sabairu thinks the best thing is not to give him an argument, which he is prepared for, but to turn it around and pass it back: 'Yes, but if you take all the health measures that we recommend, dig deep latrines, use mosquito nets at night and only drink clean water from the borehole you will not be affected by the smoke.'

The way *not* to answer him is to say that if what he claims is true then white people will also die. His response would be that it is a special smoke which only affects black people. The secret, evidently, is not to attempt to use logic to refute illogic. What is logic to us is not logic to him anyway.

'Local troublemaker', I soon discovered, was a recognized occupation in Bunyoro, as the professional fool had been in the Middle Ages. Some were quite perceptive and by no means were they mere nuisances. In another *gombolola* at another time I had a question put to me by a well-known practitioner and to this day I have not thought of a completely suitable reply. 'Sir,' he said, 'I have heard that white men sit upon horses and race each other for swiftness. I cannot believe they would indulge in such foolish behaviour and I am hoping you will tell me it is not true.'

There is a word for horse, *effalaasi*, although I never saw one during my time in Uganda. I replied by speaking about the cattle ranchers of western Canada and their dependence on their horses. This didn't answer the question but they found it interesting.

That afternoon we began with a visit to Bugungu's full primary school which had six classrooms and a hundred and fifty students. The headmaster, like Stephen, spoke excellent English and explained that most of his pupils would end their education there with only six years of school. The best he could do was to teach them to read and write their own language together with some simple mathematics and the rudiments of fishing and farming which would help them to fit into their little world. A very few would go to one of the secondary schools at Masindi or Hoima but these were the lucky ones like himself.

We walked into a classroom and the children stood up and stared at us. The master said he was teaching the history and geography of Bunyoro so I asked him to continue as though we had not been there. There were thirty children in front of me, alert and lively, and it was obvious that discipline was no problem since they were so attentive and well-behaved. To them school was an adventure and a delight; it was written all over their faces. It was the master who next captured my attention, his voice was theatrical and his gestures extravagant. He held the children spellbound and did no less for myself and the sober officials who were with me. What a born teacher, I thought, no wonder they love school. I wished some of my own teachers had been so eloquent.

We stepped out into the sunlight and I found myself agreeing to come back the following day to address the children and answer their questions. Sabairu said it could be fitted into our programme and that it would be of greatest interest if I should speak about my own country. In the event, I talked to them for an hour and their attention never faltered. They asked questions for another two hours. If the occasion was a success the credit must go to Stephen whose interpretation, according to Sabairu, was perfectly clear and well suited to the children's level of understanding.

Two subjects seemed to catch their imagination: our western marriage customs and our use of trained animals like sheep dogs and dogs for leading the blind. They were mesmerized by these ideas – more so than when I spoke of scientific or technical accomplishments. The idea that I had not paid a bride-price for my wife seemed to strike a very special chord and I was deluged with questions. A small boy who was sitting on the floor nearby held his hands to his face for the full three hours, not quite daring to believe what he heard. I could see his eyes moving from Stephen to myself as we spoke.

I made a note afterwards to the effect that this was the first time in my life I had spoken to a group of schoolchildren in any country. My own schooldays had given me a rather jaundiced view of the teaching profession and I held the unflattering opinion that most schoolmasters were not adventurous, observant, or even well read. My own approach to children is to treat them like grown-ups and on this occasion, I think to my surprise, I learned that I could make myself understood and rather enjoyed watching their reactions of wonderment and surprise.

During the days that followed we toured the villages of Bugungu from the lake to the escarpment, from the delta where the Nile emptied into Mutanzige to the torrent of the Weiga river. We walked through the cultivated land and saw the precautions that were being taken to combat soil erosion. We were invited into people's houses to see how they lived and we inspected their cattle, including the Mukama's herd of white, long-horned yet delicate creatures which could have stepped from the paintings of an Egyptian tomb. Every day we ate lunch with the *muruka* chief in whose area we had been touring and it took me no time to accustom myself to the food and the manner of eating. Their generosity was beyond anything and their kindness truly remarkable. They never pressed food on me that I didn't want and I never felt ill-at-ease in their company. I would have difficulty saying the same of some white people at whose tables I had sat.

At the medical dispensary I spent an hour in conversation with the medical assistant, a paramedic as we would call him in North America. He had undergone two years training in Kampala and had subsequently acquired a wealth of experience in dealing with the common maladies of tropical life. His out-patient register told it all: malaria, jiggers, yaws, snake-bite and, among the women, cases of burns, evidently from their rather haphazard cooking fires. Pulmonary problems were also common which he attributed to the fact that mothers carried their babies tied tightly to their backs so that the baby was wet from the mother's sweat. They even cultivated their gardens with the baby on their backs because in many places they were afraid that if they laid it in the grass it might be seized by a leopard. A woman had told him that a young leopard watched her from a tree as she dug her potatoes. She knew that it wanted her baby and was waiting for her to untie it and put it on the ground.

I asked him about arthritis which was so common in Europe and America but which seemed non-existent in Bunyoro. He said that he had never come across a case and had been told that Africans in the country districts did not suffer from it. There was a theory that bee stings were the antidote and the fact the Africans were often stung by bees and paid almost no attention to them provided immunity.

Before leaving we toured his little six-bed hospital and found a poor fellow who appeared to be on the point of death. The medical assistant wrung his hands and said there was nothing he could do. The patient had been in Masindi town and bought a bottle of Jeyes Fluid which he thought was cough mixture. His neighbours warned him not to drink it but he was stubborn and drank half the bottle. His condition was now beyond help and his family and friends were sitting on the floor waiting for him to die.

I turned to Stephen and reminded him of what he had said about the responsibilities of literate people in a society that was largely illiterate. Something had gone sadly wrong in this instance and I asked Sabairu, if the man should die, to investigate and report with emphasis on how it could have been prevented. Should there have been some sort of pictograph on the bottle which would have warned him?

Outside the dispensary was an old man whom Stephen introduced as Kaijumurubi, a retired bone-setter. I asked what a bone-setter was. Stephen gave me a pitying look and explained that when someone broke a bone Kaijumurubi would set it and the medical assistant would then apply the plaster cast. He had worked for many years at Mulago hospital in Kampala and was highly regarded for his skill. Sometimes he would work for a few moments on a broken bone, at other times for an hour or more pressing shattered pieces back into place. He had received no formal training but the Medical Department employed him just the same.

I made a note about the little brown dogs which were to be seen in every village. They seemed alert and intelligent but were sadly neglected by their owners and their necks often ringed by bulbous ticks which fed on their blood. How much better they would be if cared for properly. These dogs are called '*shenzies*' by the expatriates, an insulting word not unlike 'pi-dog' as applied to the miserable, half-starved Indian variety. *Shenzi*, a Swahili word, means useless, rotten, or something of the sort, and was probably coined by the Arabs who have an historical and religious aversion to dogs. But these same dogs, *shenzy* in Africa, have become '*basenjies*' when they reach the elegant dog-shows and breeding kennels of the west. A puppy that could be had for a few cents in East Africa gains all sorts of status and a price tag to match.

Who, I wonder, tacked that '*ba*' on the front, which always refers to 'people' in these languages. To call a dog *ba*-something is not merely incorrect but actually insulting to the human race which possesses sole rights to *mu* (singular) and *ba* (plural). Animals have their own class with the *n* and *m* prefix (*njojo* –elephant; *mbwa* – dog), so that if one wanted to use the *shenzi* word it should come out as *enshenzi*, or *ensenjy*.

The most exhausting day we spent at Bugungu was when we walked the western boundary of the game reserve. Subsequently the reserve was transformed into the Murchison Falls National Park and by now it must have been visited by thousands of tourists, which is as it should be, but then, in 1951, it was wild and little known. We began very early by walking southwards toward Butiaba, well away from the game reserve, to determine the track that would be taken by the access road when it came to be built. The Weiga river would have to be crossed, then the smaller Waisoke and Sonso rivers. All three had their headwaters high on the escarpment to the east and if there had been a gentle year-round flow the road and bridges would not have been unduly difficult. The rainfall, however, was seasonal with massive downpours interspersed with periods of drought. For part of the year the rivers were raging torrents and for the remainder dry gullies. The plain itself was of sand so that it was going to be difficult to anchor the bridges' abutments and even more difficult to be sure that the river would not change its course from one rainy season to the next. It was a question of risking the expenditure of government funds on a river that might alter course and abandon its bridge.

The alternative, which kept returning to my mind, was not to have a road at all but a ferry on the lake of sufficient capacity to carry passengers and their produce. Yet an all-weather road was inevitable in the long run; people would always clamour for it and sooner or later a way would have to be found. Anyway, we noted what we thought were the best places for the bridges and took some measurements of the spans required.

Next we walked inland to the boundary of the game reserve and then turned and followed it northwards. The boundary itself was marked at quarter-mile intervals with white posts stuck in the ground or white-painted tires hanging from tree branches. To our right, eastwards, was the reserve, to our left the plain of Bugungu with its scattered villages and herds of cattle. It seemed astonishing that so many wild animals could live in such close proximity to mankind and I was thrilled at the spectacle that unfolded as we moved northwards. Most surprising was the fact that the game animals seemed to have a sense of where the boundary was located and if they found themselves to the west at our approach they moved eastwards and watched us pass from a place of safety.

There were elephants which were spread out at this time of year, not in large herds, browsing and fanning themselves with their huge ears. Quite rightly they fascinate modern man by the sheer improbability of their size and prehistoric appearance. People can watch their gray shapes for hours, binoculars glued to their eyes, and the better one gets to understand them the more interesting they become. Buffalo were also to be seen in herds of about a hundred animals, black and antagonistic, seeming to be the very antithesis of friendliness. Their horns leave little room for the ears, which flop downwards like those of certain dogs.

There were many other species, the woolly-looking waterbuck, kob, like heavyweight impalas, each male defending its selected territory, topi and kongoni with their looks of perpetual surprise, and warthog, those least beautiful of creatures with their spiky tails held aloft like radio aerials. At one point the guides came upon a small pride of lions which had been resting under an acacia tree but went grumbling off at our approach.

Bird life was so abundant that I can do no more than list some of the varieties we saw: vultures descending like dive-bombers intent on cleaning up after a kill; guinea fowls rattling and clucking; a honey bird frantic in its desire to lead us to a bee's nest; and a great bateleur eagle swinging easily across the hot plain.

Toward evening, as we approached the Nile, the plain gave way to more broken country. We were tired by this time, having been walking since dawn and having covered a distance of just over thirty miles, but the sight of the spray rising above the falls in the evening air quickly revived us. The government launch had sailed round in mid-afternoon with the safari equipment and we found Kazimir and half a dozen of Sabairu's men with the camp ready in a small meadow.

I stood on a rock and watched the falls until it was too dark to see. The uniqueness of the Murchison is not that the water falls a great distance nor even that it is of great size but rather that it never appears quite the same for two consecutive moments. The water gushes through a cleft, scarcely twenty feet across, more like a jet than a fall, then boils downward over the rocks to the pools below. It was that jet of water that was fascinating, an entire river constricted between rocks that one might almost jump across.

In camp I found that Kazimir had pitched my small tent and had hot water ready for the canvas bath. Sabairu and Stephen were tired, perhaps more so than I was, but not the half dozen men who had accompanied us as guides and porters. A huge fire had been lit on high ground to ward off animals and a smaller one on which they were cooking their supper. It was beside the smaller one that they sat laughing and joking about the day's activities.

One of their favourite forms of humour was to mimic the animals as to the noises they made, their movements and facial expressions. It was an innocent form of humour which often produced gales of laughter and I wondered if it would be possible to use some variant of it when talking to the villagers and answering questions. Could one say 'as lazy as a hippopotamus' or 'as inquisitive as a colobus monkey'? Would they accept it or regard it as an invasion of their own private way of looking at the world? Stephen would know and I would have to ask his advice.

I slept that night with the muted roar of the Murchison Falls not a hundred yards distant. It drowned out the sounds of the night, the idiotic laughter of the hyenas, the grunting of the lions and the assorted shrieks and whistles of the African bush. Thousands of animals came to the Nile to drink but would be warned off our little meadow by the sight and smell of fire. In the morning it was still burning and Kazimir boiled the kettle without adding more wood.

The return journey to Bugungu was undertaken at a leisurely pace in the government launch. It was fifteen miles to where the river opened out into the lake, fifteen miles of hippo and crocodile, elephants and every game animal imaginable, including a lone rhinoceros. The profusion and elegance of life along that stretch of water must have been what Africa had been like a hundred years before, a panorama like the very fingerprint of God. Here was nature subtle in its interrelatedness, lavish beyond comprehension.

The hippo alone were present in their thousands. These two-ton caricatures of some vast prehistoric pig had spent the night feeding on shore, each animal stuffing its huge frame with up to two hundred pounds of green food. At daybreak they returned to the water on their short dachshund-like legs and would spend the day basking and snorting in the river. When defecating they wagged their tails violently so that it was spread in the water, hundreds of tons of it, which meant that any body of water which they inhabited became a fertile field capable of sustaining a huge ecological chain of life. Even the grainfields of Egypt, almost four thousand miles northward, benefited when the river flooded and deposited a film of silt and hippo manure as its annual gift of fertility. The ancient Greeks bestowed the name hippopotamus, meaning river horse, but the Egyptians, one of whose characteristics was their fascination with animals, called it the river hog which is a more accurate description.

Hippo society is female-dominated with herds of cows and calves occupying the most desirable stretches of river. The old males live in solitary banishment away from the herds and are the most dangerous to the fishermen. They will occasionally attack a canoe without provocation, their technique being to come up beneath it and lift it almost clear of the water, then bite it with their huge jaws. Their tusks, which are of an exceedingly hard ivory and often weigh about ten pounds, were used at one time for the manufacture of artificial human teeth. In the cathedral of the little town of Pavia in northern Italy a few miles south of Milan, there is a carved altar covering of hippo ivory. One is left wondering where the artist obtained his material and why he should have chosen hippo ivory in favour of the softer and more easily obtainable elephant ivory.

We spent the following day at Ndandamire, the northernmost *muruka* which we had passed on our return from the Murchison. It was hot and the soil infertile but most of the inhabitants were fishermen who seemed to be making a good living. Many of the houses had corrugated iron roofs, bicycles were much in evidence and the women wore bright coloured clothes.

One of the local councillors was a woman, a person of decided views who questioned me closely about the restrictions imposed by the Department of Fisheries. The nets the fishermen used were made of nylon and the smallest size allowed was four inches. This was measured by grasping opposite corners of the mesh and pulling them apart until the square had become a straight line. With this size of mesh a one-pound fish would be trapped by catching its gills in the soft nylon while smaller fish would escape. Nylon nets were new at that time and were credited with much greater catches of fish than the older hemp or cotton, due, it was said, to its softness in the water and the fact that the fish did not feel it until it was too late to extricate themselves. A smaller mesh size would have taken less mature fish which the Department was anxious to avoid.

The woman councillor insisted that taking immature fish would not deplete the quantities of fish in the lake and as proof she said that although wars are fought there was no reduction of the human population. I replied that I found her reasoning difficult to follow. In many parts of Europe where the war had been particularly savage whole villages were deserted, houses empty and fields neglected. The people who had died would not return to life and the countries in which they had lived would be the poorer for their absence. It would take many years for others to come and establish themselves and raise children. The Fisheries Department, I told her, had experience which extended far beyond the fisheries at Ndandamire. Fish were caught in lakes and rivers and in great oceans of salt water and there was no question but that fish stocks became depleted by over-fishing and by the catching of immature fish. One of the many duties of the Fisheries Department was to apply its knowledge of other fisheries and not allow the mistakes that had been made elsewhere to be made again.

'Your greatest gift to your children and grandchildren,' I said, 'will be Lake Mutanzige full of fish, not empty and lifeless.'

'You say that there are oceans of salty water,' she replied, 'But that cannot be because no fish could live in them.'

I often wondered at our policy of encouraging people to speak up, criticize and ask for what they wanted. As long as we white men were there criticism was admirable, it was seen as political sophistication, but what would happen when our backs were turned and the likes of Idi Amin took our places? Then it would become subversive and dissident to criticize, a disloyal assault against the government in power. What had earned merit badges with us would earn a bullet and a shallow grave with our political successors.

That evening, setting off from Ndandamire, I went out on the lake with Sabairu and his two sons. We paddled the heavy canoe a mile or two northwards into the estuary, then turned east to follow one of the many channels where the water still bubbled and foamed after its wild escapade at the Murchison Falls. A brilliant moon illuminated the surface of the water with its little floating plants. The dark walls of papyrus which flanked the channel were impenetrable and forbidding. Occasionally a pelican or giant heron would sweep past the canoe, or a shoebill atop the papyrus would solemnly observe us pass.

The night air contained a thousand sounds, from the heavy grunt of the hippopotamus to the incessant drumming of frogs. A crocodile on the bank would cough while the mosquitoes whined like chain saws. It was reminiscent of a crowded theatre as the lights were dimmed and the musicians tuned up their instruments. In the middle of it all was the heavy dugout canoe and the four of us toiling at the paddles.

The two young men had set their nets the night before and now found their way with pinpoint accuracy and hauled them in. The *tilapia nilotica* (*ngege* fish) were neatly secured by the gills, unable to move forwards or backwards and had to be dislodged by hand and thrown in the bottom of the canoe. One of the nets had been torn by a crocodile, a fact which was greeted by gentle whistles of disapproval from Sabairu and his sons. The Lunyoro language contains no real swear words or blasphemies and only mild expletives, which I thought was much to its credit. When we turned down river a little before midnight there was more than a ton of fish in the boat.

My respect for Sabairu had grown as I saw him in his own surroundings and came to know him better. He was a man of character and energy whose lack of book learning never seemed to act as a disadvantage or cause him any loss of respect. His word was law to the people of Bugungu but it was not a capricious law because he wedded it so intimately with the problem at hand. That day I had heard him refuse tax exemption because the man had a marriageable daughter for whom he would soon receive a bride-price. 'Pay your taxes,' he said, 'when you receive a bride-price. For a long time you have eaten and drunk every shilling you gained and now you cannot even pay a small goat to your country. As soon as the girl is married and a bride-price paid you must come and report to me.'

The surprising thing was that the chiefs rarely, if ever, met with hostility from their people. They broke up fights, arrested thieves and gave orders for communal work to be done; they were the subalterns and non-commissioned officers of African life, the agents of progress and, most important, the representatives of the Mukama. It was a system of government which had worked for centuries and continued to work, not with the harshness of former years but with modern touches such as elected councils in each *gombolola*.

Sabairu turned and asked, '*Eshaha, sebo*?'

Eshaha meant the hour, or time: twelve-thirty by my watch. Time was calculated as it had been in the Bible, in two twelve-hour episodes, beginning with dawn or dusk. In biblical times it had always been 'about the third hour' because they had no timepieces and it was only a rough calculation based on the position of the sun. At night the calculation was even rougher. A little rapid arithmetic showed that twelve-thirty was five and a half hours past sunset so I replied: 'Five and a half hours of the night.'

We returned to Ndandamire where my tent had been pitched some way back from the lake and Kazimir had lit a fire. A dozen willing hands helped us out of the canoe and the two young men went to work cleaning the catch. I stumbled off to my tent and as I fell asleep I realized that I could hear drumming from the Congo, perhaps to confirm that fish buying would take place at daybreak. I wrote 'hear', but hearing is not quite the word because the sound seems to penetrate the mind without really being heard.

At each *muruka* we visited on this safari there had been a formal *baraza* or meeting. The *muruka* chiefs did not have meeting halls so they were convened under shady trees and were open to all who cared to come. The *gombolola* chief, Sabairu, would begin by introducing me and I would then stand up with Stephen and talk for twenty minutes or half an hour. I knew that some officers did not give detailed consideration to what they would talk about or how they would express themselves. The Banyoro, however, liked a good speech, and I was sure that the more care I took the greater the chance of creating the right impression and ultimately of achieving real improvements. I always discussed with Stephen beforehand what I would say and asked his advice as to how best to express it. The rules I developed were these:

1. Be formal, respectful and grateful. The casual, folksy approach so beloved of North Americans did not go down well in Bunyoro. These people thought of themselves as aristocrats, not country bumpkins.
2. Turn your remarks around what has been seen in the villages, whether good or bad, and don't be afraid to mention names. 'Daudi Kituntu has a very productive field of cotton. He has taken trouble to prevent soil erosion and his farm prospers.'
3. Bring in at least one item of news from outside Bugungu. 'His Highness the Mukama would prefer it if the Banyoro were to buy all your fish but, as you know, the roads are not yet good enough to carry the catch to markets in Masindi and Hoima.'
4. Don't be a jackass politician and make promises that can't be kept. Of course they want a first class road, a higher price for their fish, a secondary school, a twenty-foot high fence to keep the animals out and they are right to want them but the finances of Bunyoro are like those of a family – your family or mine. We cannot spend money we don't have.

On my final day at Bugungu a formal *baraza* was held at the *gombolola* headquarters which lasted most of the day. It was attended by over five hundred people which brought to at least two thousand the total number to whom I had spoken during the week. The Banyoro enjoy nothing more than a day of talk followed by a night of beer drinking and dancing. Talk is taken with earnestness and self-importance and while there may be humour the proceedings must never be permitted to degenerate into farce. When answering questions I learned to avoid the smart answer, the put-down, the impatient reply that teaches nothing. To that hardy perennial question: 'Why does not the Native Government print its own money instead of collecting taxes?' I first complimented the questioner and then used it to go into a good deal of detail about the District's finances.

If the *baraza* was something of an endurance test I was at least complying with Amory's second dictum, namely, that all complaints should be listened to patiently and answered reasonably. This was not to say that my answers were not brutally honest but the main thing was to listen and hear them out. 'Could they have a hospital with doctors and nurses? A modern boat-building workshop with trained instructors? A wire fence along the game reserve boundary that would be strong enough to keep elephants out?' No, I saw no prospect for any of these things within the foreseeable future yet inwardly I sympathized and if unlimited funds had been available I would have recommended all of them.

It was during these *barazas*, both the formal affair at Sabairu's headquarters and the more relaxed ones under the trees at the *muruka* headquarters, that some lingering doubts were set to rest in my own mind. I had not, up to that point, fully answered the question as to what I was doing in Africa and whether I had right or reason to be there at all. Then I saw their poverty, their misdirection and their need of help and encouragement. I saw the harshness of their lives, the dangers of disease, fire and wild animals, and the cheerfulness with which they faced the world. So much could be accomplished in small ways: better agricultural methods; food and cash crops; better health by improved houses and hygiene; better education; proper conservation of natural resources. What would they do if left to themselves?

There is no need to answer that question because history has answered it for me but I knew then that I was committed. There was a task there of colossal proportions.

6

The White Community

The question we were often asked on our return to Canada was how we had lived in Uganda and with whom we had been friends. To recount the way we lived is fairly straightforward, but speaking of our friends is more complex because they were not of our own choosing but simply the result of finding ourselves among a dozen white people, 'Europeans' as we were called, surrounded and outnumbered ten thousand to one by the African population. We were thrown together rather like travellers who find themselves in the same ship or aircraft. Our destinations were all pretty much the same but there was not always agreement as to the route to be followed. In such a group, where personalities were often writ in large letters, we found that we either made friends easily or not at all.

To begin with the house where we lived. It was a government-owned house, the only one vacant at that moment and was located conveniently close to the District office. As Mr Amory explained, however, it had been condemned as uninhabitable a few years before and had been written off the Public Works Department books. This created a problem because if it did not officially exist he could not devote any government money to having it repaired. I spent the first night in the visitors' Rest House and in the morning, when the Public Works Department clerk had been found and had located the key, we opened the creaking door and looked in.

The location and the magnificent old jacaranda tree in the garden were clearly offset by a number of disadvantages. There was a massive ant-hill in the living room and a snake of moderate proportions in the roof, both of which caught my attention at first glance. A few moments later I discovered that the kitchen, which was an outhouse at the back, had no stove and the bathtub no taps. The whole house, which consisted of a living room, bedroom, bathroom and store, was dirty and run-down. At this point Mr Amory appeared and having peered inside and sized up the situation announced, 'Well, that's Africa for you.'

We walked back to the office and Amory, wishing, apparently, to appear bold and resourceful said that three or four labourers from the township work force might be spared for cleaning up and the petty cash could be raided for a couple of gallons of whitewash. Not to be outdone in largesse the Public Works Department clerk thought he knew where some old government furniture could be found, plus a kitchen stove.

I had heard a good deal about Mr Amory, District Commissioner, before I left Kampala. The overall impression was that he was well-intentioned but that details seemed to elude him. In the months ahead I discovered that he was far more complex than this. He was in his forties and had considerable experience in Africa. Physically a large man, one would have guessed that he had been an athlete in his youth and that rugger had been his best game. To borrow a phrase from North American football, he had the 'middle linebacker' look about him. His manner was jovial and straightforward, characteristic of a schoolmaster accustomed to dealing with boys. He seemed to regret that he had missed both world wars and felt in consequence that he could not hold his head quite so high. He had been too young for the first and was rejected for the second on the grounds that his work in Africa was essential to the war effort because East Africa comprised a vast reserve of manpower. Inwardly I think he was jealous of the younger ones, like myself, who had been privileged to wear our country's uniform.

His handling of the situation relating to my house was Amory at his most incomprehensible. He had known I was coming and could easily have had the place cleaned up if he had put his mind to it. Perhaps he thought I should be taught a lesson about Africa. In any event Hassan, the township headman, appeared with four men and in a couple of days it was clean enough to move in. The Public Works Department clerk found some basic furniture and a wood stove and he installed two taps on the bath, both of which said HOT, only one said it in larger letters than the other. Until the fire had been lit beneath a forty-gallon drum of water out in the garden the water they both produced was cold.

I have always held the view that one can often learn as much when things are done badly as when they are done well. The ships in which I served at various times during the war years were captained by officers who were superlative individuals and a credit to their profession, but I didn't appreciate just how good they were, or what exactly they were doing so well until a ship came alongside in which everything habitually went wrong. It was described as an unlucky ship and the officers made all sorts of excuses but the fault was bad organization and lack of discipline. Where the house was concerned, while it was perhaps a trivial matter, it created a negative first impression. If it had been ready for me I could have unpacked in a couple of hours and started work in the office the day following. As it was I had to unload my rented vehicle at the Rest House, store my kit while the house was being cleaned up and then move again a couple of days later. The Public Works Department furniture did not arrive for a week so I slept on a camp bed until it came. A little forethought and a word spoken to Hassan and the Public Works Department employee would not have changed the fact that it was an unsatisfactory house, but would have created a far better impression.

I determined that if ever I found myself in his position I would not make the same mistake and went a step further and asked myself what a District Commissioner's wife might do in such circumstances. Could the lady not have shown some interest, gone to the house and made sure that the cleaning process was being carried out? Later, when I found myself in the more exalted position of being in charge of a District, my wife Jean did more than merely supervise the cleaning of a house when new arrivals were expected. She took her own team of servants, all the necessary materials, cleaned and aired the house until it met her standard, then put food in the larder and flowers on the table. If the new arrivals were just out from England she lined up servants and went through their letters of reference.

Another lesson which I learned from this incident was that when moving anywhere in Africa the basic household cleaning materials should be in a box by themselves. Buckets, scrubbers, broom, window cleaner, soap, detergent and plenty of clean rags should be within reach. People can't work with their bare hands and they can't work in the dark either and Africa becomes dark at seven o'clock in the evening. A box containing lamps and kerosene should always be at hand.

My first piece of business was to employ servants and within half an hour the dozen or so who had presented themselves at the office were reduced to three. Aberi, a corruption of the name Abel, became my head boy. He was about fifty years of age, quiet and well-mannered and I knew that Jean would like him. He had no trouble understanding my Luganda, having worked for Mr 'Pilli-Pilli' Robertson for many years and seen a good deal of the rest of Uganda.

'Pilli-Pilli' is a nickname meaning peppery, or something of the sort, and Mr Robertson, who retired at the war's end, was never called anything else by Africans or Europeans. I was told a story about him which gives an idea of the kind of man he was. On safari at Butiaba on Lake Albert he went out early one morning to fish from the government motor launch. He was trying for a Nile perch, called *mputa* in Uganda, but he used tackle that was appropriate for salmon fishing in Scotland. He hooked one just outside the harbour entrance but could not put much pressure on it or he would have broken the line. The battle lasted twelve hours, sunup to sundown, in great heat and with blinding glare from the water. As it grew dark the fish came up and the boatman secured it with a rope through the gills. There is a store in Butiaba with a weigh-scale and the fish was duly carried there by some people who had gathered on the jetty. It weighed two hundred and two pounds, which stood as a record for many years. Pilli-Pilli, a very strong man, collapsed from fatigue.

The cook I engaged was Kazimir, not an uncommon name in Uganda where the names of saints and martyrs are pressed into service at the urging of the missionaries. His letters of reference announced him as 'a plain cook, very willing and capable of doing the marketing,' which sounded promising enough. Finally there was

Heneriko (Henry), the gardener, whose duties would include lighting fires and being generally useful.

All three lived nearby, which was important because the house had no servants' quarters. They would come in the morning at seven and worked through till lunchtime, after which they would be free until supper. Immediately after hiring them I sent them to an Indian shop, Hassanalli's, where they were measured for their uniforms, white for Aberi and Kazimir, khaki for Henriko. Besides two pairs of shorts and shirts for working, Aberi was also fitted with a long white *kanzu*, a sort of ankle-length outfit resembling the gown worn by the clergyman's assistant in church. With a broad coloured belt and a red fez he would add some dignity to the proceedings at mealtimes.

More important, I sent the three of them to Hoima's little hospital with the request that they be physically examined. Many Europeans failed to take this rather obvious precaution thereby adding another element of uncertainty to their lives. Much later in my service in Uganda I took on a servant but before he began work sent him for medical examination. A note came back from the doctor saying that he had an advanced case of venereal disease and that on no account should we employ him. A few weeks later I recognized him working in the house of a young officer and his wife who had three small children. On being informed they sacked him on the spot.

Looking back it might seem that for a young couple like ourselves three servants were unnecessary. However, a few weeks later we took on a fourth and at some point after that an *ayah* (nursemaid) to help with the baby. It must be remembered that without electricity and without running water, not to mention the temperamental wood stove in the kitchen, a western woman simply could not cope with the house. To do any washing, for instance, a fire had to be lit under the water tank which first had to be filled from the roof tanks. In the dry season when the tanks were empty water had to be brought by hand from the borehole. Water being a valuable commodity the roof tanks were kept padlocked. Having heated the water, which also served the bathroom, the clothes would be washed in a tub, rinsed and put out to dry. Ironing was done under a tree in the back garden with a large charcoal iron which was heavy and difficult to handle.

The kitchen was dominated by a stove that smoked like some ships at sea and needed constant attention. The kerosene lamps and refrigerator also had to be cleaned and trimmed on a daily basis, and all the things that people in the west take for granted: plugging in an electric kettle; dropping bread in the toaster; using an electric shaver or any one of a dozen kitchen gadgets, had to be done in a far more painstaking and inefficient manner.

Our servants were well paid by local standards, Aberi receiving the same salary as was paid by the Native Government to its *muruka* chiefs. The others got slightly less. They were kept reasonably busy and they looked after us well. Some Europeans complained endlessly about their servants but we had nothing but praise for ours.

Anyway, I was able to move into my little house within two or three days of my arrival. I worked thereafter to make small improvements and kept a list of the things that would have to be purchased on my first shopping trip to Kampala. When Jean arrived three weeks later the place was looking considerably better than when I had first walked through the door. By that time Mr Amory had learned that Major Wyndham, the game warden, was to be posted to another District and would not be replaced. He occupied a brand-new house higher up the hill which was promised to us when he moved.

When Jean arrived we decided to employ someone who would accompany me on safari and make himself useful around the house when I was in Hoima. Exactly how he came into our employment I cannot recall, but somehow Georgi found his way onto the payroll. In all probability he was one of Aberi's relatives. The surprising thing about him was that although he had never worked for a white man he possessed a lexicon of words and mannerisms that seemed to have been copied from an English butler. He was given to flourishes and fine gestures with overtones of pomposity: the archetypal African Jeeves. I think he longed to be a courtier but couldn't find a king and had to make do with us. When told to do something perfectly simple he bowed gravely and when asked a question he replied as though he were the Lord Chancellor.

Georgi, like so many Africans, imagined himself a godsend to the cooking profession. One day I returned to camp at lunch time, hot, tired and hungry and sat down at my camp table. With a flourish he placed mashed potatoes in front of me and poured custard all over them.

He was also very concerned with the minor proprieties of life, correct dress being a fetish. One evening Mr Amory came to our house on a matter of urgency and I emerged from the bathroom wearing only a towel. A moment later Georgi appeared with a dressing gown which he held while I put it on. Once the cord was tied he stood back and surveyed me and his expression changed from one of faint disapproval to something closer to bemused tolerance.

He could also be infuriating. On safari I heard him berating a couple of men, older than himself, who had been sent by the chief with firewood and water for our camp. I didn't understand all that was said but it was his tone that caught my attention.

'Georgi,' I said, taking him aside, 'you can't talk down to these people. What makes you so much better than they are?'

'Because I have shoes on and am better dressed,' was his reply.

There were occasions, however, when he redeemed himself, such as when we had guests for a buffet supper. He stood behind the table, helped them fill up their plates and explained what the various dishes contained. At a mixed party of Europeans, Asians and Africans with differing dietary observancies this was an important task and he always did it well.

Another thing that redeemed him was his sense of humour. One evening I arrived at a *gombolola* headquarters, unpacked the Landrover and began to set up camp. Georgi appeared at my side, cleared his throat and announced that the *gombolola* chief was approaching. I straightened up from my task and went to the doorway to find the chief, a rather fat man, dragging a reluctant sheep across the grass in our direction. The sheep was plainly intended as a gift, but it was excessive, only governors qualified for whole sheep, not junior officers; for me a few eggs or some fruit would have been quite enough. Georgi caught the situation perfectly.

'I imagine you will wish to check his books rather carefully,' he said in an undertone, clearly implying that the chief had done something wrong.

The European quarters in Hoima consisted of eight bungalows set within their own gardens on a small hill, the District Commissioner's house being located, appropriately, at the summit. Just below, in a circle, were the houses occupied by Major Wyndham, the game warden; Warren Thorpe and his wife Rachel, he being in charge of Co-operative Societies which were numerous in Bunyoro; and Henry Berunga, the Agricultural Officer. Henry, a Munyoro himself, had been trained in the United Kingdom and was qualified as an agricultural officer. Next to Henry's house was the young English doctor, a bachelor, whose full title was District Medical Officer of Health. Doctors do not normally have a pious reputation but our doctor was a born-again Christian of a persuasion which in Uganda was known as Balokoli. He was attentive to his medical duties and one could not have wished for a more devoted doctor but he also found time to attend every prayer meeting held for miles around. I was invited to one of these but having been warned by Amory I made my excuses. Amory had said that the doctor possessed an astounding knowledge of the Bible which he liked to show off to anyone who would listen.

I reflected that this was the second time that I had found myself in a small community with a doctor. In a wartime destroyer there had been a surgeon-lieutenant among the ten officers in the wardroom whose problem had becn that the minor injuries suffered by two hundred and fifty men gave him hardly any work to do. Indeed, they were potentially the healthiest body of men to be found anywhere because they almost never came in contact with disease and so the doctor's dilemma was to find enough work to do. For a District Medical Officer in an underdeveloped country it was just the reverse. We had only two qualified doctors in a District of 150,000, the other being in Masindi in the north of the District. In some Districts there were mission doctors, but not in Bunyoro, so he was alone at the small Hoima hospital without even a trained nurse.

Many of Uganda's younger doctors had elected to do their two years' National Service in an underdeveloped country rather than in the armed forces. Most were just out of medical school and were none too pleased by the situation they found and the conditions in which they had to work. As our doctor pointed out, the basic research had been so negligible that he was treating patients for diseases that didn't even have names, never mind an approved treatment. One day I went to his office feeling suddenly feverish and weak. He poked and prodded for a minute, gave me some pills and told me to go to bed.

'By the way,' I said as I left, 'what's the matter with me?'

'I don't have the faintest idea,' he replied.

Two other houses were occupied by the two women officers, Miss King, Education Officer, and Miss Hastings, Community Development. This latter was a fairly new idea in Uganda and I think the incumbent, a most dedicated person, was still feeling her way. The idea of Community Development was to get into the villages with a small staff of African assistants and help the people in practical ways. Miss Hastings tended, quite naturally, to concentrate on the women because that was where she felt the need was greatest. She said that until she came to Africa she had imagined that women, whatever their colour, would automatically know certain things such as how to pick up a baby, but that nothing could have been farther from the truth. Banyoro mothers would grab the baby by an arm as a monkey would do and dislocate the arm; she had seen this many times. Head injuries to babies were also common. The women were careless and allowed the babies' heads to get bumped.

Her biggest problem, however, was teaching the mothers to feed their children. Traditionally the Banyoro weaned their babies far too late, sometimes at the age of two or three years. When the milk dried or when another baby came along the infant would be given adult food which it could not digest. They had no idea how to cut up or soften food or cook it in goats' milk in a suitable manner. Sometimes she found that a village had milk, tomatoes, oranges and a good variety of vegetables but none of it was reaching the children because no one knew how to prepare it. It was common for children to die just after being weaned because of this ignorance and yet, she said, the older villagers resented her presence and thought that her work was offensive to their tribal customs.

My house at the foot of the hill was the eighth. It was the oldest, the smallest and the least desirable, but since I was the latest arrival in Hoima I could scarcely complain. A ninth house, situated near the police station, was specifically assigned to the police inspector and did not come under the District Commissioner's authority. The others he could assign at will and no house was the property of a department or individual. We paid 'economic rent' which was very low and which I did not pay since my house had been written off and one could scarcely pay rent on a house that didn't exist.

It was always said that the first thing that two or three expatriates would do when they reached Africa was build a club. Strangely, however, Hoima did not have one and it must have been the only up-country headquarters in Uganda without. A club would have been the focal point for officers to meet for an hour in the evenings to exchange news before going home to bath and supper. It would have been the obvious place after a game of tennis and a good spot for people visiting the District to meet the officers informally. The only person whom it would not have suited was the doctor, who was an aggressive teetotaller. Erik Andersen, on the other hand, our water driller, would have made excellent use of it. He came in at weekends from wherever he was drilling and stayed in the Rest House, and would have enjoyed a club where he could pay for his share of the drinks and talk to other white people.

I myself am not an avid club person, preferring my own house and family in the evenings, although I was well aware that Hoima lacked the focal point that a club would have provided. Unofficial information didn't always circulate and the team spirit among the officers left room for improvement. My recommendation was that my own house be converted to a club as soon as we moved out, but nothing came of the idea.

I have never resolved my ambivalent attitude toward up-country clubs. At best the club would organize the sporting and social life of the station, draw people together and allow them to exchange useful ideas. At worst it was a drinking den where bored misfits could complain endlessly of the heat, the lack of facilities and the bloody Africans. There were always a few Europeans who spent every evening, all weekend and probably more money than they could afford in the club.

The question of membership was always hotly debated. Aside from the expatriates, should Africans and Asians be included in club membership and, if so, who? If there had been a club in Hoima,

Henry Berunga would presumably have been invited to join because he was a fully qualified government officer. The Mukama would have been asked to become patron, or permanent president, or something of the kind, but what about his senior officials, the Chief Accepter of Bribes, the Handkerchief and the Keeper of the Royal Tombs? Their wives, many of whom could not speak English, would have compounded the problem. As an alternative, should African membership be restricted to those who had some chance of joining club activities, which means they must be able to speak English and possess a bit of education. In a country heading toward self-government and preaching a policy that Africans must become involved in all aspects of their own future, a lot of difficult decisions would have to be made. A certain type of political African could not be appeased whatever was decided and up-country clubs were an easy target for such people's attacks.

My favourite club story was from Fort Portal which had some non-government Europeans living in the vicinity, all of whom were members of the local club. An elderly man with a red face and white hair who had practically taken root by the bar confided to Jean and myself that this was the finest club in East Africa. We looked round at the bare walls, rickety furniture and bar that wasn't level.

'How so?'

He gave me a triumphant look. 'During the earthquake no one spilled his drink.'

Bunyoro at that time was part of Uganda's Western Province which included, besides Bunyoro, the Districts of Toro, Ankole and Kigezi. The provincial headquarters was at Fort Portal where the organization included a Provincial Commissioner and a complete set of officers at the provincial level who were supposed to supervise their specialist staff in the four Districts. Only the Game and Fisheries Department had no provincial representative and supervised its officers directly from Entebbe. It was a top-heavy system, wasteful of staff and questionable in another sense because individual officers in the Districts tended to divide their loyalties between the District Commissioner and the provincial specialist. The average officer had enough loyalties to contend with if he devoted himself primarily to his District and its people, with a secondary loyalty to the central government which paid him and issued the broad policies outlining his work. To add another layer of government, the Province, was too much supervision, particularly at a time when communication between the central government and Districts was rapid and efficient. Worse than this, the Province could be a divisive influence because it enabled officers to play off their District Commissioner against the provincial specialist. Anyway, a few years later the whole provincial organization was abolished and the fifteen Districts were, from then on, administered directly from Entebbe.

So there we were, a small and not very select group of expatriates, plus Henry Berunga the Munyoro, trying to work through the Native Government to improve the quality of life of a hundred and fifty thousand Banyoro. Warren Thorpe tried to get them to form co-operative societies, to undertake in groups what they could never achieve individually. Inspector Frisby had more murders in any one year than the police had in the whole of London, England, and an outlaw whom he couldn't catch. Miss Hastings had about thirty thousand women of childbearing age who didn't know how to pick up their babies or feed them. The doctor had to treat diseases that didn't have names. Miss King had to organize education when there were not enough schools or teachers. Major Wyndham had to keep thousands of elephant and buffalo out of people's cultivated land and put a stop to cruel methods of snaring game with wires and traps. Henry Berunga's job was to get the Banyoro, who thought of themselves as cattle owners and aristocrats, to take farming seriously and cultivate the soil. My job was to get into the villages and ensure that the chiefs were administering their areas in an honest and humane manner, that law and order was maintained, taxes collected and money accounted for. In addition I had court work to do and I had to keep Hoima town clean, tidy and an example to all. Finally, Mr Amory had to co-ordinate everyone else's efforts, know what was going on and transform the antiquated Native Government into an efficient, modern administration. Besides this he had to represent the Governor, explain policy, carry the responsibility when things went wrong and prevent the Mukama from doing anything particularly outrageous.

One thing we shared was a feeling that we were privileged to be doing that very work on which we were engaged. It was a serious, life-and-death struggle with nothing frivolous about it. Later, when I joined the Canadian Public Service, I realized that the low morale was a consequence of public servants having work that was trivial and uninteresting and which, in many cases, did not need to be done. The pettiness of the challenge produced a pettiness of response so that people became consumed with trivia – the hours of work, the coffee breaks, the overtime. I heard that a fairly senior and well paid officer in the Treasury Board had spent two years writing a policy paper on the subject of who pays for the coffee served at government conferences. In Bunyoro I never once heard the word 'overtime' used in the government although everyone worked longer than the standard hours. Coffee breaks or tea breaks just didn't happen because we had enough stamina and interest in the work to last from breakfast to lunch without them. Nor did I ever hear anyone discussing their pay and allowances; to have done so would have been thought of as bad manners.

It would be wrong to think that our little group was invariably harmonious and there were no differences of opinion. However, at the end of the day nothing prevented us from playing tennis, entertaining each other to dinner and helping in small ways. Whenever someone went down to Lake Albert it was understood that he or she would bring back fresh fish for everyone else and when the game ranger shot a buffalo there was supposed to be a distribution of fresh meat. Anyone driving down to Kampala was expected to go shopping for the others.

Living in a small community was hard on some people. To anyone who had served in the war, as both Wyndham and I had, it came fairly easily, but it was more of a strain to those who had not been in a military service and had no experience of being thrown in with people whom they might not have chosen as friends.

A few of the expatriates we met in Uganda were there because they had not been able to solve their personal problems at home. Much later, when I was in the Public Service Commission of Canada selecting people for duties in the far north we were doubly cautious about this kind of person. If they could not solve personal conflicts in Toronto, or wherever it was, the chances of their doing so in a small northern community were less. The strain of life in the north and the hardships were an unfair burden on people who were contending with emotional difficulties.

Looking back I must say that the selection process used by the British Civil Service Commission for staffing in Africa seemed in need of overhaul. My own interview and medical examination, carried out in Canada on behalf of the Colonial Service, was amateurish. The questions they asked me came close to being foolish and it was obvious to me, the candidate, that the board itself was not agreed as to what constituted acceptable answers. Later in my service in Africa, when I had charge of a District, officers arrived who openly expressed their dislike of the Africans. Bad enough were the ones who were merely lazy or indifferent but it seemed incredible that those who disliked being there at all had passed through all the stages of selection and been appointed. Thankfully such people were few in number.

In Canada the Public Service Commission took infinite trouble to match a candidate to a job. There would be background checks and the candidates would be asked to provide detailed curricula vitae which would be followed up in detail. There were often written tests, examples of work were asked for, sometimes wives were asked to accompany their husbands, or vice versa. The heart of the selection process, however, is the personal interview which, when conducted by experienced interviewers, is a more subtle and revealing process than outsiders can imagine. The candidates who tried to bullshit never stood a chance, the ones with gaps in their experience or knowledge would be exposed immediately. Some managers claimed to have intuition where the selection process was concerned but the best interviewers didn't need intuition because there were more reliable ways of revealing the facts.

It is tempting to point a finger of scorn at the British Civil Service Commission in relation to its more notable lapses. How on earth could the famous traitors of the 1930s have got in the door if the selection for those sensitive posts had been working even moderately well? My own feeling was that by the 1950s the selection process for sending candidates to Africa was not much improved. If only one in twenty who arrived in Uganda had been a misfit it was still too many.

7

Mulisi Alideki

A favourite story told about Mulisi Alideki was that he shot an elephant that had lost its tail. Mulisi had been a game guard in Uganda's Game Department, known formerly as the Department of Elephant Control. He had shot hundreds of elephants and buffalo in the early days when cultivated land was being expanded, and he was one of the Department's most trusted hunters. One day he shot a bull elephant that was on the rampage in a banana garden but when he went to cut off the tail he found that someone else had been there ahead of him. The game guards always took the tails of animals as proof that they had shot them. At the end of the month they would pedal to Hoima on their bicycles, lay out their collection of tails on the grass, present their rifles to the District Commissioner for inspection, collect their pay and pick up a fresh supply of ammunition.

'How did it lose its tail?' asked the District Commissioner, who had been one of Amory's predecessors.

'From what the local people said,' replied Mulisi, 'about a month ago a white man came from another country with a visitor's licence to hunt an elephant. This particular elephant had been in the area and had been doing damage in the villages so they followed the tracks and came to where it was resting under some trees. The hunter fired and the elephant fell down. The hunter then gave his rifle to his companion and cut off the tail, smearing blood on his face as a token of his bravery, and used *kodaki* [camera] to make pictures. The hunter looked very fierce with blood on him and his foot on the elephant's trunk. He unloaded his rifle but at that moment the elephant got up and walked away because it had only been stunned by the bullet. It is a common mistake to shoot into the bone at the front of the elephant's head whereas the brain is located farther back. The hole made by the earlier bullet had healed but I could see that it was not in the right place for a deadly shot.'

The District Commissioner laughed at the thought of the fierce hunter who smeared blood on his face and had his picture taken, and the elephant that got up and walked away. The African clerks laughed and were joined by the normally rather taciturn cash accountant, whence the joke spread to the office messengers and bystanders. Finally the story reached the Mukama's palace and he laughed as he had never laughed before.

Not long after that something had gone wrong with Mulisi. The laughter stopped and he had left the Game Department and become a poacher and an outlaw. People said that his descent into a life of crime coincided with his having contracted venereal disease. The same was said much later about Idi Amin. Mulisi acquired a stolen army rifle of .303 calibre for which ammunition was obtainable on the black market and he roamed the forests of Bunyoro hunting and selling the meat. Mulisi Alideki, the brave and trusted hunter, guardian of poor people's homesteads against maurauding animals, had turned to a life of crime.

The name Mulisi is a corruption of the English word Morris and was commonly heard in Western Uganda. It had a pleasant cadence to it and was copied, obviously, from a renowned District Commissioner named Morris who served in the early years of the century. Alideki was a tribal name.

Stephen spoke movingly about Mulisi whom he had known since childhood. Mulisi had been one of nature's gentlemen, courteous and brave, the hero of schoolchildren and on good terms with the Mukama. He had taught European officers to hunt, had crouched beside them as they shot their first elephant or buffalo, and had gained the respect that is due to those who have special talents in a dangerous occupation.

At one point he was nearly captured in the Budongo forest by another game guard. His illegal rifle was taken but he slipped away and within weeks had managed to obtain another. His next brush with the law reduced him to the status of common murderer. On 20 July 1950, game guard Erinayo Muno and some men were on duty in a forested area a few miles north of Hoima. Quite by chance they ran into Mulisi who must have assumed that they had come to arrest him. He killed Erinayo with a shot, took his rifle, a game department .404, then pulled Erinayo's body into a grass-roofed hut and set the hut on fire. The government immediately posted a reward for information leading to Mulisi's arrest.

When I arrived in Bunyoro Mulisi had been at large for eighteen months following the murder of game guard Erinayo. He lived by shooting buffalo and selling the meat or bartering it for the things he needed such as food, clothing, beer and ammunition. People were afraid of him and any information that reached Inspector Frisby at the police station as to his whereabouts was always several days old and therefore of no use. He kept on the move, never slept in the same place for two nights consecutively and displayed all the cunning of a hunted animal.

Mulisi, however, was also a master at the art of propaganda. He and his two sons spread rumours about themselves which were eagerly believed by the Banyoro. He was invincible, employed witchcraft and could disappear at will. He would kill the police if they approached him; he would never be caught.

It was understandable in Bunyoro that the people should be afraid of him yet be loyal customers where his buffalo meat was concerned. There was never enough protein in the local diet and buffalo meat was an obsession. To make it worse, the chiefs were not to be relied on any more than the rest of the populace and Inspector Frisby learned that a *gombolola* chief who was related to the Mukama had bought an entire leg of buffalo, 150 pounds of it, for a wedding feast. Even the Mukama had not spoken publicly against Mulisi and it was assumed that he did not actively oppose him.

The final blow was the fact that Frisby's police were showing signs of hesitation in their duties. Most of his *askaris* were northerners, self-reliant men from the dry, northern parts of the Protectorate whose tribal discipline was legendary and who regarded the Banyoro as soft and degenerate. Erinayo Muno had been a northerner from

Acholi and the northern police had every reason to hate Mulisi, but they too were becoming hesitant and afraid. Searches were not carried out thoroughly; they got lost in darkness or dense bush; pathways that were supposed to be watched were abandoned and Mulisi had at least two escapes when he should have been caught.

From Amory's point of view the situation was disastrous. The whole policy in Bunyoro had been to leave the old institutions and usages undisturbed, to build on what was there and not interfere unduly. His task was to prepare Bunyoro for self-government and, indeed, the District already possessed a wide measure of self-determination. Yet here they were with a murderer in their midst who was undermining the authority of the Native Government and making everyone a laughing stock. What Amory would have liked to do was to step in himself, sack the offending chiefs and take charge, yet that would have been an abandonment of his mandate. The heavily populated areas round Hoima were the worst and the five *gombololas* which Mulisi was reputed to frequent were descending into anarchy. Taxes were not being collected, Native Council laws were poorly enforced and the police were the objects of mockery. It was known that when police parties were in the area drumming would start up and it was not difficult to guess what the drums were saying. Only at night could the police operate in secrecy but at night they needed local men to guide them down the winding pathways and local men could not be trusted.

How was it, Amory asked himself, that one man could get a District into a mess like this? Was it connected with the fact that Bunyoro had low morale to begin with, was enfeebled by the loss of its territories and had little resistance to offer against the blandishments of a petty tyrant? And what was the Mukama's position? Why did he tolerate this affront to his authority? Could he not see that his efforts to regain his lost territories would be ridiculed as long as Mulisi was at large? Mulisi had shown that the Mukama and his government were incompetent and couldn't govern the land they had, so the authorities would hardly be disposed to award them any more.

Amory also had to reckon with the fact that the Uganda police were not taking the situation seriously. It did not seem to be asking too much for a special contingent to be posted to Hoima: six men, say, specially armed and supplied with a Landrover. He had proposed this to the Commissioner of Police and had been fobbed off with the argument that Mulisi had been a game guard and had murdered another game guard so it was proper that the Game Department should be responsible for catching him. This was nonsense, the police were there to catch murderers, but then the police and Game Department at that moment were on uneasy terms.

What had happened was that one of the game wardens in another District, John Mills, inquiring as to where all the illegal .303 rifles were coming from, made a discovery that showed up the Uganda Police as hopeless incompetents. The rifles had been systematically stolen from the Central Police Armoury in Kampala. Of course it was an inside job, the Sikh armourer and his African assistant being responsible, but that didn't lessen the police's responsibility. To make the story even better, a police board of survey had been deluded by the fact that dummies had been substituted for the stolen weapons. Instead of insisting that each rifle be taken from its rack and the serial number checked against the record book, the board members contented themselves with counting what they could see in an ill-lit dungeon of an armoury.

The Uganda Police force was a large and well funded department. There was a commissioner and assistant commissioner, forty or fifty expatriate officers and an army of African police *askaris*. The Game Department, by contrast, which included fisheries, had a chief game warden, four or five expatriate wardens, two fisheries officers and about sixty game guards and fish guards. The police were highly organized, dressed in proper uniforms and drove around in dark blue Landrovers or three-tonners. The Game Department on the other hand seemed determined to appear poor and inconspicuous. For the police to have their faults called to public attention by these scruffy bushwhackers was a humiliation of colossal proportions. They simply had not reckoned with John Mills, a game warden who should have been an undercover police officer. He was not a great hunter or naturalist nor would he have wanted to be thought of in that light, but it was said that he operated an efficient spy network and had been responsible for recapturing a large number of illegal firearms. We never discovered how he found out that the police weapons were being systematically stolen and sold on the black market but it was a remarkable achievement. The weapons in question were finding their way into the hands of murderers, poachers and desperadoes all over Uganda and the police were spending thousands of pounds and using thousands of man-hours to recapture them.

People who have been made fools of are not easy colleagues. The first rifle Mulisi had possessed was one of those stolen in Kampala. He was known to have a second illegal rifle in addition to the Game Department .404 taken from Erinayo, so he evidently had connections with the black market. Inspector Frisby was doing his best, of course, but he was a young man with little experience. On one occasion he almost caught Mulisi. A house had been surrounded at night and Frisby ordered his second-in-command, a sub-inspector, to enter with a flashlight. The sub-inspector refused and Frisby went in himself. A man ran out another door but the two *askaris* who were supposed to be guarding it were not there so the man escaped. The following day Frisby learned that the man had been Mulisi. The day after that the sub-inspector and the two *askaris* were dismissed with disgrace from the Uganda Police, yet in spite of this incident the police commissioner would not reinforce Frisby's contingent.

The Game Department was Amory's next consideration. If they were to post six more game guards in the District he could have them work in pairs in the areas which Mulisi was known to frequent. They could shoot buffalo and give meat to the villagers which would undercut Mulisi's operations. Surely the villagers would not pay for meat if they could get it free. The price was reported to be somewhere about a shilling a pound although it was doubtful whether it was properly weighed; more likely to be sold on a basis of guesswork and haggling. A big bull buffalo carried a thousand pounds of edible meat, six to seven hundred for the average beast, and if Mulisi were to lose his income he would not be able to buy ammunition on the black market. The Game Department, however, had not liked the idea and claimed that they were so short of trained men that even by raiding other Districts they couldn't come up with six men, or even four.

The Game Department, as Amory knew, was a bit of an enigma itself. For years it had been the only department of government that paid its way and did not cost the taxpayer a penny. This was done by the sale of elephant and hippo ivory and the sale of licences to visitors and residents. Now that Fisheries had been added to Game Control they were having difficulty balancing their books but in Amory's view should have concerned themselves less with a small deficit and more with providing really effective game control. To say that there was a shortage of game guards was difficult to accept because there were plenty of returned soldiers who had served in the Far East and who could have been trained as game guards in short order. The Acholi, in particular, were hunters and trackers by instinct and had joined the Kings African Rifles in their hundreds during the war. What were these men doing now? Cultivating their gardens?

There was something else that worried Amory about both the Police and the Game Department. They had a tendency to treat the whole Mulisi affair as a sort of game – his wits against ours –all very sporting and well-intentioned. They couldn't see it as a fight to the death and they missed the fact that he was causing so much damage within the District. The disruptive aspect, the weakening of authority and the fact that the place was becoming ungovernable was not their concern.

Roy Wyndham, the game ranger, knew exactly how to catch Mulisi and said that he could get him within a week if he was given a free hand. Mulisi would not be likely, he pointed out, to let the powerful Game Department rifle out of his own hands. Not only was it more lethal than the stolen .303 but ammunition would cost more and be harder to obtain. Very well then, fill a couple of cartridges with high explosive as opposed to the normal slow-burning charge which, in effect, would shatter the weapon at the breach when it was fired. There might also be some damage to the person firing it, but so what? It would not be difficult to feed the ammunition to Mulisi by way of his accomplices who were well known to the police and still at large.

This suggestion was greeted with howls of dismay. Mulisi, they pointed out, was presumed innocent until proven guilty and so far he hadn't even been charged with anything. Besides, the doctored ammunition might find its way into the hands of some perfectly innocent person, although innocent people don't usually buy their ammunition on the black market. Anyway, the whole idea was unsporting and neither the police nor Game Department would go along with it. 'Which shows,' Wyndham had said, 'they are not serious about catching Mulisi. It's being treated as a joke.'

A point of disagreement between Amory and all the others was the fact that Mulisi's two sons were still at large. They pedalled their bicycles around the village tracks, went shopping in Hoima bazaar and were generally thought to be Mulisi's contact with the black market. Amory wanted them arrested if only to prove that the authorities were not altogether impotent. Frisby, on the other hand, thought they would be more help in the long run if he left them alone. They might speak too loudly at a beer party and lead him to Mulisi's hiding place and, in any event, if he took them to court too early he doubted whether he could make any charges stick.

What is it, Amory kept asking himself, that afflicts these people when they get their hands on a gun? Why does that primal core of evil erupt and change them into bullies and murderers? The secret of governing Africa, he thought, was never to let the Africans have guns. Only a few months earlier a missionary had asked to licence a firearm, a cheap single-barrelled shotgun, so that he could knock over a few guinea fowls for the mission dining room. Inspector Frisby had given him a crash course in the safe handling of a firearm and he himself had spoken to the man about the need to keep the gun in a secure place. He could not have been more emphatic about the need for constant vigilance in not allowing it to be stolen. Yet three weeks later that is exactly what happened. The missionary went to inspect a school somewhere off the road leaving the gun in the back seat of his car. When he got back it had disappeared together with a box of ammunition.

Amory, of course, was furious and wanted the man charged in court with negligence. At this point the Father Superior of the mission came to the office and made, as Amory described it, the statement of the year. 'You must realize,' he said, 'we do not obey the laws of men, only the laws of God.'

Within a few weeks a *muruka* chief had been murdered a couple of miles from the mission. He had gone out of his house at night and been shot full in the chest at close range by a shotgun blast. The shot size corresponded with the size purchased in Kampala by the missionary.

Inspector Frisby had a suspect, not much of a suspect, but a suspect nevertheless and sent a sergeant and three or four *askaris* to search the man's house. The basis of his suspicion was nothing more than the fact that he had a bad reputation and someone had reported him spending money rather freely, money that could have been paid to him for committing a murder. The *askaris* entered the hut and a drama of infinite subtlety was enacted. As the suspect protested his innocence his wife stole the tiniest glance at the thatched roof above. One of the *askaris* saw it, climbed up and felt around with his hand at the spot where he thought her glance had travelled. His hand emerged and in it was the missionary's gun. The missionary never got it back because Amory decided that one of God's laws said that a gun that had been used to kill a *muruka* chief would get thrown into the deepest part of Lake Albert.

Amory looked out of his office window at the bed of brilliant scarlet lilies and the open fields beyond. Fear, he thought, was such a potent and pervasive factor in these peoples' lives. White men don't fear all that much, but Africans were closer to the natural catastrophes of life and lived on the edge of the abyss. They feared the darkness, disease, the witch doctor and, most of all, their enemies who could set their house on fire, pull out their young cotton plants, cut down their bananas and reduce them from affluence to poverty in a single night. Englishmen spoke of fearing God and honouring the King but one of the Lunyoro titles by which superiors were addressed was *o'wekitiinisa*, 'he who is feared'. Back in the Middle Ages our forefathers probably feared more than we do, but they had adopted religion as the antidote and accepted its promises and comforts. These people were not the same; religion or not, they were gripped by fear which was why Mulisi and his rifle could tyrannize them.

Amory was sure that Mulisi would be caught eventually but what damage might he do in the meantime? A plan was forming in his mind, a plan to win the propaganda war or at least deprive Mulisi of his status as a hero. Somehow the people had to be convinced that

Mulisi was a sham and that his threats and boasting were meaningless. It was not merely the hearts and minds of the Banyoro which were at issue but their stomachs also. That buffalo meat was real and tangible and fulfilled an agonizing need for protein so that Amory had somehow to find his own weapon to counteract it. Posting a monetary reward, he realized, was the worst thing they could have done because it had given Mulisi status without producing results. 10,000 shillings – 500 English pounds – was beyond the imagination of those who bought his meat. Five hundred shillings would have done admirably, the price of a new bicycle.

8

The Bachwezi

At the time the first Queen Elizabeth sat on the throne of England and her sea captains attacked the Spanish Armada, when the quill pen of Will Shakespeare scratched across the parchment, a people known as the Bachwezi entered Uganda and passed through the country. According to legend they were fair-skinned and bearded and they built encampments on the tops of hills. The Bachwezi belong to the misty realm of prehistory and they left as mysteriously as they had arrived, an enigma upheld by the legends told about them in the places through which they had journeyed. If the Bachwezi had caught the attention of the Banyoro alone their very existence would have been suspect but they also figure in the legends of Bunyoro's neighbours, the Baganda to the south-east, and the Batoro and Banyankole to the south-west. The evidence indicates that they came through Acholi and moved southwards but their identity and their purpose is uncertain because they left nothing tangible behind. All that is known is that they created a deep impression on the minds of the tribes which they encountered.

Possibly the Bachwezi were westerners and represent Bunyoro's first contact with a white race. This theory is supported by the fact that Muchwezi is not an uncommon name in that part of the world and implies that the person possesses a fair skin. Not all persons with that name necessarily carry the blood of the Bachwezi in their veins because any child born with fair skin could have been given the name. These people are, after all, Nilo-Hamitics and not as black as true negroes. However, at the turn of the century an observer did find at least one individual called Muchwezi who might have been a true Muchwezi descendant with characteristics that seemed to him decidedly European. The Banyoro and Banyankole tribes did their visitors the honour of copying them, creating a sort of Bachwezi cult. The Mukama, when dressed in his ceremonial robes, wore a false beard of white hair from a colobus monkey, almost certainly in imitation of those tourists some twelve to fifteen generations earlier who had so impressed his forebears.

It is tempting to leave the Bachwezi undisturbed by historical speculation until more evidence comes to hand. However, it has been pointed out that they could conceivably have been nothing more than a band of Portuguese missionaries fleeing from persecution in Ethiopia at the end of the sixteenth century. Perhaps they were following the Nile or perhaps they were lost. This theory does fit the puzzle reasonably well and is supported by the possibility that the word Bachwezi is a corruption of 'Portuguese'. The *Ba* would be affixed to mean 'people' and '*chwezi*' substituted for 'guese' which to speakers of these Bantu languages sounds plausible.

What is not known is how many there were, how long they took to pass through the country and what their organization was like. One of my friends in Uganda studied the Bachwezi legends with a great deal of care and pointed out that there were essentially two subjects of controversy, the Bachwezi themselves and the response to them by the tribes whom they encountered. He conjectured they were harmless people, somewhat disorganized, which suggested they were not soldiers but missionaries. The fact that they were travelling in the wrong direction, southwards, rather than eastwards toward the Indian Ocean is bleak evidence in itself.

Some rather amateur archeological digs were being undertaken in Uganda during those years in places where the Bachwezi were supposed to have camped. Mubende hill, in particular, attracted some interest, but nothing was found, no ring or crucifix that might have identified the Bachwezi beyond dispute. Nor has evidence emerged from Portugal in the form of diaries, letters or African artifacts that would have laid speculation to rest.

An important point is that the Bachwezi were said to have promised to return to Bunyoro, a promise that is easy to make but difficult to honour, and this suggests that they were on friendly terms. Again it leads to the conclusion that they were missionaries rather than soldiers or adventurers. In that century soldiers were rarely welcome for a return visit. Furthermore, when the white faces of explorers were first seen in Bunyoro in the closing years of the last century, Samuel Baker, for instance, he was hailed as a Muchwezi who had at last fulfilled the ancient promise.

There is a further piece of negative evidence which suggests they were refugees. We know that the Banyoro at that time were a powerful tribe united under the rule of the Mukama. If the Bachwezi had been able to make a gift or presentation to the Mukama it seems probable they would have done so and the Banyoro with their sense of history would have kept the object. The Mukama's regalia and the tombs of dead Bakama are all meticulously preserved so that a chain, ring or dagger would still be in existence. If the Bachwezi had been refugees fleeing for their lives they would scarcely have been in a position to offer a gift. Furthermore, the fact that no cross or inscription has ever been found carved on rock or tree, no simple tombstone or graffiti, might lead to the conclusion that they had no tools with them.

What the Bachwezi did leave behind, however, was a cult which was not unlike the adulation which attaches itself to present day individuals or groups who seize the imagination of youth. Stories about them took root and flourished, they were venerated and their deeds told and retold. The outcome seems to have been a stirring of the national blood which sent the Banyoro outward in conquest. They challenged the Baganda who may originally have been a tribal offshoot of Bunyoro and the title of whose king, Kabaka, means delegate or ambassador. For two or three hundred years the Banyoro were the tribe most feared in western Uganda, proud cattle-owning people armed with spears and supported by a disciplined organization.

Besides their spears, the Banyoro also carried something else – salt from the mines at Kibiro to the south of Hoima. Salt is still mined there by the local people in considerable quantity and its scarceness in Uganda made it valuable to the point where the Banyoro were known at great distances as suppliers.

The discipline of the Banyoro during those years of conquest may be adduced from one startling piece of evidence. The early explorers who entered the country during the 1880s and 1890s and in the very early part of the present century were unanimous in describing the mutilations ordered by the Mukama as punishment for misdeeds. They could scarcely find an adult Munyoro man who had not suffered the loss of a hand, ear, eye or nose. The slightest infraction was met by this barbaric exercise of authority and there must have been many others whom the explorers did not see who had been put to death. The Mukama's power was absolute and he did not lack chiefs and soldiers to carry out his will. His brand of savage discipline held the tribe together and while it must have weakened them ultimately they were more than a match for their tribal neighbours until the dawn of the present century.

At this point the Banyoro made the mistake that history did not forgive. As the British marched inland from the Indian Ocean with their *askaris*, their firearms, their bibles and their very laudable desire to suppress the slave trade, the Baganda on the northern shores of Lake Victoria were their first contact. The white men, adventurous but few in number, accepted whatever allies they could find and teamed up with the Baganda who helped them in the task of exploring and pacifying the remainder of the upper Nile. It follows that Luganda words like *saza* (county), *gombolola* (sub-county) and *muruka* (hillside or group of villages) – the Buganda district organization – became common outside Buganda. It follows also that individual Baganda were appointed as chiefs in backward areas outside their own borders and even that the country as a whole came to be called Uganda, although the U has no meaning and the Ganda refers only to a quarter of the whole. ('Upper Nile' would have been a more appropriate name.) Finally it follows that the Banyoro, smouldering with long-standing animosities, should reopen hostilities, not against the British with whom they had no quarrel, but against the Baganda who by that time enjoyed British protection. In the eyes of Captain Lugard, soldier, adventurer and *de facto* ruler of the country, the Baganda were quick learners, friendly and more or less reasonable while the Banyoro were quite the reverse.

There followed a sorry little war in which the Mukama of those days, Kabarega, was defeated and took refuge in the forests. It was the low point in Bunyoro's fortunes, the Mukama being hunted in his own dominions by his traditional enemies. He was eventually captured and deported to the Seychelles Islands in the Indian Ocean. Not only did the Banyoro lose their rightful Mukama but they lost a part of their territory to the victorious Baganda. The two large and populous counties of Bugangadzi and Buyaga in Mubende and much of northern Mengo were Lunyoro-speaking and remained so but became part of Buganda. It was a settlement which settled nothing because it was unfair and a violation of historical fact and it was not corrected until the time of Uganda's independence.

A phrase we often heard in Uganda in those days was that the various tribes hated each other more than they hated us. It came almost as a surprise to discover the absence of resentment toward white people, the warmth of their welcome and their generosity towards us who, like the Bachwezi, were intruders in their country. Their relationship with other tribes, however, ranged from merely unforgiving to blatantly hostile. The animosity which existed between the Banyoro and Baganda, for example, we found difficult to comprehend. We would say to ourselves that they all lived in the same country, faced similar problems and were all Africans, so why couldn't they forget their tribal differences? To them, however, those tribal differences were the rock on which their world was built. Their land, their language, their tribal customs, their king and their history set them apart in their own eyes from all others.

The intensity of these feelings can be indicated by trying to imagine a combination of the Russian love of their land which they call Holy Russia; the French concern for their language, the language of princes and lovers whose purity is a national obsession; the American mania surrounding their political system; and finally the British adulation of their royalty combined with their sense of history. Take all these extremes, Russian, French, American and British and their sum comes close to the tribal passions of the Banyoro.

Tribal differences were a fact of life in Uganda and hampered the pace of progress. When independence was achieved in the 1960s it was essentially tribal animosities that were at the heart of the country's subsequent decline in the years that followed. Uganda had not come to terms with its tribalism nor emerged from its tribal past. Bunyoro, deprived of almost half its traditional territory, could reflect on the fact that if the British had arrived in the country from the north as the Bachwezi had done, its boundaries would have been enlarged, not reduced. It was happenstance that brought Captain Lugard and his *askaris* from the east, the Indian Ocean, whereas the Nile route southwards from Egypt was just as plausible. The Banyoro would have welcomed Lugard as they welcomed Samuel Baker as a reincarnation of the Bachwezi and would have rallied round him in his task of exploring and pacifying the remainder of the country.

There was one final disaster in store for the Banyoro, one last catastrophe that cut to the heart of their economic and tribal organization. In the early years of the century sleeping sickness entered the country and people began to contract the disease and die in large numbers. The areas hardest hit were those bordering the lakes and rivers where the tsetse fly, *Glossina morsitans*, found a favourable habitat. The governor of those days, Sir Hesketh Bell, undertook to move the inhabitants of the affected areas to safer ground as a way of breaking the human link with the tsetse flies which carried the disease. These vast population upheavals were bad enough but they did not halt the spread of the disease among cattle and thousands of animals perished. The herds in Bunyoro were almost wiped out and the people, from being the proud owners of great herds, became cultivators by necessity, an occupation which they considered inferior.

The tribe that loses its cattle loses its very soul. Cattle are not a mere possession, an adjunct of human life, they are woven into the thread of daily existence. The people of Ankole to the south, also Nilo-Hamitics like the Banyoro, were partly spared by the tsetse fly and provide a picture of what the Banyoro would have been like when they were a cattle-owning society.

Each individual animal has its name which is derived from its colour, horn shape and other characteristics. They come when they are called and some develop into household pets which follow their master on his daily rounds. Cattle-owners are fearless in defence of their herds against lions, sing to them and compose poetry in their honour. They build earthen water troughs which hold a hundred gallons or more so that the animals can drink without fouling the water supply. The herd is halted a few yards from the trough and the animals stand patiently while four or five are called by name to come and drink. The herdsman positions himself in the trough and with his stick holds back any that try to tread down the wall. By watering the animals in small groups he is assured that all get their share and the water supply is not fouled.

At night the animals are driven inside a kraal of thornbush to protect them against predators. In the morning, if one were stolen or had escaped the herdsman would know immediately, even though he owned hundreds. They notice an absence by the behaviour of other animals which demonstrates the rapport between the herdsmen and his charges. When greeting a herdsman it is proper to ask after his cattle first, his children second and his wives last.

When on a visit to western Canada during our first leave my wife and I learned that a well-known cattle breeder regularly lost ten per cent of his animals during the winter months as a result of cold and starvation. In my ignorance of such matters I enquired why it was not possible to build shelters where the animals could be protected from the wind. I had seen cattle in northern England huddled behind the stone walls which are such a feature in that area. I also wondered why the owner could not carry emergency food rations to his animals by using a snowmobile and trailer. The answer to my question was simple: he also owned a house in southern California where he spent his winters, and his cattle were left to fend for themselves.

The herdsmen of western Uganda had not learned to treat, or maltreat, their animals as a mere business proposition. They were good shepherds and it was as easy to admire their devotion as it was to deplore the indifference of a Canadian cattle owner.

In the days when the Banyoro had cattle their diet was better than it is today. Although reluctant to slaughter animals for their meat they would kill one that was on its last legs and appeared to be about to die and they would finish off a beast if it became injured. They also had milk and occasionally fresh blood which was taken from the neck. A herd of cattle, however, was more than a source of food but a bank account. Bride-prices were paid in cattle, debts settled and fines exacted. Cattle were the hundred dollar bills of commerce; cowrie shells from the sea coast were the pennies. Any animal that was pure white belonged automatically to the Mukama but some other colours, gray for instance, were much prized.

These Banyoro among whom we laboured were, therefore, doubly stricken by misfortune. Their rich properties to the east were compromised, although perhaps not irredeemably so, because there remained a glimmer of hope that history's injustices would be reversed. Where their cattle were concerned they had been assured by the Veterinary Department that progress was being made against the tsetse fly and when eradicated they would be able to reintroduce the beautiful long-horned animals which were their pride and joy. These beasts, esthetically pleasing but not very productive in the economic sense, are usually called Ankole (rhymes with Man-Holy) because the plains of Ankole to the south carried vast herds. They are depicted in exquisite detail in many of the tomb paintings of ancient Egypt whose artists truly captured those very characteristics which the present day herdsmen continue to treasure – the tall but not bulky frame, the huge spreading horns, delicate nose and soft eye.

Their hopes, however, were distant and hardly reassuring. Morale among the Banyoro was poor, an indication of which was the fact that the birthrate was just about steady from year to year, neither increasing nor declining. In every other District of Uganda the birthrate had the effect of doubling the population every thirty years but in Bunyoro the figure remained steady.

The Banyoro, therefore, were an inward-looking people whose feet were heavy with the irony of history and this was nowhere more apparent than in their memories of Mukama Kabarega. He had been a fugitive in the forests, a hunted man, yet he was the true Mukama, the chief milkman of his tribe, an aristocrat whose place was the open grassland among his pure white cattle. A fugitive mentality had developed, a glorification of the outlaw escaping his pursuers by the narrowest of margins. Robin Hood, according to improbable legend, had at least stolen from the rich and given to the poor, but the Banyoro adulation of Kabarega possessed no salutary overtones. He was pictured only as a fugitive surrounded by enemies, an animal eluding pursuit. As a hero figure he did not point in any discernable direction or express any values. He was cruel, cunning and he used witchcraft to obtain his ends.

People have the heroes they deserve and it is not hard to see how Mulisi Alideki, also a fugitive in the forest, inherited the mystique of Kabarega. The Banyoro sympathized with him, aided him and warned him of the approach of police parties. He was their hero and while they knew he would be caught eventually it was all part of the sad cycle of history which could not be disputed.

9

Hoima Headquarters

Hoima was the administrative headquarters of Bunyoro District and from it the roads radiated outwards to Masindi some thirty miles north-west, to Butiaba on Lake Albert due north, to the Kafu river and the Kampala road south-eastwards, and Fort Portal in Toro District to the south-west. The town itself was 4,000 feet above sea level and enjoyed an almost perfect climate, warm by day and one-blanket-cool by night. Being only 1.5° north of the equator the sun rose in the morning and set at night at almost the same minute throughout the year, and since the sun was bisecting the horizon at right angles twilight was brief. On the tennis court in the evening you would think there was enough light for one more game but a few serves later you could scarcely see at all.

The annual rainfall was quite heavy, 60 or 70 inches falling in two rainy seasons. The remainder of the year, although called the dry season, had occasional showers. In former times the Banyoro measured the year as one rainy and one dry season together so that their year was of six months duration.

No one who had been there could fail to be impressed by the beauty of Hoima, an oasis of flowers, rolling lawns and red-roofed houses set amid the villages and cultivation round about. There was an orderliness and sanity in its layout, an air of organization which contrasted with the papyrus-filled valleys, the jungle and elephant grass through which one had travelled to reach it.

As in India, an up-country headquarters like Hoima was referred to as a 'station'. In the early days when all movement was by foot safari this must have meant a stopping place for the porters, a way-station where one group of men would be paid off and a new group taken on. When we went on our first leave in 1954 my young son confused his relatives by referring to Toronto as a 'station'.

The first duty conferred on me after my arrival in Hoima was to be put in charge of the station. Mr Amory explained that it was more than just the headquarters of the District, it was a showplace and an example that was to be seen and copied. The Banyoro were great travellers within their District and sooner or later every chief, schoolmaster and council member and about half the male population would visit by bus or bicycle. They would see wide roads with ditches to carry off the rainwater; there would be cut grass giving the place a park-like appearance dotted with flowering shrubs. The flower beds would be a mass of lilies and roses, the tall jacaranda trees spilling over them in cascades of blue flowers. Magnolias, oleanders, poinsettia and bougainvillaea would be everywhere and, as Hoima's speciality, there were magnificent rows of avocado and loquat trees. They would see the bazaar area swept and clean; no banana peelings littering the streets, no naked children relieving themselves, no clouds of flies round the public lavatories. They would find order and cleanliness at every turn, particularly in such mundane matters as garbage disposal, and they would be inspired to do likewise in their own corners of the District.

It is well known to teachers that pupils do not always learn the lesson that is intended to be taught. One of my first initiatives in Hoima was to order a bush saw and show a labourer how to trim and tidy the trees. Where branches were trailing on the ground making it difficult to cut the grass underneath or where the tree looked unbalanced or untidy he cut off the offending branch close to the trunk and painted over the scar. The fallen branches were then dragged away and used for firewood.

A month or two later I found that several of the chiefs had picked up the idea of trimming their trees but instead of cutting the branches neatly and close to the trunk they were lopping them off leaving a foot or two sticking out. It looked terrible so I enquired and was told that the projections could be used as a ladder in case someone needed to climb the tree.

The labour force at Hoima consisted of Hassan, the headman, and about thirty men. They would arrive at the store on their bicycles at seven in the morning and start work shortly after. If the weather was fine they did quite well until about ten o'clock but slowed down after that and at midday brought their tools back. The doctor attributed their leisurely work habits to what he described as centuries of malnutrition and a bit of malaria thrown in. Amory pointed out they had no tradition of performing what we would call a full day's work because the cultivation of their crops didn't call for it.

All this may have been true, but there was another consideration – their physical stamina. Young Banyoro men were strong in the legs and could walk all day with little fatigue. They could also carry heavy weights on their heads, a sixty- or seventy-pound load for ten miles being nothing remarkable. When it came to working with their hands and arms, however, they were weaker than their western counterparts. They lacked strength for the arm-chest kind of activities such as sawing a piece of wood, and they were not good at lifting things, obviously in consequence of the fact that they were not accustomed to such work. In the result they were not particularly productive labourers but with encouragement and some buffalo meat once in a while they got the work done. I learned their names quite rapidly and whenever I asked for a couple of men to go hunting with me they all volunteered.

Hoima bazaar consisted of a dozen Indian shops which faced each other across the main street. These *dukas*, as they were called, were built of sun-dried brick with iron roofs. All had three-foot-high verandahs on which sacks of produce were piled and it was on these verandahs that the Indian or African tailors worked at their foot-pedal sewing machines. The interiors of the *dukas* were dark because they had no proper windows so any job that required good light was done outside.

If Hoima bazaar excelled in any one thing it was the tailors who made up clothes in a matter of hours. This did not apply to Jean's clothes, she having come out from home with a good collection of summer dresses; however on my uniforms and the servants' work clothes the local *derzi* did an excellent job.

Some officers wore boots in Uganda either because they had been in the army or because they were frightened of stepping on a snake. I never liked boots on the African footpaths because the paths were narrow, no more than a foot or eighteen inches wide, and were usually eroded by rain so that they formed a sort of trench. In those days there was not the same variety of sneakers, sport shoes and generally comfortable footwear that there is now but I found that soft leather shoes served best. The trick of walking down the village paths was to step from side to side of the path and only walk down the trench when the jungle pressed in on both sides. African paths were narrow because most Banyoro at that time went barefoot and always in single file. It made good sense for a man to walk ahead of his wife and children in case of snakes, soldier ants or any other pests that might be encountered.

Our office attire was non-uniform and consisted of khaki slacks, a white shirt and tie. We were not expected to wear a jacket at our desks but always had one handy in case we were called into the courtroom or in the event of a visit from the Mukama, who often dropped in.

I rapidly became friends with Hassan, the township headman, and together we walked round the township at least every two weeks. When it rained the people coming into Hoima would pull down banana leaves and use them as primitive umbrellas which they cast aside when the rain stopped. It infuriated Hassan to see his beautiful township littered with banana leaves eight feet long. It occurred to me that in some parts of the world a certain humour had grown up around banana skins that get discarded but in Hoima the entire leaf was the culprit.

The hardest place to keep clean and tidy was the area round the township borehole where the Indians and others drew their water so I got Hassan to build seats and plant flowering shrubs. An empty forty-gallon drum was given a coat of paint and the word 'Rubbish' written on it in different languages. Hassan insisted on making holes in it because he said it would be stolen if he didn't. The holes made it useless as a water container or cooking pot. When Amory saw Hassan's handiwork and the seats in particular he said that we were encouraging people to idleness and gossip.

My wife Jean was trained in fine art but instead of setting up her easel in the garden she took to bird-watching. One of the frequent sights was a group of crested cranes, tall elegant creatures walking the open lawns in search of grasshoppers or dancing their elaborate minuet. As Uganda's emblematic bird they had a reputation to maintain and they always attracted an appreciative audience of another two-legged species.

They are large birds, gray and white in the body with a rufous tail touched with black. Behind the feathered head the golden crest stands like the decoration on a Roman helmet, the head being a contrast of black, gold and red. When dancing they would form a circle, bow their heads and trail their wings, five and six together, although there was always one that stood confused and sorry for itself, having apparently not mastered the choreography. Unfortunately for them crested cranes had a reputation for flavour and were probably not difficult to snare so that many must have found their way into African cooking pots.

Another species we often saw in our jacaranda tree was the hoopoe bird whose antics in the top branches always brought pleasure to the beholder. They were probably doing nothing more than catching insects but they made a great sport out of it.

My personal favourites, however, were the black and white crows which were early morning risers. They welcomed the dawn vociferously if not tunefully from the top of the tall eucalyptus tree by the tennis court and when I appeared early, as I sometimes did, to practise serve a hundred tennis balls they kept up a torrent of comment, not to say abuse, at my efforts below. It was good practice for me, not only in acquiring a lethal serve but also for maintaining my composure in face of the foolish chatter of the other players.

One of the *dukas* in the bazaar, Hassanalli's, stocked a small amount of groceries and other things suitable to the needs of Europeans, but their main business was directed toward the African trade. They bought produce in the villages: coffee, sim-sim, beans, groundnuts and chillies, and sold the things that Africans needed: cloth, tools, implements and the minor luxuries of life such as sugar, tea and salt.

Most of the dozen or so Indian families in Hoima came originally from the Gujarat coast of India with a few from the Punjab. At that time there were still a small number of older men who had immigrated in the early years of the century to work on the Uganda railway or set up small businesses in the wake of the British explorers, but the majority had been born and raised in Uganda and thought of Uganda as their home.

The most remarkable thing about them was their clannishness and the fact that in such a small bazaar there were so many different 'communities'. There were two or three Patels, a Sikh and some others who represented the differing Moslem sects. One might have supposed that the very circumstances of life in an up-country bazaar would have blurred their differences and reduced the emphases on such matters as dietary prohibitions. However, each community followed its own observances, customs and dietary rules. There was very little intermarriage between the communities and absolutely none between Indian and African.

From Amory's point of view, the fact of having so many communities, each jealous of its own prerogatives, meant that he could not approach any one individual as the acknowledged spokesman of the bazaar. If there was some information to be passed, or co-operation sought, he had to invite representatives of each community who would have great difficulty settling anything among themselves. He tried, for instance, to get something organized on the anniversary of Indian Independence but each community decided to go its own way. The ideal arrangement would have been only one community and this was said to have been the situation at Moroto in the northern District of Karamoja. The story was told of there being six Patels so the District Commissioner, a bachelor who greatly loved his curry tiffin (lunch), ate with each of them in turn on weekdays and only had his lunch in his own house on Sundays.

Only in the education of their children did the bazaar manage to forget its internal divisions. There was a primary school in a back room presided over by one of the married women which all the Indian children had to attend. After that they would be sent to one or other of Hoima's secondary schools, preference going to the Protestant school where, as Amory put it, they didn't ram it down the children's throats quite the way the Catholics did. Some of the Indian families were wealthy enough to send their children to the boarding schools in the highlands of Kenya, but never did so. The idea of a boarding school was alien to their way of thinking and it would have seemed inhuman to part with a child for the length of the school term.

Only one of the Indians, the manager of the cotton ginnery, joined with the Europeans in the social life of the station. He didn't play tennis, or sing at the piano, but he would take a glass of beer and was not out of his element in European company. He could not stand the bland nothingness of European cooking and I suspect that his popularity was due in part to the fact that his wife made magnificent curries.

At Christmas the Indian communities in Hoima were gripped by a primitive urge to give lavish gifts to the officers. I came in for more than my fair share because I was in charge of Hoima township and was responsible for issuing trading licences. The government rule was that if the gift was small and consumable you might keep it but if it was valuable and non-consumable it had to be returned. The Indians knew this and arrived on Christmas day laden with things that were essentially consumable, like Scotch whisky, crates of beer and Christmas cakes.

I rapidly developed a technique which involved thanking the Indian for his gift and saying that since I did not need so much for my own use I felt free to send part of it to the hospital and elsewhere. We kept anything home-made such as dishes of Indian food, but the remainder, such as canned cakes and biscuits, would go to our servants, the prison and hospital; the beer to the police and labour force. On Amory's suggestion I also kept three or four bottles of whisky because neither Jean nor I ever drank it and it would only be used for entertaining visitors, an expense for which we were never properly reimbursed.

One of the things I quickly learned about the Indians was that their names disclosed useful information. With a name like Abdul Aziz the man would clearly be a Moslem; Gurdial Singh would be a Sikh and Shah Karam probably a Beluchi. Among the Africans it was much the same. Okot would have been an Acholi, Walusimbi a Muganda and Kasaijja a Munyoro. These minor subtleties became second nature and saved embarrassment such as not offering to shake hands with elderly Hindus who prefer to press their own hands together rather than shake someone else's, or keeping the dog locked up when Moslems came in the house since Moslems don't like dogs.

A story that was doing the rounds when I was in Hoima provided an explanation for the fact that baby food was never stocked by the Indians. It seems that in some out-of-the-way place an Indian shop owner had put baby food on his shelves and the local Africans had seen the baby's face on the outside of the can. They assumed that the contents of the can was that which was described pictorially on the outside. This was not unreasonable because a can of corned beef always had a bull's head on it, a can of baked beans showed beans boiling in a pot. At this point the stories varied a good deal but at very least the villages seized the offending cans and buried them.

Hoima had a post office, a hospital and an African housing estate for government servants. Then there was the police station and police 'lines' – rows of small houses occupied by the *askaris*. Finally there was the rest house where travelling officers could put up for the night. There were no mud and thatch buildings within the township, this not being permitted, and the Native Government buildings, schools, missions and cotton ginnery were outside the boundary, as was the market.

To list what Hoima did not have would occupy more space than saying what it did possess. First, there was no hotel or motel for visitors, which meant that people who arrived from Kampala not equipped for up-country travel became an immediate burden. Visitors would turn up at all hours of the day and night and having looked over the Rest House would complain that it had nothing in it and would we please explain. All we could say was that as government officers it wasn't our business to build hotels or restaurants for about one visitor per night. To seasoned East African travellers it was quite adequate and when, for instance, a High Court judge came on circuit he would bring his own servant and everything he needed.

The next most obvious shortcoming was the shops. Hassanalli's had a few items that were of interest to Europeans, some cans of food, soap, cooking oil and household items. With no drugstore or chemist one had to go to Kampala for such obvious needs as baby food, toothbrushes or razor blades. With no hardware store you couldn't get a bit of wire to hang a picture or the fixtures for curtains and there was no way one could get any of the things needed for making improvements around the house and garden. Of course there was no bank, barber, restaurant, movie house, laundry or dry cleaners. There was a filling station but no garage.

The thing that worried us least of all was the absence of imported food. Unlike many Europeans Jean and I made do with game meat that I brought home and the produce that could be found in the market. In addition, we had a loaf of bread which Kazimir baked on a daily basis. There were always potatoes in the market, not 'Irish' potatoes but a slightly sweet variety, and there was a great assortment of beans and lentils. Our favourites were a small purple bean with a distinctive flavour which I have never seen outside Uganda. When served to visitors from other countries they were always appreciated. Tomatoes, avocadoes and some other vegetables were also to be had locally although the tomatoes grown in the tropics never really became red. The eggs were small and frequently stale but Kazimir held them up to the sun and scrutinized them, then spun them on a smooth surface, which helped him, so he said, to decide if they were good or bad. His failure rate was in the order of five per cent but with eggs at one cent each, albeit quite small ones, there was little reason to complain. He knew enough never to boil an egg or break it directly into the pot, but break it into a cup first.

My best egg event occurred one morning at breakfast. Why, I wanted to know, had Kazimir put hot chillies in the scrambled eggs. Aberi summoned him from the kitchen and I asked the question rather forcefully, but he pleaded not guilty. The eggs, he explained, had come from our own chickens of which we had a few behind the garage. Intrigued by the mystery and with my mouth burning I went and looked at them pecking around in the early morning. The solution to the problem was staring me in the face. There was a bush of small red chillies which I had not noticed and the chickens had been eating them and spicing up their own eggs. As I said to Kazimir, it would have been worse if the eggs had been used in a dessert.

A bush or two of small red chillies was often planted in European gardens to manufacture a brew called pilly-pilly ho-ho. Sherry drinkers will tell you that the last quarter of an inch of sherry at the bottom of the bottle may not be drinkable owing to the sediment. Instead of throwing it away it is put in a special container and loaded up with hot red chillies and then used, a few drops at a time, in soups or stews. This, of course, accounted for the presence of the bush behind the garage. We always had a bottle of pilly-pilly ho-ho in our own dining room although we liked it rather mild so that the sherry flavour was not lost.

Milk was unobtainable in Hoima except for condensed milk in cans or powdered milk. The doctor was emphatic that if ever we succeeded in getting fresh milk we were to pasteurize it by bringing it to a low boil for twenty minutes. Much better, in our opinion, was the dried milk from Kenya which was less trouble and perfectly safe. Our young son thrived on it and I personally would not have cared if I never saw milk at all. I didn't drink coffee, never put it in tea and we couldn't get breakfast cereals. It is a constant source of amazement to me to witness mature people in the west drinking milk until they grow from six foot two inches to six foot four. The Batussi of the Ruanda-Urundi likewise drank great quantities of milk and were likewise very tall but it did not seem to be an advantage except for looking down on others. It rather saddens one to think that so many mature people drink milk unnecessarily and so many children have none at all.

When we first went home on leave in 1954 and told my wife's family that we made a point of subsisting on local produce we were showered with sympathy. They told us that it must be such a relief to be in a civilized country and have a decent meal after suffering those years of privation. We laughed at this and, looking back, I am not sure that our diet wasn't better than theirs. All our vegetables and fruits were grown without artificial fertilizer and were never sprayed with chemicals or poisons. We had fish from Lake Albert, the waters of which were brimming with good hippo shit but which contained no pesticides. The meat we ate was game meat and therefore lean because game animals have no fat. We got coarse brown sugar produced in Uganda, tea from the mountains of Toro a couple of hundred miles to the south and butter from the farms of Kenya. To people who knew something of dietary matters and enjoyed their food it was a wonderful opportunity to adapt local, inexpensive foods to our own tastes and local food was truly inexpensive, being exactly what the Africans themselves ate. A small market chicken was from fifty cents to a shilling, remembering that four shillings made up a dollar. The flavour of an African chicken was much superior to the flavour of a western supermarket chicken. The African chicken feeds on grubs, insects, seeds, even on small red chillies, so that the meat acquires real flavour. By comparison western chickens raised in batteries taste of very little.

Eggs and avocado pears were always one cent each; tomatoes, onions and local potatoes a few cents a pound. Beans were never more than five or ten cents a pound, while yams, chillies and ginger root were only slightly more. The green bananas which were the staple diet of most Banyoro were two shillings for the whole bunch, which weighed something like a hundred pounds. Ten or twelve bananas, comprising a 'hand', would cost about twenty cents and would form the basis of a meal for a family of six.

These food bananas, or plantains, did not have much nutritive value but were acceptable once in a while in place of rice, noodles or couscous. They would be peeled with a knife since the skins didn't just tear off, then wrapped tightly in five or six layers of clean banana leaves. They were steamed over a low fire for two or three hours and finally unwrapped to reveal a slightly yellow mashed-potato-like dish. The flavour was faintly nutty, said to have been imparted by the leaves, and while most visitors quite liked it the usual criticism was that it tended to be a little gluey in one's mouth.

This dish was called *mattooke* (ma-tow-kay) and was what the Banyoro called 'food'. Rice, potatoes, spaghetti and carbohydrates generally were also 'food', but vegetables and meat were not. This seemed to confuse many Europeans who wanted to stick the label 'food' on everything that was edible. However, the Lunyoro language is perfectly clear in classing carbohydrates as 'food' while meat or vegetables come under different headings. If I were to ask Aberi what had been cooked for supper he might say, 'Food': potatoes. 'Vegetables': beans. 'Meat': guinea fowl'. In other words there was a sharp distinction to be maintained between the various categories.

This was by no means the only difficulty for people who did not understand the tribal languages. I read a book by an intrepid explorer and his valiant little wife who were invited to a meal by the local chief. Using an interpreter who probably wasn't very skilled in his craft they thanked him and enquired what sort of meat they had been eating. The reply was 'arm' which they assumed to mean a human arm. To put it mildly the lady was discommoded, she thought she had been eating game meat, she cried all night and she would recall the occasion with revulsion for the remainder of her days.

What she didn't know was that the word 'arm' also means the front leg of an animal. In these languages an animal, whether it be an elephant, monkey, dog, or cat has two legs and two arms. To refer to the arms as front legs would sound to them just as silly as if we were to refer to our legs as our 'back arms'. My guess is that the lady had eaten the 'arm' of an ordinary bushbuck so the only thing to cry about was her poor comprehension of the language.

Hoima's most conspicuous disaster area was the butcher's stall in the market. The butcher was a local Munyoro whose knowledge of his craft was rudimentary, probably because he had so little practice. His only tool was a *panga*, a broad-bladed slashing knife about two feet in length which he used for taking animals apart in chronic disregard for the way they had been put together. There was sometimes sheep or goat meat to be had but very rarely any beef because cattle could not survive in Bunyoro. On one occasion in the south of the District I came across a cow that was being butchered at the roadside. The owner explained that he had been driving it to market but it became so weak it could go no further. He managed to obtain a two-shilling slaughter permit from the chief just before it expired, so there he was cutting it up and selling the meat to the local people. I was in no doubt that if it had dropped dead first he would have sold the meat just the same.

We had our own vegetable garden behind the house and in it we concentrated on salad greens which could not be bought in the market. It was a rule that Jean would wash the salad leaves herself in a mild solution of permanganate of potash and that the servants would not handle it. Much the same principle was applied to fruit; the servants would wash the paw-paw or mangoes which would be cut open by ourselves in the dining room. People who did not abide by these rules usually paid a hefty price in upset stomach or intestinal disorders. Some old hands went to the extreme and refused to touch any food that had not been cooked, but we thought this was going too far. We ate our salads and fresh fruit but were careful in the way they were handled.

One or two of the Europeans in Hoima used to get weekly parcels of food from Nairobi. There was an organization which made the arrangements and forwarded them by rail to Kampala then onwards by bus to the various up-country stations. Nairobi to Hoima was just over five hundred miles, but it was a hot and bumpy journey judging by the appearance of the parcels on arrival. In our opinion they were too expensive and often in dismal condition when they arrived, assuming they arrived at all. The clerks who packed them made mistakes and you were either charged for what you had not received or received what you did not want. For the sake of ham, English potatoes, cheese, bacon, sausages and a box of dates it simply wasn't worth the trouble and we found it more interesting to experiment with local foods. Besides this, it was only a three-hour journey to Kampala where we did our shopping every two or three months.

A rather strange peculiarity which I developed in Bunyoro was that when suffering from over-exertion I developed a craving for certain foods. There was a lot of sheer physical effort in life: walking long distances in arduous conditions, hunting at weekends and tennis in the evenings. Sometimes I would get a sudden craving for tomatoes and eat ten at a sitting, or half a dozen eggs. No one else seemed to share this outrageous peculiarity and it continued to haunt me as long as I was in Africa. The probable explanation is that the body knows what it needs and tries to tell the owner, if he will listen. Pregnant women are well known for sudden food cravings, obviously related to the adjustments their bodies are making.

At about that time, in late 1951 or early 1952, packets of dried soup began to make their appearance in the Kampala shops and these had an effect on the food we ate. My recollection is that they were salty and not very good but were a godsend when it came to a quick meal, particularly on safari. When faced with a chicken still squawking, Georgi would deal with it as only an African can: skin, feathers, head, feet and insides flying in one direction and the meat going into a pot with some water and a packet of chicken soup. He would add a couple of potatoes and an onion. In half an hour it had become a tasty meal, more so than if the soup had not been there. Even at home Kazimir would use a soup packet in the cooking once in a while. Nowadays, of course, packets of just about everything are found in all the grocery stores but at that time they were a novelty. On safari they gave flavour and variety to the food with the advantage of being easy to carry.

The fresh fruits available in Hoima were pawpaws, passion fruit and a few oranges which, like the tomatoes, never really became red. There were also limes and loquats from the trees behind our house, mangoes which were small and not very good, and sweet bananas. The traditional dessert was fried banana with lime juice, but Kazimir could also do wonders with passion fruit. Loquats, which have a vague taste of apples, were an excellent accompaniment for wild pork. I am not sure whether avocadoes qualify as fruit or vegetable but they were nearly always available. Very occasionally there would be pineapples in the market but bananas and paw-paws were the year-round staples.

Our visitors, of course, were not always such adventurous eaters as we were. In the early stages we made the mistake of telling people what they were eating, banana porridge and warthog for example, and we would see the fork hesitate and the smile fade. We learned to tell them after dinner even though it meant they turned pale and took a quick gulp of coffee.

On the whole, therefore, we lived on local foods and lived well. It was a challenge to make interesting, balanced meals but between them Jean and Kazimir made a huge success of it. Had there been such a thing in those days as a deep freeze unit operated on kerosene it would have made a great difference because we could have kept meat much longer. As it was I had to go out hunting at least every two weeks and if, let us say, I got a wild pig weighing sixty or seventy pounds, we found ourselves eating it in some form or another for about two weeks. In fact we kept only ten or twenty pounds for ourselves and gave the rest away. Selling game meat was absolutely prohibited. A kerosene refrigerator helped but a freezer would have been perfect because then we could have kept a bit of everything – buffalo, bushbuck, pig, guinea fowls and even fish from the lake.

10

The Up-Country Office

Early in the century some intrepid administrator must have covered his desk with green baize (a kind of felt cloth), which is not such a bad idea in a hot country where there is glare from the sun and where your arms perspire, particularly the arm of your writing hand. In Uganda, however, things changed slowly and our office desks were always covered with green felt: not blue felt, not brown, but green, like a billiard table. There might have been differing in-trays and out-trays, different ink wells and, wonder of wonders, a telephone, but that green felt was unchanging and I never saw a desk without it. When we were on safari we were khaki-clad administrators touring a green countryside; when we were at headquarters we sat behind green desks.

Amory's office was large, comfortable and cluttered. There were maps on the walls, half a dozen hard chairs, a waste-paper basket, the contents of which the office messenger cleared out at intervals and burned in an incinerator. There was also a large and antiquated safe which contained about a dozen 'Secret' files under his personal care, some gold dust that had been confiscated in a court case and a bottle of sherry. When my law examination papers were received from the Registrar of the High Court the sealed envelopes were lodged in the safe until I found time to sit and write them. There was, of course, in Amory's office the mandatory poster-sized photograph of King George VI, by the grace of God, and of the Queen, formerly the Lady Elizabeth Bowes-Lyon.

The court room was next to Amory's office at the end of the building, a large whitewashed room with raised dais for the magistrate, a prisoners' dock, witness box, tables for prosecution and defence, and seats for about twenty spectators. One of the first cases which I heard was prosecuted by Roy Wyndham, the District Game Warden. He had rounded up a dozen poachers in the game reserve and he and his men marched them into the courtroom with its limited size and sluggish air circulation. The accused were in their filthiest clothes and the game guards not much better, while the exhibits consisted of horns, skins and piles of rotting meat. I recognized forcefully at that early point in my judicial career why English judges, my great-grandfather among them, carried nosegays of flowers and sweet-smelling herbs. My great-grandfather had been a judge of the Northern Assizes of England and was credited with having devised numerous remedies to alleviate the population shortage in Australia.

Afterwards Roy Wyndham said that during the hearing, while I had been writing down the evidence, he had enjoyed ample time to study the coat of arms behind the magistrate's chair. The unicorn was well depicted, he thought, but not the lion which he described as an impotent disgrace to the proper administration of justice. The secondary sex characteristics, namely mane and beard, appeared to him sufficient, but elsewhere the lion was so poorly endowed that it set a bad example to the litigants. It was the kind of detail, he said, that Africans would notice and they would ask themselves what power and majesty resides in the law when so hermaphroditic a symbol was exhibited.

My own office was next to Amory's but appropriately smaller and less cluttered. There were no electric lights because Hoima did not have electricity, which meant that we could only work by daylight, seven in the morning until seven at night. At year's end, when pressed to get our annual reports completed, I suggested to Amory that it might be useful to keep a lamp at the office so that we could work for an hour after supper.

'Certainly not,' he snapped. 'I don't want it advertised that we are so inefficient that we can't do our work during twelve hours of daylight.'

On another occasion he saw me carrying papers to my house.

'Take those back to the office where they belong,' he shouted, 'and meet me on the tennis court in half an hour.'

Later he told me that the most useless District Commissioner in Uganda was an office workaholic. He laboured for twelve hours every day and did twelve hours' worth of damage. He wrote letters that didn't need writing, created difficulties where none existed, invented problems for which there were no solutions and was a menace to his superiors and subordinates. No Provincial Commissioner wanted him in his province, the Chief Secretary wouldn't have him at headquarters and he'd end up on 'Special Duties', because such nuisances always do. 'The main thing,' Amory continued, 'was to keep him away from the Africans because that's where he could do irreversible harm.' He glared at me. 'Twelve hours of useless office work every day of the year. Never become like that!'

Amory had been a teacher early in his career and was planning to return to the schoolroom when he reached retirement age. He tended to oversimplify problems but I felt instinctively that his ideas were backed by common sense and that I could have done worse than be appointed to his District during my first tour of service. Most of the other Districts were somewhat larger with a District Commissioner and two or even three assistants; two of them were smaller with a District Commissioner alone. The advantage of Bunyoro was that when Amory was out of the District I was left with full authority. The regulations made provision for this because the moment he drove his car across the river into the next District I automatically became a first class magistrate with full powers under the law.

Even when he was in the District but away from Hoima I had to fill his shoes. On one occasion when the District Council was in session I received an urgent note to the effect that they did not understand the relationship between the *saza* councils and the *saza* chief. In case of disagreement whose will was to prevail? It was unfortunate that Amory had chosen to be absent from Hoima during a meeting of such importance and it left me with no option but to go to the Council chamber and try to answer their questions.

It was said in East Africa that the first District Commissioner's office had been an old railroad car abandoned during the building of the railway. All subsequent District offices, and hotels, for that matter, seem to have been modelled after that railway car with the offices, hotel rooms or whatever leading off a straight passage. The Germans, on the other hand, made everything square like a fortification and their District headquarters in Tanganyika came to be known as *bomas* which means fortress or defensive position, a word sometimes heard in Uganda. Our offices in Hoima were of the railway car variety, straight, one-storey with a concrete platform running round. The clerks and interpreters, about six of them, had a large office near mine and the accountant, a Goan by nationality, had his office at the end. This latter individual, Mr Fernandez, was a rather severe person who grudgingly paid people on pay day and gathered in the revenues at other times.

One day I received a request from an Indian in the bazaar to inspect a consignment of goods that had been damaged in transit. I did so and issued a magistrate's certificate detailing the extent of the damage, the whole task having occupied me for an hour. Subsequently, to my complete surprise, I received an honorarium from the company of ten English pounds. No sooner had I endorsed the cheque than Mr Fernandez was standing there with his hand outstretched.

'All such monies,' he intoned, 'to be paid into General Revenue and not one penny to be kept by officer concerned.'

In his thirty years' service he had learned a great deal about the inner workings of government and everyone relied on his store of knowledge. All the same I was sorry to part with those ten pounds.

On my arrival in Hoima I was not a complete novice at office work, having had some introduction aboard a wartime destroyer. It was Stephen, as might be expected, who put me through the preliminaries and explained that when letters came to the office they were opened by one of the clerks and placed on a clip-board, then passed immediately to Amory or myself. If they were written in Lunyoro or some other tribal language a clerk who was proficient in that language would make a brief translation in red ink. I was called on to translate letters from the Belgian Congo which came in French. Sometimes a half page of writing would be reduced to a couple of lines such as: 'Disgraceful animal in banana garden so people dare not approach.' At other times they told a sad story; a *gombolola* chief wrote to say: 'Three people killed by lightning while drinking beer,' or a humorous one like: 'Snake attacks bicycles but does not harm pedestrians.' One day there was a letter from an Indian who said he had been buying chillies in a village and when his back was turned the bumper was removed from his pick-up truck. He complained about it to the chief who told him it would be used for making spear blades. 'Is there not some law,' he enquired, 'which would prevent them making spears out of my bumper?'

Letters addressed to the District Commissioner from within Bunyoro usually contained the rather strange-sounding salutation 'Omunyoro, District Commissioner Bunyoro'. Omunyoro in this sense did not suggest Mr Amory was Munyoro by tribe but was used with the implication of 'Sir' or 'gentleman'. When I left Bunyoro the Mukama appointed me as an honorary Munyoro which meant I was an honorary gentleman. Amory thought that it was better to be an honorary gentleman than not to be one at all.

When addressing the Mukama in correspondence his subjects would frequently use the phrase: 'You are appointed by God,' which was sometimes included in letters to the District Commissioner. I would have to admit I was struck by the simplicity and directness of the assertion.

Letters that were in English were passed to us with nothing added and one day I chided Stephen for a letter which he had not translated.

'But it's written in English,' he replied.

I looked at it again and on being read aloud the unorthodox spelling began to make sense. The man had paid a visit to the neighbouring territory and been robbed of some possessions: *esarti*, *sueta*, *sapo*. I looked at it for a moment and finally the penny dropped. *Esarti* was a shirt, *sueta* was a sweater and *sapo* was a hat, not a nice English hat but a French one, *chapeau*.

With the clip-board of letters in front of Amory or myself it was our job to read through each and write simple instructions for the clerks. The letter about the disgraceful animal, probably a buffalo, would get a handwritten instruction: 'Inform game warden immediately.' The one about three people killed while drinking beer would be passed to Inspector Frisby so that he could open an inquest file. I really can't remember what we did about the snake which attacked bicycles, but recall that the villagers who manufactured their spear blades out of someone's bumper were duly brought to book.

Letters from the Provincial Commissioner or the Secretariat were designated 'Register and Return' which meant that the clerks would write the details in the Correspondence Register, then place the letter on the appropriate file and pass it back. They did more than this, however, because many letters referred to previous correspondence, sometimes on a variety of different files.

If there was more than one file involved the whole lot would be tied together with red office tape. Until I worked in a government office I didn't realize that there was such a thing as red tape and that it really got used to tie things. Like most people I thought of it merely as an expression, a form of speech which had no basis in reality. The red tape itself was of good quality and the clerks often used it to lace their shoes so that their feet were literally tied up with government red tape.

Here is an actual case which will illustrate how the office system worked. A letter from the Chief Secretary was received asking the District Commissioner what progress had been made in the matter of the young woman Ruth, daughter of Kopita, resident of the Eastern Province of the Belgian Congo. The clerks would look through the file to find the antecedents. First, on letter No 18 (all letters on the file were numbered in sequence), was a complaint from the Belgian *administrateur de territoire* in Djugu to the effect that the girl had been kidnapped at knife point by a fisherman and conveyed protesting to Uganda where she was being held against her will and subjected to vile indignities. Vile indignities sounded even more vile in French than they did in English. The letter began: '*J'ai l'honneur de porter à votre connaissance* . . .' (I have the honour to call your attention . . .) and ended, '*Veuillez agréer, Monsieur le District Commissioner, les assurances de ma considération la plus distinguée* . . .' which prompted Amory to acknowledge it in the same sort of florid prose and add that the matter was receiving his personal attention. He also sent a copy to Uganda's attorney general, Mr Ralph Dreshfield, because this was an international affair.

The next memo on the file was from Amory to myself. At the moment of writing he was in Hoima, I was away somewhere. 'Walter,' he wrote, 'you will be in Bugungu and can look into this. Speak to the girl and find out the story.'

Next on the file was my report which read: 'I refer to the alleged kidnapping of Ruth, daughter of Kopita. I saw her on January 12th and interviewed her with Stephen interpreting. I can say emphatically that she was not kidnapped and is not being held against her will. She said that she chose to come to Bugungu with Tommasi (her husband, a licenced fisherman) to escape being beaten and maltreated by her father. She showed me marks on her back which could have been caused by a stick and are now healed. She was carrying a small baby and said that Tommasi was the father. She implored me not to send her back to the Congo. Even though no bride-price had been paid I recommend that she not be forcibly returned.'

The next letter on file to which the clerks called attention was Amory's to the Attorney General enclosing my report and asking for a legal opinion. Amory had put in a few shots of his own to help Mr Dreshfield compose his legalistic opinions.

'By no stretch of the imagination does the girl qualify as a fugitive offender under the Fugitive Offenders Ordinance. The only person conceivably at fault is Tommasi, who circumvented native custom by not paying a bride-price. However, I cannot see how Tommasi can be extradited as a criminal for doing something that is not in our criminal code and I endorse the views expressed by my assistant.'

Now here was the Chief Secretary asking about it and Amory wondering how the hell the Chief Secretary got to hear about the case. He sat down to draft a reply using the file with its orderly sequence of letters and reports. As Amory pointed out, the advantage of the system was that if we all dropped dead and a totally new District Commissioner walked in the door he would not have any difficulty understanding the case as long as he read the letters on file. No time would be wasted and there would be no duplication of effort.

Much later in my career I took over a small District from an officer whom I met only briefly as he was being loaded on an aeroplane strapped to a stretcher. His filing system had been well kept and all the problems and difficulties of the District were set out so that a lengthy verbal turnover between the two of us was not needed.

The filing system we followed in Bunyoro was part of a Uganda-wide system and worked with all the genius of simplicity. Civil servants normally have a mania for complication and proliferation but the filing system of Uganda was a work of elegant straightforwardness. A letter from the Chief Secretary asking something about the District's cotton production would be marked AGR 6 (Agriculture six). It would be filed in our AGR 6 file and our letters going out to the five *saza* chiefs asking for information would also be marked AGR 6 and would likewise go on their AGR 6 files. The secretariat probably had hundreds of AGR files, with subdivisions; we had a dozen or so and the chiefs no more than one or two. The point was that AGR was immediately recognizable as Agriculture and of course there were others, equally simple; TAX meant taxation matters, ADM was administration. I recall that when I ordered tools and equipment for Hoima Township the requisitions were placed on the MIS (Miscellaneous) 13 file.

When I was on safari I always asked to see the chiefs' letter files and Stephen would help them if there were any problems. During my safari in Buhaguzi *saza* in early May I looked over the cupboard of neatly stacked files and picked one at random which happened to be the VET file (Veterinary matters, livestock etc.) and leafed through it. I knew that Amory had sent Christmas cards to the five *saza* chiefs in mid-December because he mentioned it to me, but I did not expect to see his Christmas card on the *saza* chief's Veterinary file. The chief was an elderly man, very respected, and I was determined not to say anything tactless, particularly since his two clerks were in the room.

I turned to it again, a plain card with the words 'Christmas greetings and all good wishes; Cecil Amory, District Commissioner.' Handwritten underneath was the same thing in Lunyoro, obviously the work of one of our clerks. Then I turned to the centre page and all became clear. It was the familiar Christmas scene of Mary, the baby Jesus, Joseph, bearded and dumbstruck, as fathers tend to be at such moments, and an assortment of livestock looking on. It had been the livestock, camel, cow, sheep and goats which had persuaded them to put it on the 'Veterinary' file.

Later I told Stephen to mention it casually to the *saza* chief, not in any sense as a reproach, but merely to say that a Christmas card was different from an ordinary letter. The animals didn't matter so much as the good wishes and compliments that were being conveyed. Stephen discovered that this was the first Christmas card the chief had ever received and on my next visit to his headquarters I noticed that it had been put up on the wall of his office.

To return for a moment to the story of Ruth, daughter of Kopita, it is pleasant to record that the matter was laid to rest by a letter written to the Belgian *administrateur*. The attorney general advised us to state that the information on which he relied was false and misleading and make it clear that we were not interested in pursuing it. Amory outdid himself and we got it translated into really elegant French, not my sort of schoolboy French, by someone who had been in the Diplomatic Corps. It was a hard-hitting letter accusing him of 'blatant disregard for the facts of the case', 'inhuman treatment of an innocent young woman', and a good deal more. We never heard another word about it.

Some of the matters that reached the District Commissioner's office called attention to problems for which there were no solutions. We received a letter from the East African Currency Board pointing out that coins of small denomination were being hoarded and taken out of circulation to the detriment of their operations. They noted that it cost them four cents to manufacture a one-cent coin and yet millions of them were being buried in the ground by African farmers and not passed from hand to hand. The Board believed that as soon as the growers had received cash for their crops of cotton, tobacco and coffee they hid the money and the Currency Board had no option but to produce more at considerable expense. They suggested that the District Commissioner instruct the people in better numismatic habits.

'You deal with this,' was Amory's note to me. He had underlined 'better numismatic habits' and written 'Ye gods' beside it.

The East African Currency Board had a difficult problem. Cases were always being reported of African farmers who had saved coins of small denomination for many years and buried them in their gardens. If the man were to die suddenly his family might not know where the money was hidden and would be cheated of their inheritance and at the same time the Currency Board would be the loser. Clearly this was not a problem that was confined to Africa but must have been worldwide and one wondered how it had been dealt with elsewhere. A possible solution was that if all currency were paper, none of it metal, people would be afraid to bury it for fear of its being eaten by the white ants. In other words the fact that paper was so destructible might mean that they would be reluctant to hoard it.

The only other solution was to open small, government-run banks and teach people to have enough confidence in them to deposit their money, although this seemed a long distance off. At that time Bunyoro had not a single commercial bank and there were no plans to open one while I was there.

A peculiarity of East African currency was that coins had holes through them so that they could be strung together and carried round the owner's neck. In the backward Districts of Northern Uganda this was an advantage to people who did not have too much in the way of trousers and therefore no pockets for their money.

One of Amory's many responsibilities was in relation to the finances of the District. This meant that he drew up the estimates of expenditure for the forthcoming year and, when they were approved, ensured that the money was spent precisely as it should have been. The unforgivable sin was for a District Commissioner to move money from one 'vote' to another and use it for a purpose other than that for which it had been approved. To keep us honest, audits were conducted by gangs of hawk-eyed individuals from the Finance Department who descended on us without warning armed with their distinctive green pencils. No one in the government except auditors was permitted to use a green pencil. It was, of course, the solemn duty of an up-country officer to outwit them, which happened when one of our chiefs, visiting the Belgian Congo, was arrested for no offence whatsoever and managed to obtain his release on payment of a two hundred shilling bribe. Amory was furious and determined to recompense the chief from government funds. He searched through the Vote Book and stopped at 'Entertainment of Visitors and Foreign Dignitaries'.

'Make out an expenditure item,' he shouted to me, 'and mark it down as *Entertainment of Corrupt Congolese Official*. What's more,' he added, 'make bloody sure the Belgians get to hear about it. You can write in French and ask them for a receipt.'

Unbelievably, the auditors did not question the entry although I didn't get a receipt.

I scored a minor triumph of my own when called upon to pay for a wooden leg which had been fitted in Mulago Hospital, outside Kampala, to one of the victims of the Bunyoro bus accident. It seemed astonishing that the hospital would not pay for such an item, but there it was, an account for sixty shillings for an artificial limb. Of course the District had no vote for prosthetic devices but I thumbed through the book and allowed my imagination to run wild. There was a little money left in 'Sports Equipment', no, that would hardly do. Then I came across the Furniture Vote: 'Office and Other Furniture Supplies', and decided that a wooden leg might fairly be described as an item of furniture because it did say *other* furniture supplies, not just office ones. In the event, the man hobbled away with his leg paid for and the entry was spared the attentions of the auditor's green pencil.

Quite frequently one met goverment officers who deplored the amount of paperwork that was forced on them and invented ingenious ways of getting round it. The game wardens, for instance, prided themselves on being naturalists and hunters who didn't bother to answer letters from headquarters until they had received at least three reminders. One of them, a somewhat eccentric but well-intentioned character who was game warden in Toro District, submitted his monthly car mileage claim on toilet paper because he had run short of the proper forms. If he answered a letter at all it was by turning it over and scratching the answer on the back. On one occasion he didn't have a pencil handy so he wrote the reply with the tip of a soft-nosed bullet.

A report which we were all required to make at the end of each month was our Touring Return which showed how many nights we had spent away from heaquarters, Hoima in our case. A daylong trip did not qualify; it was spending the night away that counted and many officers set themselves a target of ten to fifteen nights a month. To my mind there was a striking parallel between being on safari and being at sea, and equally between being in harbour and being in Hoima. Often I inadvertently said, 'I'll be at sea on that date,' when I meant that I'd be on safari.

Accompanying our touring reports were the monthly mileage claims on which we detailed every journey undertaken, the distance and the means of travel. The form itself was the soul of helpfulness and listed the possible means of conveyance as 'foot safari, bicycle, horse or mule, camel or motor vehicle. (Cross out whichever is not applicable.)'

The most pestiferous correspondence was always that which called for information or answers that we did not have and could not obtain. We knew that the chiefs, for instance, occasionally compelled tax defaulters to work on the roads in defrayment of their taxes but it was infrequent and there were no records. It was impossible, therefore, to answer a question about 'Forced Labour' from some international body because they wanted to know the number of man-hours worked. If I recall correctly the question came from the International Convention on Forced Labour which I am sure was an admirable organization with worthy objectives to which we would have subscribed. However, we had no means of answering their questions fully or accurately.

Likewise a letter asking for details of infanticide left us at a loss. It was generally assumed to occur on the rather negative evidence that one never saw a malformed or diseased baby except for one or two born in hospital. The doctor said that the evidence, or lack of it, suggested that if the baby was born in the village and there appeared to be something wrong it was disposed of quietly. The *gombolola* chiefs' Register of Births would have no entry because it would not be reported as a birth by the father and no inquests were held when persons died, old or young, unless the police specifically intervened. Ninety-nine out of every hundred deaths were followed by immediate interment in the village with no outside interference. Most of us were fairly certain that infanticide was practised, just as abortion is practised in the western world, but if we had asked questions we would have received denials.

In this connection it was interesting to study the records of early explorers and missionaries. They recorded native custom as they saw and heard it before western education had taken hold and in consequence people were not ashamed to disclose all kinds of details. Now, of course, they are embarrassed by those aspects of native custom, like infanticide, that appear savage or uncivilized. Even someone as truthful as Stephen would not answer directly if asked about the ancient burial customs, for instance, as applied to a dead Mukama. All the older writers reported that the body of the Mukama was wrapped in a white cowskin and placed in a large grave with milk poured over it, and a few bystanders were then hacked to death and thrown in before the grave was closed up. When asked, Stephen would adopt his most refined air and say that there must be some mistake, nothing like that had ever taken place. Likewise with infanticide; they knew enough to deny it, but not enough to put a stop to the practice.

The letters and reports prepared by Amory and myself were drafted by hand, translated if need be, and typed by one of the clerks. If the letter was addressed to a chief who did not understand English a Lunyoro version followed the English. Two of our clerks possessed beautiful handwriting, both of them having been appointed before the office had any typewriters, so that it had been their duty to write fair copies of letters. When one has seen the sheer elegance of a handwritten letter, the character it possesses and absence of mechanical overtones, only then does one realize how much is lost by using a machine. Sadly, we have no time for this kind of thing in the modern world and are reduced to the plainness of mechanically produced letters. I was glad to have had a glimpse, however briefly, of the older and more personal style that preceded the typewriter.

Amory, surprisingly for a former schoolmaster, had the worst writing I have ever seen. The clerks simply could not make it out and would come to my office and ask for help if he had written a batch of letters and then gone on safari. Sometimes it got so bad that I sent them to his house to see if his wife could do any better than I could. At least she knew his pet phrases and expressions, which were often in Latin, a language of which the clerks had absolutely no knowledge. A page of ill-written *quid pro quos* and *status quo antes* is pretty hard to comprehend if you have never seen any Latin in your life.

One day when he was in the office I heard a bellow of rage and went to see what had gone wrong. Amory had written 'the onus now falls directly on us . . .' but on being typed the 'o' of onus had changed to an 'a' so it was something very different and less attractive that now fell directly on us.

One of the abiding problems in up-country Africa was the isolation and shortage of news. It was perverse that by subscribing to the *Times of London* air mail edition we could be well-informed on English and world affairs, and by reading the *Uganda Argus*, the English language newspaper printed in Kampala, we could be rather less well informed of happenings in Kampala and Entebbe, but when it came to knowing what was going on in the other Districts of Uganda, there was a blank spot. There was no internal information, no exchange between Districts and the only time I ever met the government information officer was when he came trailing around with the governor's safari. The truth was that the Districts were too compartmentalized and no one at headquarters took it upon himself to inform District Commissioners of the trials and errors of others. There was not even an annual District Commissioners' conference which would have been an admirable vehicle for passing information.

In Ankole, for instance, the rich cattle District to the south, we heard vaguely that a resettlement scheme had been undertaken in the wake of tsetse fly clearance. Settlers from the overpopulated and mountainous areas of Kigezi District had been offered inducements to migrate and take up free, empty land which was fertile and had excellent water supplies. For some unexplained reason it didn't work and people didn't move. Inducements were increased to the point where they were almost bribing them to migrate: a preliminary tour of the new land to see if the prospective settlers liked it; tax exemption; free food for the first year and transportation paid for – and still the potential settlers remained precisely where they were in overcrowded, land-hungry Kigezi where the fields were the size of ping-pong tables. The only way we got to hear about it was because Mrs Amory ran into the wife of Ankole's District Commissioner in Draper's store in Kampala. There must have been lessons to be learned but no one took the trouble to write a few pages and pass it to the other Districts.

Likewise in Toro District the development of the copper mines would have made fascinating reading. The mines were supposed to have been discovered by the Italian Duc d'Abruzzi who led a mountaineering expedition to the Ruwenzori which is one of the very few mountain ranges in the world that has no foothills. The problem was, of course, that access to the mine was exceedingly difficult, but they solved it somehow and although we lived within a couple of hundred miles we never discovered the details.

In the Eastern Province it was known that considerable advances had been made with local government and local councils but we were never informed. In wild and backward Karamoja it was said that the annual cattle-stealing match between the two main tribes had been, well, not stopped but adequately refereed by police in Landrovers and a helicopter, which would have been interesting since we had problems with poachers in the game reserve.

Visitors used to drop in at the District Commissioner's office in Hoima, although the numbers mysteriously declined after the polio outbreak in May of 1952. Most were officials or semi-officials attached to some government department. A rather jolly fellow with a loud voice came to ask if we wanted instructional films to be shown in the District on such matters as cotton production, soil erosion and house building techniques. Amory pointed out that we had no electricity for him to operate the machine and, just as important, the Banyoro couldn't comprehend moving pictures anyway. I didn't want to display my ignorance by asking him what he meant and questioned Stephen later.

'Yes,' Stephen said, 'I went to the moving pictures myself when I visited Kampala and could not understand any of it. A lot of pictures seemed to be moving but it made no sense and I could not tell what the story was about. I don't think we are the only Africans who have this difficulty. Mr Amory is right, it would be a waste of time to show movies to the people in the villages although I think after a little practice we would learn to see them as white people do.'

I had often wondered about the Africans' ability to understand pictures, which they are not brought up with as children. I had noticed that they did not take in a picture at a glance like Europeans. Copies of the *Illustrated London News*, having spent a week in our living room, would always be taken down to the office where

Mr Fernandez would claim them first and after him the clerks and office messengers. They loved the pictures, particularly those of the King and Queen, but they studied each one for minutes at a time and I wondered how their eyes really saw them.

Anything in the nature of a cartoon was totally foreign to their comprehension. Stephen came to me one day and the conversation went as follows:

'Sir, the clerks do not understand these pictures and have asked me for an explanation.'

'Very well, Stephen. This figure is a stuffy old colonel who has retired from the army.'

'How can you tell that from a few lines?'

'I am interpreting the essence of those lines. And here is an empty-headed young woman.'

'Is she married?'

'I don't know, but I think not. Here the colonel says that his grandfather was killed at Waterloo. The battle of Waterloo was fought in the year 1815.'

'It is sad to think of battles,' Stephen mused.

'The silly woman knows that there is a railway station in London called Waterloo but she does not know about the battle. She says, "which platform?"'

Stephen looked pained but I struggled on.

'Here the colonel is talking to an older woman, probably his wife. You can see she is older by the size . . .'

'She has had many children,' Stephen said primly.

'Exactly, so she should know that the railway station was built after the battle and was named after it, not the other way round. The colonel tells her about the silly young woman and what she said. The older woman says, "What a silly girl; as though it mattered which platform," which shows that . . . are you following me, Stephen?'

11

Biseruka

One day I drove with Stephen to the village of Biseruka, which clung to the top of the escarpment overlooking Lake Albert. It was a collection of homesteads spread over an area of two or three square miles with cultivation where the soil was rich while in other places the bush had been left undisturbed. The amount of cotton produced at Biseruka seemed to justify expenditure on improved roads, a cotton store and other amenities so Amory told me to have a good look and report back to the Council with my recommendations.

We were driving in the Landrover westwards along the jungle track when Stephen turned and said, 'Sir, at Biseruka they use a very bad word when they see me.'

'What do they say?' I asked.

'They say "goddamitman".'

'Stephen,' I said, 'They don't say "goddamitman" because they thought of the word themselves. I am sure there is a story behind it. Why not tell me about it.'

Stephen grasped the metal rail in front of him and began.

'It was some years ago, before the war, when I was a young interpreter. A great doctor had come to Uganda to study a blood condition which was thought to be prevalent. For reasons I cannot fully explain he found it better to take samples in isolated villages where he could be sure of getting blood from every person in the village and not miss any. The District Commissioner sent him to Biseruka and ordered me to accompany him as interpreter. The village chief at Biseruka had been asked by letter to have all the people in readiness.'

Stephen paused and stared at the elephant grass which formed solid walls beside the track.

'He was a very important person and ill-tempered. He cursed the bad road and seemed to be saying that it was the fault of the driver of the vehicle which, by the way, was like a large ambulance with a red cross on it. The doctor spoke in a strange accent and used expressions that I could not understand.

'When we reached Biseruka we stopped under a tree and the village chief came forward to introduce himself. The doctor, however, was too important to greet him and shouted at me to get the bastards lined up. He told me to step on the gas, which made no sense at all. With the people in a line he indicated that he wished to address them and explain what he was about to do. This is where my difficulties began.

' "Your government boys have flashed me the green light," he said, and I translated into Lunyoro: "The sons of government offices have shown me a green lantern."

'He could not understand any Lunyoro so he did not know what I was saying.

'He went on, "You guys are gonna be the guinea pigs."

'I told them they would be pigs from Guinea. I had not the faintest idea how to say these things properly, but I spoke anyway.

'The villagers were slow to react but with some grumbling they allowed the doctor and his assistants to draw blood from each person's arm. The place where the needle penetrated the skin was cleansed with a piece of cotton which, with a little blood on it, was thrown into a bucket.

'The village nuisance and troublemaker at that time was a man called Asahi. He began to say that it was disgraceful that men and women should be required to form up in a single line one behind the other. Such a thing did not conform with native custom and the men should have been in one line and women in another. What was more, the doctor had made blood brothers of all the people in the village by throwing the pieces of cotton in the same bucket. The doctor had shown himself contemptuous of the dignity of the people and he had failed to explain what he was doing. Only if the people had agreed should he have taken their blood. The chief and older men should have been asked to decide how the lines were to be formed.

'He was applauded and the shouting grew loud. I explained to the doctor what Asahi had said and he told me he would reply:

' "Right off the bat you guys are nuts."

'I had become bolder and said to him that I could not understand what he meant. Right off the bat, what bat? I could see no bat. And guys meant nothing to me. How was I to translate such a word? We had words for people, villagers and cultivators, but no word for guys.

'"Goddamitman!" he shouted at me, and the people all began to say "Goddamitman". Some laughed, others were angry and led by Asahi they pushed his ambulance down the hill and into a swamp. Asahi then took mouthfuls of dust from the path and blew it into the air. It is difficult to explain exactly what is meant by such a gesture but it is intended as an insult. There was no violence done to the doctor or his assistants but after a lot more shouting and argument we were compelled to leave the village on foot. No one would lend us bicycles, not even the village chief, so we had to walk ten miles to the main road where we were able to get a ride from an Indian. As we left the village there were shouts of "goddamitman".'

'How did it end, Stephen?' I asked. 'Did the doctor get his vehicle back?'

"Well, the District Commissioner at that time was Mr Dauncey Tongue and when he heard the story he laughed. Of all the District Commissioners we have had, I believe Mr Tongue liked the Banyoro and understood them the best. He was a brave man, rather "Kapere" as we call it.'

'I have seen his picture in the Mukama's office,' I interrupted. 'He has his hat on one side and a smile on his face. I think we would use the French word "debonair". It means having a pleasant manner, being vigorous and well disposed to people. You are right to call him "Kapere", a captain, because he was a soldier.'

'Well, Mr Dauncey Tongue went to see the Mukama and what they discussed I do not know. However, he left the doctor in Hoima and we went to Biseruka the next day with ropes in his car. He held a big *baraza* which lasted a long time. He said that he did not blame the people for their anger because they had been abused and he promised that there would be no punishment provided they pulled the ambulance out of the swamp. As far as the blood brotherhood was concerned he agreed that this was a serious matter. He proposed to discuss it with the Keeper of the Royal Tombs and take whatever steps were needed to reverse the ceremony that had turned the people into blood brothers.'

'But since coming to Bunyoro,' I said, 'I have heard little about the ceremony of blood brotherhood; in fact I hardly knew it was practised. Did the people really believe the doctor had made them into blood brothers and if he had, what difference did it make?'

"Well, Asahi was correct about blood brotherhood and no one could argue with him. It was what you might call a technicality but at the same time their anger had been roused and they had to agree with him that the action of combining the pieces of bloody cotton was binding on everyone. But yes, you are right that it is not much used these days since tribal wars are no longer being fought. It is a very private ceremony in which young men pledge help to each other right up to their deaths. They still do it sometimes when two young men join the army because it gives them confidence in face of the unknown. It is totally inappropriate for a whole village to be made blood brothers and would lead to a lot of trouble.

'You must also remember that a person like Asahi, the village troublemaker, is an actor and orator and he was putting on a show which people expect from him. Since the doctor had behaved badly and abused them it was his job to make difficulties in return. Anyway, they pulled the ambulance out of the swamp with the ropes that Mr Dauncey Tongue had brought. That was not the end of the story because Mr Dauncey Tongue spoke with the Keeper of the Royal Tombs and between them they decided what should be done to negate the blood brotherhood.'

'In other words,' I suggested, 'the Keeper of the Royal Tombs was acting in his capacity as chief of protocol and high authority on native custom.'

'Right. They decided on the form that the ceremony would take and how it would be conducted. We all came here again about three weeks later with Mr Dauncey Tongue in his white uniform and the Keeper of the Royal Tombs and Chief Judge of Bunyoro in ceremonial robes. A police *askari* blew his bugle while the British flag was laid on the table in front of Mr Dauncey Tongue and the Bunyoro flag in front of the

Keeper of the Tombs. There were fine speeches and the cotton with blood on it was thrown on a fire. It ended with a feast and was such a noble ceremony that it undid the blood brotherhood of all the village.'

I tried to imagine the scene; a blue sky overhead and Lake Albert shimmering in the distance. Under a spreading tree the District Commissioner in white uniform with medals and sword playing his solemn part among a people for whom he felt such deep affection. His speech would have been well prepared, courteous and dignified. Then it was the turn of the Keeper of the Royal Tombs of Bunyoro in his black cotton robes edged with gold lace and a decorated red fez. He was acting in his capacity as guardian of native custom, custodian and high priest of those dark, inward secrets of the Banyoro people. He would call attention to their history and ancient heritage, their long dynasty of kings, their warlike exploits and inviolate customs. He would pronounce in this ancient and sonorous language that the blood brotherhood which had been inflicted on them was to be expunged, that they would be free to conduct their lives unhampered by its restrictions and penalties. The police bugle would sound, Dauncey Tongue would salute and the offending cotton swabs be cast upon the fire. The chiefs would murmur their approval, the people clap their hands and thoughts would turn to the fat ox that had been roasting for the past two days. Stephen had said that Asahi and his kind were born actors, but Asahi was not the only one who knew how to put on a good performance.

I wondered what the doctor had learned from it. His mistake was to show insensitivity to the personal dignity of the villagers and I remembered that back in London Margaret Mead, the anthropologist, had lectured us to be eternally careful of two things, their dignity and their land.

'People in third world countries possess so little,' she had said. 'They don't have our education, they don't have our physical or intellectual freedom and none of our vast material wealth. What they do possess is an unquenchable personal dignity and, of course, their land, and these they treasure to an extent that is difficult and yet very necessary for us to understand. Err on the side of formality and deference, be patient and listen to their side of every story.'

I had learned from the Native Court registers in each *gombolola* that personal insults in Bunyoro were treated in the same way that a savage blow would be treated. To be called a fool would justify a violent response and at such times one could only hope that no spear or other weapon was within reach. The Lunyoro had a word for 'fool', the commonest insult, but they also seemed fascinated by the expression '*biruddifuru*', their rendering of 'bloody fool'. It seems odd and a little unfortunate that this epithet should have found a niche in their language when they had their own word which was more than adequate for creating trouble. When I first saw '*birrudifuru*' in a court register I stared at it for a few seconds, realizing that it was not a Lunyoro word. Turning to Stephen I began, 'What does this word biruddi . . .' then recognized it even as I said it. The trick, of course, is to say it out loud.

The Lunyoro language has a saying that demonstrates their sense of outrage at being verbally insulted. It is one of those stitches-in-time-that-save-time, enough-is-as-good-as-a-feast phrases that goes something like this: 'If your wife insults you, send her home and reclaim the bride-price. It is better to be without a wife than to keep a woman who destroys you with abuse.'

The lesson to be learned, therefore, is that an assault against his dignity is, to a Munyoro, an attack where he is most vulnerable and his reaction is often violent. His personal dignity and his worth as a human being cannot be assailed with impunity.

If the doctor's first mistake was bad manners and insensitivity, the second grew naturally out of it and led him to disregard the subtle process of communication between English and Lunyoro. He made no effort to converse with Stephen before going to Biseruka to discover the range and capability of his mind, nor did he try him, in advance, with the sort of things he wanted to say. His use of slang phrases which Stephen could not understand was inexcusable. Having said that, however, it is only fair to add that there are many people who have such a poor grasp of their own language that they thumb a ride on every passing cliché. It is a form of mental lassitude, eternally taking refuge behind those ghastly phrases whose meanings have become vacant as a consequence of endless repetition.

When translating from English to Lunyoro, even mere carelessness is bad enough. A judge who sat in Hoima to hear a murder case used the phrase: 'So far as I can see he gave assent . . .' The court interpreter looked perplexed and translated: 'So far as the judge can see he gave a cent.' Later in the same case the judge asked: 'How on earth did you get into the picture?' This came through as: 'How did you get your picture taken?' The rule is to use only simple and basic English but there are many so-called educated people who cannot do this.

Stephen, when I knew him in the early 1950s, was an experienced and very capable interpreter. When he was interpreting for Mr Amory at a meeting following the bus tragedy Amory used the phrase: 'They were packed like sardines into a can.' Stephen shot him a quick glance and hesitated. There were not three people in the audience of five hundred who knew what sardines were or what they would be doing in cans. 'They were packed in,' Stephen finally said, 'like grasshoppers into a bag.' It was a perfect translation because it conveyed the meaning precisely and no one there could have failed to understand.

There is an important difference between translating for a group of villagers and translating in the formal circumstances of the courtroom. In the village the interpreter's duty is to convey the meaning, to understand what is being said and put it over by any means he can. In the process he must somehow express the tone and mood of the original and be able to exude warmth or humour or whatever is needed. To help him, the person using the interpreter must make each sentence contain a single, clear thought. It is no use rambling on with subordinate clauses and modifications of what has just been said. He must also learn to drop his voice at the end of a sentence so the interpreter knows when to begin. With close attention it is not difficult to produce a polished performance which has some chance of appealing to the audience.

In the courtroom the interpreter's duty is different. If he is not careful he will find himself taking sides, tidying up witnesses' answers or slanting it one way or the other without being fully aware that he is doing so. If the witness answers a question with a foolish or irrelevant reply he must give that reply in all its folly and irrelevance so that the judge, defence lawyer and prosecutor will know that it is foolish and irrelevant and draw their own conclusions. He must never be an interpretive interpreter but rather a machine translating exactly from one language to the other. He must scrupulously avoid forming ideas about the case such as the credibility of a witness or culpability of an accused.

It helps beyond measure to know something of the other language when using an interpreter. You can appreciate the difficulties and know instinctively what can be said and what is beyond the capacity of the interpreter and the language. A phrase like: 'It is better to light one small candle than to curse the darkness,' would cause Stephen not the slightest difficulty. The phrase: 'It's a white elephant,' would leave him baffled. You also get better continuity from knowing a few words and if you have, for instance, ended your sentence with something about soil erosion you listen for the words and know when to start a new sentence.

I have no idea what happened to the doctor but I do remember that my recommendations concerning Biseruka were accepted by the Council. With the head of Public Works I returned and camped for a few days while we laid out a chief's headquarters, new roads, a medical dispensary and primary school. Asahi, the professional troublemaker, had died some years before but I was determined to preserve the tree under whose branches so much drama had occurred in years gone by. This was accomplished by building a camp site for visiting officers, so that those who came to visit Biseruka would be camped beside it, would take their meals under its shade and it would come to be regarded as part of the camp and not just a tree that anyone could cut down and hollow out for a canoe.

I remember Biseruka for the magnificent views across Lake Albert. The weather was cool and sunny at that time of year with a few sharp storms. Using binoculars I could study the creviced mountains brooding on the western side of the rift. It was thirty miles to the plateau just east of the town of Djugu in the Congo but after the rain the air was so clear that the metal roofs of farm buildings could easily be seen. Lake Albert lay below in its trough reflecting the changing colours of the surrounding mountains. Geographically it is part of the western arm of the Great Rift valley which begins somewhere in Syria and runs southward three-quarters of the length of Africa.

There was a rock on the slope below the camp, a monolith the size of a cathedral which could be climbed and which was a sort of crow's-nest from which the whole valley of Lake Albert could be seen. One morning I was up early watching the animals on the plain emerging from the shadows: kob, waterbuck and congoni, when my eye was attracted to a fish eagle soaring upward in the clean morning air with a fish, probably tilapia, in its talons. It alighted in a tree where it had its nest and I could see the fish struggling. The eagle must have carried it five miles across the plain and just over a thousand feet up the escarpment, a fish that I judged to be a pound in weight, and yet there it was, as fresh as the trout that swim in tanks in French restaurants. The eagle could not have been much assisted by thermals at that early hour and it was the sheer power of its wings that had brought the fish eagle family a breakfast that I would not have scorned myself.

Another memory of the Lake Albert Rift was a shower of meteorites. The stars were clear with no moon and the meteorites streaked through the earth's atmosphere in a cascade. Sometimes they left a smoke trail in their wake which lasted a few seconds and they were so bright they looked like starshell during the war. It is almost a disappointment to know that the whole magnificent display is caused by particles no larger than a pinhead. They were at their best during the hour before dawn owing, presumably, to the angle of their approach relative to the earth's rotation.

During the few days I was there I decided to go down the escarpment to the two fishing villages of Tonya and Kaiso. We started early so as to benefit from the cool morning air but the grass was wet with dew and our clothes were soaked before we had gone more than half a mile. The local chief led the way with his *askari*, I followed carrying my rifle, then half a dozen men from Biseruka carrying our camp kit. In the rear came Stephen and Georgi. I mention this because we heard later that we nearly ran into Mulisi Alideki. He was also going down the escarpment that morning by the very same path that we had chosen and, indeed, I pointed out the fresh tracks on the pathway to the chief who thought it was a group of fishermen returning to their lakeside villages. When Mulisi realized that people were behind him he and his companions stepped off the path into the long grass and allowed us to pass. He and one of his companions were armed and were not more than a few yards distant. He evidently supposed that we were following him, hunting him, in other words, and the moment we were out of sight he doubled back up the slope and into the jungle to the east of Biseruka.

In retrospect I can only blame myself for inattention and poor organization. I was rather enjoying my few days at Biseruka which was not considered to be one of Mulisi's hunting grounds. I had not taken the trouble to get information as to his movements, nor did I have a policeman or game guard with me. Furthermore, if I had been truly alert I might have paid more attention to the tracks and noticed that they ended abruptly at a certain point. Lastly, it was a calm, still morning and I had not eaten any breakfast so my sense of smell should have been at its best. The smoked buffalo meat which Mulisi and his companions would normally carry as rations should have been evident if I had had my wits about me.

Anyway, blissful in our ignorance, we descended the escarpment and crossed the flat plain to the villages of Tonya and Kaiso on the shore of the lake. The number of inhabitants was small, about a hundred people in all, and there was no other habitation on the plain because it was hot and unhealthy and the soil poor. Nor was there any cultivation because hippos ambled out of the water every night and ate or trod on any attempts to plant gardens. Hippos feed their huge bodies at night and return to the water at dawn. I once shot a troublesome old male which was terrorizing a lakeside village at about nine o'clock in the morning. On examination it turned out that it was blind as a result of fighting with other bull hippos and did not know that the sun was up and that it ought to have been back in the water.

With no food crops grown locally there was considerable foot traffic across the plain and up the escarpment with fish, and down again with potatoes, food bananas, maize and vegetables. It was all carried by head-load, about sixty pounds per man and on average, they made the journey once a week. The two villages, therefore, were not places where people lived on a permanent basis but were more in the nature of temporary camps from which they conducted their fishing operations. In consequence the houses were poorly built and unhealthy. A few goats and chickens shared their master's accommodation at night, there were no deep 'privies' because the soil was sandy and caved in when attempts were made to dig, and the whole place had a primitive air and a bad smell. There were very few women and no children, the men claiming that they had proper houses and gardens in the Biseruka area. From an administrative standpoint, therefore, it was unsatisfactory, but the thing to remember was that valuable fish was being provided to a few thousand people. For this reason the Biseruka chief had not demanded compliance with the Native Council by-laws on house-building, sanitation, the growing of food crops and so on.

A simple answer to the problem would have been to build a road down the escarpment for wheeled traffic. However, the escarpment, clearly visible five miles distant across the plain, was over a thousand feet high with a steepness of forty-five degrees so that the cost of a road would have been prohibitive. All we could do was to persuade the fishermen of both villages to make gradual improvements to their dwellings and replace grass and mud shacks with something more permanent.

We decided to spend the night at Kaiso so Georgi put up my tent just outside the village. He made a fire and asked what he should cook for supper. As though in answer, a fisherman appeared with a twenty-pound Nile perch, called *mputa*, which he wanted to sell. It was large enough to feed all ten people who had accompanied me, the chief from Biseruka, Stephen, Georgi, and half a dozen young fellows who acted as porters. The only problem was that I hadn't any money and while I could have bartered some of our rations I did not want to lose my supplies in case we had to spend an extra night below the escarpment.

Suddenly I had an inspiration. Somewhere in my kit I had a couple of large fish hooks. In the navy they are called cod-hooks and when the ship is at anchor the chief boatswain's mate hands them out to any sailor who asks for one. The reasoning is that you might as well encourage the sailors to catch their own supper if it only costs the price of a hook. Anyway, I produced them from the tin in which I kept a few odds and ends. The fishermen seemed delighted at the exchange and we had a magnificent supper. The only one upset was Stephen.

'Sir,' he said in an aggrieved voice, 'Two hooks is too much and the man would have been satisfied with one. You spoil people with your generosity.'

The next day we broke camp early and walked south-westwards along the lakeshore and across the dry Ngema river. The flat land carried plenty of game animals and it soon became apparent that the fishermen of Tonya and Kaiso were not confining their activities to fishing but did some poaching on the side. There were pit-traps covered with light brush and leaves so that an animal treading on it would fall in and be impaled on the sharp sticks that were set in the pit with their points upward. As Stephen pointed out, the fishermen had claimed that they could not dig privies in the sandy soil but were digging pits to snare animals. We also found dozens of wire snares which were set to catch animals by the neck. They were looped at a place where an animal might push its way through a bit of jungle or between trees; the wire would tighten and the animal die a slow death from thirst and starvation.

The official attitude toward game poaching by Africans was that it was cruel and that females and young animals suffered the most. The male waterbucks, for instance, with their long horns, were rarely caught because the horns did not get through the loop and where pit traps were concerned they seemed more cautious than females. Technically it was the game warden's task to deal with poaching but Roy Wyndham couldn't be everywhere and his staff of African guards was small. The one thing we could do was to uncover the pit traps and fill them sufficiently to cover the sharpened sticks and to collect the wires and take them away with us so they could not be used again. It was a considerable task and by the end of the day we were all tired and had added to our burdens with a huge coil of wires. I think we had covered twenty miles and had done much hard physical work so when we reached the foot of the escarpment below Biseruka we decided to camp for the night and climb in the morning. The sun had gone down behind the Congo mountains as we halted and made camp. I told Georgi to cook rice and beans in a big pot.

I want to describe rather carefully the events that followed because they left a deep impression on my mind. I made notes at the time but

I don't need them to recollect how I might have killed myself by sheer stupidity. The little river Lwamaronga was dry and the stream bed made a cut in the ground twenty feet deep and twenty or thirty feet across, a sort of miniature Rift Valley. I could climb down the bank, I thought, and put up my tent on the clean white sand at the bottom. It looked inviting by the fading light and would have given me a comfortable night because I had no camp bed and my sleeping bag would lie directly on the soft sand. However, it was getting too dark to see my way down and I found another spot on level ground at the top. I put up my tent, the Lunyoro expression for this being to 'increase' a tent, rolled out the sleeping bag and laid my rifle beside it. The process of 'checking in' was about as simple as that. Next I went to see how Stephen and the others were doing and help Georgi with the supper. He had a fire going and had started cooking the food with water we had carried with us. A small fire is much better than a big one for cooking in the bush. If the fire is too large you burn the food and burn yourself trying to stir it. The most sensible arrangement is to have a small cooking fire about the size of a hat and a larger one for keeping mosquitoes away.

At about two in the morning I awoke to hear a storm raging on the plateau above. For seconds at a time the thunder and lightning was continuous although we were getting no rain at the foot of the hill. Then I heard it come down the mountainside, a noise like a thousand stampeding elephants, the noise of trains in tunnels. I realized that a wall of water was on its way down the mountain; water, trees and rocks in massive confusion. I rolled out of my sleeping bag and pulled on my shoes and for half an hour stood in the dark and watched it pass. The water rose to within a foot of the top of the bank, an astonishing confusion of water and debris, and the ground actually shook under my feet. I thought how I had considered putting my tent in the stream bed and now felt exceedingly foolish because no one could have survived that torrent. I simply had not used whatever brains I might have possessed, this being the cardinal sin in Africa as elsewhere.

I had heard Amory speak of the difficulty of building roads and bridges on the flat land below the Lake Albert escarpment and now I had seen the problem at first hand. An ordinary bridge of the kind that could be constructed at reasonable cost by local labour would scarcely have lasted a minute against that mass of water, rock and tree trunks. What was almost as bad was the fact that the rivers, when they reached the plain below the escarpment, had a tendency to change course from year to year. Bridges built with every good intention in a certain place would be found later at a distance from the river and meanwhile the road would have been washed out and become impassable. The only motor road in the District which led down the escarpment was the one running westwards from Masindi to Butiaba, about twenty or twenty-five miles north of where I was. The escarpment was not steep at this point, thc road having been built in the early days to connect Uganda with the northwards-flowing Nile.

On the western side of the Rift, the Belgian Congo side, the situation must have been worse. The escarpment rose five thousand feet from the level of the lake to the plateau above, this being four times higher than on the Uganda side. Day after day we saw storms raging about those mountains and the rainfall must have been immense, making it impossible for the lakeside villages to be approached by road. This would in turn mean that the fish, once caught, could not be moved to the population centres further inland.

Another thought comes to mind when recalling the night when an insignificant little stream raged down the escarpment toward Lake Albert. There were no people living on the side of the escarpment, no bush had been cleared and no trees cut. Only at the top among the rolling hills had the jungle been cleared for cultivation. It seems doubtful that more than one tenth of Bunyoro's land was in use and even where it was cultivated the soil was well protected by banana gardens and other crops which would break up the rain drops and reduce the erosion. Yet in spite of having trees, grass and good cover generally, the river had filled in minutes and run totally out of control.

How much more terrible it must be in countries like Bangladesh and on what an infinitely vaster scale! The heavy monsoon rains would fall on mountain slopes to the north that had been denuded of forest and every patch of soil unwisely cultivated, causing massive erosion and floods that could inundate an entire country. The agony of Bangladesh originates upstream where Bangladesh possesses no authority so that their miseries come literally from above and there is nothing they can do to correct them.

A few days later when we were back in Hoima Stephen said that he had been surprised at something a fisherman had told him. On a calm night there had been canoes out fishing and they had encountered elephants in the water. They had the impression that the elephants were crossing from west to east, that is from the Congo to Uganda.

'Surely,' I said, 'there was some mistake. The lake is twenty miles across and it's hard to imagine elephants swimming that distance. Perhaps they were hippos.'

Stephen shook his head.

'The fishermen see hippos every time they go out and would recognize them. These were elephants because they could see their trunks above the surface. Much of the lake is fairly shallow and they think the elephants walk on the bottom and hold their trunks up to get air.'

It all seemed hopelessly improbable but I mentioned it to Roy Wyndham to whom I had reported in detail about the wire snares and pit traps. In fact I had deposited the coils of wire on his verandah since he had no office.

'That doesn't surprise me,' he said. 'Elephants have been sighted in the lake by the captain of the Nile steamer. They collided with one and killed it near Mahagi Port.

'By the way,' he added, 'The best way to deal with wire snares if you don't need them as evidence is to cut them into short lengths with wire cutters and leave them in the bush. It saves carrying them.'

12

Entertaining

We had not been in Bunyoro long before discovering that entertaining was not something that we could choose to do or not to do but rather was one of life's necessary duties. For a start there were the people who arrived from Kampala, their cars covered with red dust from the murram road, expecting to find a motel or hotel with adjoining restaurant. They may have made enquiries and discovered that Hoima had a 'Rest House' which they probably assumed to be an inn with one of those names of the order of 'Travellers Rest' or 'Stay Awhile'. I saw one on the Alaska Highway which catered to the hunting-fishing crowd called the 'Booze and Snooze'.

What they found in Hoima was three bare rooms with two beds in each, mattresses and mosquito nets. There was also an outdoor privy, not of the flush variety, and a bathroom, the water for which was heated in an oil drum over a wood fire. The kitchen contained a stove but no other equipment, the dining room a table and some chairs. Hoima had no electricity so of course there were no lights, and in general the place had a Spartan appearance not calculated to appeal to tourists, even those who ventured into the dark continent.

Such people would arrive at the Rest House and be shown around by the caretaker, after which they would search out Amory or myself. The loudest complainers were the ones on motor cycles or scooters who were touring Africa and assumed that government people had no function other than to offer them every amenity at no cost. They announced that they were 'doing Africa on a shoestring' – how they loved that word 'shoestring' – and they gave us to understand that their journey was a noble undertaking and that we were fortunate to have an opportunity to be of service. They presumed to know much about the country, were writing a book about their experiences and hinted darkly that we officials ('what was your name again?') would be roughly handled between the covers of their book if we failed to live up to their expectations. In fact they were doing nothing to help Africa or its people and we, for our part, felt bound only to ensure that they had a night's rest and moved on in the morning to be a nuisance somewhere else.

On one occasion I lost my patience altogether. A couple of missionaries, a husband and wife team who should have known better, deposited themselves on our doorstep and announced that the Rest House was worse than Sodom and Gomorrah. We could scarcely put them up in our house because there was only one bedroom so we offered them bedding for the night, gave them the use of our bathroom and invited them to dinner, all of which they accepted as their due. At a certain point during the evening the woman missionary put down her fork and announced in a flat nasal voice: 'All the way from Kampala we did pray that the Good Lord would provide.'

'Dammit,' I said, 'It looks as though we are doing most of the providing.'

The people whom we enjoyed entertaining, on the other hand, were those who had taken the trouble to make proper arrangements by notifying the government offices down-country. One of the Secretariat officers would have passed the message to Amory and we could then get the Rest House ready, have a servant in attendance and an 'interesting' meal prepared. Alan Moorhead, for instance, the author, was an amusing and captivating person with a fund of stories. I also remember Admiral Norris, his wife and his flag lieutenant who were on their way home to the United Kingdom after he had served as Commander-in-Chief in the Far East. He seemed genuinely delighted to discover, first hand, what a reserve lieutenant did when the war was over and he seemed to enjoy the company of younger people. Then there was Mr Vane Moreland, a Londoner who had spent thirty years with the Greater London Transport Commission and was preparing a report on how the Uganda Bus Company might balance its books which, up to that time, had been awash with red ink. He told us that he had come to Uganda supposing that Africans were rather simplistic but had discovered that the reverse was true. They were cheating the bus company in ways that he had never even heard of. 'They have the Cockneys beat hollow when it comes to cheating,' he said.

Another visitor whom I remember was one of those irrepressible enthusiasts of the gee-whiz variety. He was writing a book and had already visited the three other Districts in the south-west of the country so that his scratchpad was bursting with information. From his conversation it dawned on me that the Assistant District Commissioners to whom he had been talking in the other Districts had been pulling his leg unmercifully. The cone-shaped containers suspended from the trees in Kigezi District he had duly noted down as native funerary bundles: 'Don't go near them because the stench is frightful,' he had been told. In fact they were bee hives. In Ankole District he had learned that the ten-foot ant-hills which dot the plains and are such a feature of the landscape were hand-built altars to the pagan god Dudu. 'Dudu' means an ant in Swahili. If he ever wrote a book based on the information recorded during his travels it would have been an instant best-seller in East Africa.

I also recall a small parliamentary delegation headed by the Speaker of the House of Commons. Amory must have been out of the District because we were notified by the Secretariat that they were anxious 'to see and experience something of native life'. That was all I needed; I had them plodding through cotton fields, peering into famine reserves and one of them was persuaded to take off his shoes and socks and tread out some banana beer. For supper we served fried grasshoppers on toast, not exactly the way Africans eat them but with their heads removed because, as we explained, they have large eyes and stare at you rather accusingly as you put them in your mouth. The *pièce de résistance* was a whole hippo tongue, the hippo having been shot by the game warden. The tongue of a hippo is quite large, about ten pounds, and most knowledgeable people consider it the best part of the animal. It seemed appropriate to offer tongue to the Speaker of the House.

Our most memorable visitors in Hoima were Sir Leslie Hore Belisha, the great English politician who had been in the war cabinet, and

Lady Hore Belisha. I cannot recall what on earth they were doing in Uganda, least of all in Hoima, but I remember them for being such charming people, easy to entertain and having a lively interest in all they saw and heard. During dinner there was some sort of hitch, Kazimir having gone slightly berserk in the kitchen garden and picked every leaf of mint, which had been cooked and served as though it was spinach. Lady Hore Belisha said she thought it was delicious and would order it done that way when she returned to England. It wasn't really very good but we ate it anyway with much merriment.

A less enjoyable dinner party took place a few weeks later. I have forgotten who the visitors were but there were four of them, plus the two of us. They were not very high in their professions, had no conversation or sense of humour and took themselves exceedingly seriously: all the ingredients, in other words, of an unsuccessful evening. All but one, that is, which I proceeded to supply. I had gone out with my gun the evening before to look for guinea fowls in the cotton fields but had come across a bird called a greater bustard. I knew that the lesser bustard was considered one of Africa's delicacies so with impeccable logic I assumed that the greater bustard must be even better. It was carried home in triumph, deprived of its feathers and other non-essentials and left to hang overnight. When Aberi bore it into the dining room our visitors brightened up a little and gave some hope that all was not lost. The carving knife was as sharp as a razor but I had trouble slicing the meat and ended up putting rather small portions on each person's plate. As I struggled with it, my back to the table, scraps of my wife's conversation came through. 'Greater bustard, not usually seen in this area; normally found in more open country; my husband goes out with his gun every couple of weeks; guinea fowls good but rather dry . . .' I resumed my place at the table and mumbled something about it not being quite as tender as I had hoped.

That greater bustard was indescribable. It was exceedingly tough and tasted of diesel fuel. The remainder of the evening was passed in a hideous and contorted silence during which our guests treated us as though we had put strychnine in the food. As soon as they had made their very subdued and 'we-are-not-amused' departure we opened the bird book: 'bustard – lesser, bustard – greater, appearance, habitat, egg-laying capability' and all the rest. At the very bottom of the page was information which was too late to be of use: 'This bird is totally inedible.' Had our guests been the Hore Belishas or Admiral and Lady Norris it would have been a hilarious evening and when they returned home they would have had their London clubs rocking with laughter about the whole episode. With lesser people, however, a lot of the fun goes out of life.

The Amorys did more than their fair share of entertaining but Amory had a rule that if he was on safari he would not interrupt his work or return to Hoima for the sake of giving a meal to visitors and listening to what they had to say. If people came unexpectedly wanting to see him I produced a copy of his touring programme and explained where he could be found. I added that if he was walking in the villages, inspecting granaries, cultivated land, water supplies and so on then they might have to go some distance to find him, or else they could wait at his camp until he returned at six or seven in the evening. I always offered to send a uniformed messenger to show the way but at that point they generally decided that they didn't need him quite so urgently. I would then listen to their problem, make notes and offer to pass it on. Quite often it was trivial stuff that could have been conveyed just as well by letter.

As District Commissioner, Amory had a small allowance for entertaining visitors but it was never enough and in any case it was not supposed to cover situations where there was no government justification for entertaining. People who had broken down or were ill-equipped or just plain disorganized, like the two missionaries, were the biggest drain on our purses because we couldn't claim a penny back. Equally, we felt we couldn't leave incompetents to fend for themselves.

Another type of visitor whom we encountered were the government specialists who were coming out from England in quite large numbers at that time. Typically, he or she would live in Kampala and drive round the country at intervals which might be anywhere between a few weeks and a year. Our sawmill in the Budongo forest, for instance, which was run by an Indian, received the attention of an expatriate 'saw doctor' whose business was to sharpen and set the various saws that were used. I wondered then and still wonder how the word 'doctor' got into his job title. It sounds as presumptuous as it would be to describe an auto mechanic as a car doctor.

I also recall a burly individual from the north of England who was carpentry adviser to the schools which had technical classes. Amory asked the man whether they were teaching the students to make simple furniture and how long it would be before we could expect to have carpenters establishing themselves in the villages. Up to that time carpentry had not been practised in Bunyoro because it was not traditional and the nearest carpentry shop was operated by an Indian in Kampala. It seemed absurd that chairs, tables and so on were not being made locally, particularly with a sawmill in the District.

His answer was not reassuring; he was teaching the four main kinds of wood joints and it wasn't his business to teach them to make furniture. The first thing, he said, was to grasp the essentials; not try to run before they could walk.

Amory reasoned with him for an hour and tried to explain what the District needed but the more he talked the more pig-headed the man became. He was not going to lower his standards just because he was in Africa; his business was to teach the four main kinds of wood joints. Amory glared at him in stupefied disbelief. There was a demand for school desks as well as furniture in the chiefs' headquarters, not to mention the demand from private individuals, and our sawmill was turning out muvule wood (not unlike mahogany) which was ideal. Yet this man, a so-called government expert brought out from Europe at great expense, was so wedded to some foolish and irrelevant theory that he wasn't producing any results. Shortly thereafter Amory laid the whole matter in front of the governor.

It may not have been apparent to us at that early stage but a sharp distinction was being created in our minds between ourselves and those who lived down-country. We thought of ourselves as the real toilers in Africa, the ones who knew and understood the people, spoke the language and were privy to the mysteries of that fascinating country. They, the down-country people, were mere suburbanites who worried about the wrong things, spoke a few words of bastard Swahili which they thought qualified them as experts and made fools of themselves when they got into the real Africa. We smiled indulgently at their absurdities: 'You never quite know what goes in the sausages, do you?' and laughed politely at their stupid jokes: 'Our houseboy didn't know that the electric toaster has to be plugged in the wall.'

We, superior beings that we were, spoke to Africans in their own language, ate buffalo meat or guinea fowl and never gave a moment's thought to electric toasters or what went into sausages. We pitied them that they lived in Africa but had barricaded themselves behind a wall of imported trivia and senseless ideas. They knew nothing of the striving and the effort, the danger and the heartache; they couldn't envisage what Africa meant to us. They lived in a town, Kampala, that had more in common with Tooting Bec than it had with Bunyoro. To us Africa was all or nothing, life or death, a total and absolute commitment, a love affair of overwhelming proportions. To them it was just another job.

One of my favourite anecdotes about an expatriate Kampala family came from the chief game warden, Bruce Kinloch. He told us that the man, his wife and child had driven a few miles out of Kampala for a picnic and had come across what they thought was a dead python. They loaded it into the trunk of their car intending to have their servant skin it when they got home. The python, however, had been in process of digesting a hearty meal and after a few miles of being bounced around it was very much alive. The trunk was opened and there followed a hue and cry in the gardens and laneways of suburban Kampala; men shouting, women screaming until finally someone had the sense to call the Chief Game Warden who came with his men and captured it.

To pass from the exotic to the mundane, I remember an indignant expatriate complaining that his golf clubs had been stolen from the roof of his car. As he said: 'They were left-'anders and 'ard to get 'old of in East Africa.'

I told him he should report the occurrence to Inspector Frisby at the police station but privately doubted whether Frisby would have much sympathy or would even take the trouble to suppress a smile.

The new governor of Uganda at that time was Sir Andrew Cohen. As soon as he arrived at the end of 1951 he made a tour of the Districts to see the country and meet the officers. Much has been written about Sir Andrew and it would be wrong to suggest that he was universally popular, but I must say that for my part I much admired him. The story always told, and one usually heard it long before meeting him, was of an event which had occurred during the dark days of the Mediterranean war when he had been the civil servant responsible for supplying food to the beleaguered island of Malta. A deputation of Maltese, so the story goes, came to his office with a sample of bread which they described as maggot-ridden, stale and totally unfit for human consumption.

Sir Andrew treated them to a discourse on the problems which faced him: continuous German air attack; the Italian navy making surface replenishment hazardous so that he was reduced to using submarines for bringing in essential supplies. He was a great walker while he spoke; perhaps peripatetic is the better word, but by the time he had finished his dissertation the inedible morsel of bread had also been finished. He had been so desperately hungry himself that he had eaten it while he spoke.

I sensed that Amory found Sir Andrew a difficult person. He had been warned by the governor's private secretary that the governor's table manners tended to be a little relaxed, but Amory did not have the soup tureen handy and was disconcerted when His Excellency rose from table and went to the kitchen carrying his empty plate and tapping the spoon on it. In fact both Mr and Mrs Amory seemed paralyzed by the incident but my wife and I preferred to view it as a compliment to the hostess and the cook.

Sir Andrew possessed a formidable mind and a disconcerting habit of being two jumps ahead of any conversation. However, there was nothing capricious about him and I thought his ideas direct and logical and at times almost simplistic. In the subsequent years of his governorship I came to know him as well as most officers at my level. I always enjoyed his visits to my District although I asked to have my name removed from the list of officers who were being considered for appointment as his aide-de-camp and private secretary. It seemed to me that I had not come to Africa to perform that particular duty and I could be more useful by remaining in a District.

On one of the governor's later visits to Bunyoro a *gombolola* chief came forward with a large basket of eggs which he presented with a gracious little speech. For some reason Stephen wasn't there and the governor turned to me and said, 'Walter, tell me what he's saying.' He paused. 'And mind you tell me literally what he's saying. No cleaning up, you understand.'

'Sir,' I began, 'Most feared governor. We look to you as we look to God Himself. You are like a great chicken who sits upon us eggs and hatches us; so I offer this humble present.'

At dinner that night Lady Cohen was in great form. 'Andrew,' she said, 'You know what the chief said today about your being a great chicken sitting on the eggs and hatching them, well, that's what I'm going to tell the Secretary of State when he comes out next month.'

'Very well,' said Sir Andrew. 'But don't forget the bit about God Himself.'

He turned to me. 'When I told you to translate literally, dammit, I didn't mean as literally as that!'

Hoima in those days had no movie house, no television, and even radio reception was poor so the evening dinner party for two or four guests was the standard form of entertainment. A maximum of six people was preordained by the size of the dining room table and we found ourselves giving or attending one at least every week when we were in Hoima. These were not lavish dinners, more in the nature of working suppers, which served the purpose of keeping us up-to-date with District affairs. They were particularly valuable after returning from a two-week safari. A more elaborate buffet meal for a larger number of people was a less frequent occurrence and was usually prompted by a birthday, someone's return from leave or some special occasion.

The servants, particularly Aberi, liked entertaining and did their part with quiet efficiency. At the first such party I attended in Hoima (I think it was at the house of Miss King, the education lady), I found myself eating with my own table silver and drinking out of my own glass. I caught Jean's eye and held up a utensil of some sort with that faint facial gesture by which married couples ask each other: 'Did you know about this?' She replied with that barely perceptible shrug which means that she had absolutely no idea. Obviously there had been collusion between Aberi and Miss King's head boy with the result that her table had been augmented with bits of our equipment.

With African servants such simple entertaining should have been easy but many of the expatriates never got it right. A common mistake was to try to be lavish or complicated with such exotica as sucking pig that looked vaguely human or ice cream desserts that melted long before they were meant to. The trick was to be simple, normal and good humoured and not attempt to outdo King Louis XIV in any particular. I can't deny that we had our share of 'greater bustards' but I think we learned quickly from experience.

Rather low on our list of favourite evenings were those houses where the hostess picked on the servants and berated them for anything that went wrong. In nearly every case they were trying their best and if they made mistakes it was because the hostess had not explained things properly. In one such house the hostess had managed to get a goose from somewhere which was served in that typically English manner on an overcrowded plate with stuffing, jelly and various vegetables slurped all over with gravy. The conversation was all about that damn goose but after a bit of searching around under the other things on my plate I discovered that I didn't have any. Later Jean told me that she didn't have any either but neither of us said anything so as to avoid an outburst of reproaches by our hostess against the servants.

Another of our aversions were those households which treated their African servants meanly and did not give them clean uniforms or indeed any uniforms at all. This almost never occurred in the houses of married couples or bachelor men but it was not unknown in the houses of bachelor women for what reason I wouldn't know. Morale was bound to suffer if an employee's mistress couldn't spend a few shillings on a white *kanzu* and, for myself, I never liked being served by someone in dirty clothes.

My own worst aversion at dinner parties is probably peculiar to me and not shared by others. My sense of smell is acute and when a lady is wearing perfume my nose seems to distinguish between the flowers in the perfume, the base on which the flowers rest and the other components used to stabilize it. The outcome is that many perfumes smell positively nauseating. So it was at one dinner party where I couldn't at first comprehend what was wrong. The soup should have tasted well enough, a chicken and peanuts combination accompanied by a glass of sherry, but it was quite repulsive. I wondered what on earth was amiss; my health was good but it seemed that I had been afflicted by some chronic ailment of the sensory system. Next on the menu was leg of lamb to be accompanied by a Saint-Julien. Not quite the elegance of Margaux, I thought, which combines so perfectly with lamb, but a good approximation. My mind wandered to the quiet, sleepy villages of the Médoc, the church spires and the lovingly cultivated vineyards. Saint-Julien is only just down the road from Margaux and its wines have much the same delicacy as those of its famous neighbour. I put it to my nose and was disappointed. I took a sip and it tasted like turpentine.

Realization washed over me that the problem lay in the perfume worn by the lady on my right. It was not merely unpleasant, no, it went much further and made everything else taste and smell rancid. It came perilously close to violating the international ban against chemical warfare. The meat and wine were uniformly disgusting while only the fruit salad came close to normality. Why, I asked myself, does such a person have to slobber that kind of mixture over herself before going out to dinner?

Another type of hostess whom we found tiresome but not fatal were those who made a fetish of etiquette and doing things according to the book. These people lived with a copy of Mrs Someone-or-other's standard work within reach; to them it was Holy Writ and their lives were lived accordingly. This might not have been too bad until they actually quoted it at you to prove that you were wrong and they were right. A certain rather thin-lipped lady was convinced that if I had a beer glass in one hand propriety demanded I should have a napkin in the other. I was handed a dainty affair which I used for wiping my brow and cleaning up the bottom of the glass. At the lady's urging the servant relieved me of it and got me another. It was a hot night and by dinner time I had gone through six of her beastly little napkins and she was fed up with me. If I would care to consult her book, I was told, and she referred me to the chapter on 'beverages', I would see what I was doing wrong.

The pleasantest houses to visit were those where people had the courage to have their own customs and do things their own way. Our Indian ginnery manager served curry to his friends as he and his family ate it, that is to say sitting cross-legged on the floor and using their fingers. We quickly got the hang of eating with our fingers and concluded that when done properly it could appear perfectly elegant and mannerly.

I am inclined to the view that the western custom of having knives on the table is uncouth if not downright barbaric. Knives, according to most eastern peoples, should be kept in the kitchen where cooks and butchers use them and by the time food reaches the dining room it should be sufficiently prepared that guests don't have to chop things up themselves. It may be that this view is gaining ground because a lot of food gets eaten these days in sandwich form, with fingers, or with just a spoon or fork.

Only one of the officers in Hoima, Henry Berunga, could not entertain his brother officers at his house. He and his wife were Banyoro with the result that their numerous relatives, following tribal custom, were at liberty to take up residence in their household without notice and for as long as they felt like it. There was little that Henry could do without offending native custom which took the view that since he enjoyed the good fortune of a government salary and the occupation of a government house he would not close his door on indigent relatives. The result was that the house was always dirty and household articles were 'borrowed' so he was invariably missing something. It was, as he explained, the tribal system at its worst, a sort of primitive communism amounting to theft which made it impossible for him and his wife to entertain their expatriate friends.

Amory's proposal for dealing with it was for Henry to approach the Keeper of the Royal Tombs who was the Mukama's spokesman on native custom and have him put a stop to it. In Amory's view Henry was being presumed upon to the point where his work as a government officer was suffering. Henry himself, however, had been promised a transfer to another District which he believed would solve his problem, or at least provide an escape from it. When his transfer actually came it had no such effect because his indigent relatives followed him on their bicycles.

Normally Banyoro were well-mannered and sensitive people but this was deeply engrained and we all felt sorry that the Berungas had it inflicted on them in the first place and could not cope with it in the second. As Amory pointed out, we were trying to encourage the Banyoro to be farmers and businessmen, but if, the moment they did well, their relatives felt free to descend on them like locusts and gobble up the profits it was going to be an uphill struggle.

There was a good deal of talk in the Districts of Uganda at that time as to how the government might be persuaded to make liquor duty-free for up-country officers. The argument was that the Diplomatic Corps had duty-free privileges in consideration of the amount of entertaining they did and the same reasoning should be applied to us. Food was not particularly expensive but liquor and even beer was a burden on the salaries we earned. Senior government officers who had served up-country earlier in their careers knew all about this and when they came to dinner they would quietly hand a familiar shaped package to the head boy who unwrapped it and placed it on the sideboard.

In the District of Toro to the south there was a small group of white expatriates, perhaps a dozen, who solved the problem imaginatively. They were self-employed, being neither government, mission, nor attached to any of the big commercial enterprises. They simply distilled their own liquor from banana beer or bought it from the Africans. The classic story is that when the governor visited Toro and asked for a gin and tonic he was given illicit liquor and didn't know the difference. One of them was subsequently charged in court with 'possession' and pleaded that his brew had been sanctioned by His Excellency who had taken a glass of it and made no adverse comment.

Jean and I recognized early that there were two quite distinct types of entertaining, the sit-down party for four or six and the larger buffet party for twenty or twenty-five which was usually an all-races gathering. The small party could be left to Aberi who took it in his stride.

The food was well served and conversation could proceed uninterrupted. We usually drank 'sangria' of our own devising, part wine, part ginger ale, with lime juice and mint leaves. It always went down well, particularly in a hot climate among young people.

The larger buffet party was more complicated because of the dietary prohibitions forced on our guests by religion or tribal custom. Moslems would not eat pork, and Sikhs (people with beards, puggarees and Singh in their names) would not eat beef. Hindus were strict vegetarians. African women would not eat chicken or eggs or anything with cheese in it. Some Africans would not eat fish, although the Banyoro as a tribe generally did so and, strangest of all, the Banyoro would not eat green salads, which they regarded as suitable only for goats. Amory's comment on the subject of an all-races reception was that his wife would never have married him if she had known about the difficulties in advance.

The trick, we soon discovered, was to have a separate table for vegetarian foods and be a hundred per cent certain that they really were totally vegetarian. This meant rice, bean and tomato casserole, salads and, of course, plenty of fresh fruit. The worst mistake was to allow any animal products on that table. A fruit pie might appear innocent but not if the pie-crust had been made with *kimbo*, a shortening containing animal fats. Noodles were suspect because eggs had probably been incorporated in them at some stage. At the end of it all, rice, beans, tomatoes, fruit and salad from the garden were the only things that were safe.

Another table would contain the meat dishes and spicy sauces. We found that buffalo stew was popular although Moslems sometimes asked which way the buffalo had been facing when it expired, northwards toward Mecca being preferred, and whether it died by having its throat cut. I had to reply that I could not vouch for the course it was last steering and that it died of a mysterious bullet. Once it was down in the grass a few drops of blood had probably been coaxed from its throat by a spear blade. Moslems generally were not too fussy over the details but there was usually a guinea fowl platter from which they could help themselves if the buffalo stew offended. African women who would not eat chicken did not have the same problem with guinea fowl (*Numida meleagris*) although I am not sure what historical factors contributed to this distinction.

The surprising thing was that one could have an all-races party in such circumstances and that it should come off so well. It brought people together, broke down the racial barriers and got everyone talking. The Africans always enjoyed themselves and were great fun; the Indians were a little more reserved.

A type of meal that we much disliked and did our best to avoid was where the genial host, probably a bachelor, plied you with drinks until all hours of the night and then ordered dinner somewhere between nine and ten o'clock by which time the food was spoiled and the guests too tired to eat. Even worse was a 'curry tiffin' held on a Saturday or Sunday which effectively ruined an entire day. The drinking would start when the guests arrived at about one o'clock in the afternoon and you would be lucky to get some lunch by four. I never solved the problem of what one did or could possibly do for the rest of the day and after enduring one or two such parties we went to great lengths to acquire a previous engagement.

At the risk of being thought unreasonable there were two other forms of weekend entertainment that drove us to distraction. The first was square dancing which some expatriates, particularly Scots, seemed to think was an activity of fundamental importance. The sight of young people prancing around like idiots never failed to bring out the venom in me. I know that Africans danced and did so exceedingly well but for white people to do it when there was so much else to be done seemed to border on insanity. Anyway, I always refused to join square dancing classes and those who passed their time in this way I cancelled off as immature.

One other activity left me at a loss for words, the motor car rally. We all had to have a car and while no one tried to organize a rally in Hoima it was quite popular in the larger stations. Some genius would work out a route and people would drive their cars round it to absolutely no purpose. I saw it as a complete waste of petrol. I never really liked driving on those corrugated roads and with so many Africans wobbling along on overloaded bicycles I saw no point in compounding the problem. One of my friends in another District had an accident and killed a small African child who ran out from the grass beside the road. I doubt whether he has ever forgiven himself, or whether any driver in the world, in the same circumstances, could have avoided the accident. My friend did, however, have the small satisfaction of knowing that he was on duty and was using the road because he had to. If he had been driving on some foolish prank like a motor rally it would have been much harder for him to bear.

13

The Court Room

I had been in Hoima about a month when the Provincial Commissioner of the Western Province, Sir George Duntze, called in on his way to Fort Portal. I made no particular notes concerning his visit, but recollect having taken my oath in front of him as a junior magistrate. I swore to do justly to all manner of men without fear or favour, without prejudice and without ill-will. On that note began my career in the court room.

I believe that I possessed one advantage from the outset. During my years in the navy I had served under commanding officers who were harsh disciplinarians but scrupulously fair in their administration of shipboard justice. They required their officers to investigate every breach of discipline and present the story at the defaulters' table. These painstaking investigations were my training ground and in nine cases out of ten the sailor, when asked by the captain if he had anything to add, would say: 'Nothing to add, sir. My officer has been very fair.' This was music to the captain's ear because he wanted to pass a message to every man on board that although strict he would never tolerate carelessness or injustice. I learned a great deal from both captains, as all their officers must have done, and when I first sat in court I found myself in a situation that was somehow familiar.

My first case was a preliminary inquiry into an accusation of murder. My duty was to hear the evidence and record it, then do one or other of two things: acquit the accused and let him go free if there was no evidence; or order that he be tried before the High Court of Uganda if the evidence was strong. If it went to the High Court, a judge would rehear the entire case.

The accused was a young man of about twenty and the evidence showed that he had been drinking banana beer with his neighbour. When both of them were drunk they began to insult each other and proceeded from there to an exchange of blows. At some point the accused reached for a knife and stabbed his opponent, striking him in the groin and severing the large artery of the upper leg.

Hearing the sounds of a fight, the villagers gathered round and held a council as to what should be done. After some debate they decided to arrest the accused and take him to the chief with his hands tied. The victim was left lying on the ground and he received no assistance until the arrival of a police *askari* from Hoima. A tourniquet was applied and the man placed on a makeshift stretcher but he died from loss of blood. In his evidence Inspector Frisby described the pool of blood where the victim had lain and the doctor said that to have saved the man's life all that was needed was someone's thumb pressed on the wound.

When the prosecution evidence was complete I asked the accused if he wanted to say anything. 'He owed me two shillings,' was the reply. 'I killed him because he would not give it back.'

I looked at Stephen's impassive face, then at Inspector Frisby. Both of them were true professionals, Stephen as a translator who never seemed to slip up or hesitate but moved effortlessly from English to Lunyoro. Inspector Frisby had prosecuted the case in a quiet, painstaking manner. There was no hint of rancour or even disapproval; it was done with equanimity and fairness. He was thoughtful enough to watch my pen moving on the paper and only when it stopped did he put the next question so that I never had to ask him to slow down or give me more time.

There seemed no point in adding any comments on the fact that the local people, by negligence toward the injured man, had contributed to his death. The wound was not particularly deep but had severed the artery and what was needed was to stop the bleeding. The people who gathered talked about it, arrested the accused and tied him up, but the victim of the attack was left on the ground to die. He must have been in such a state of drunkenness that he was unable to help himself.

I learned in the months that followed that this was no more than typical of the Banyoro. They were a race of primitive politicians who loved the sound of their own voices and believed that endless chatter somehow achieved results. They could flog a thing to death with words but were not much good when it came to getting anything done. A day well spent in the village was a ten-hour discussion. No Munyoro would describe such a day as ill-spent, even if, by western standards, the discussion was pointless and led to no action or decision. The only parallel I can think of in the western world are certain church committees. The women, of course, were left to do the work and cook the food because they were not considered clever enough to take part in these aimless parleys.

Anyway, I assumed that the judge, when his turn came, would take into account the villagers' negligence. If he concluded that they were partly to blame the charge would be reduced and a term of imprisonment would be in order. Alternatively, he might say to himself that the man had taken up a knife and struck a blow with intent to maim or kill. It was the accused's misfortune that the local people had failed to save the victim's life but to do so they could not be expected to rise above the level of their normal intelligence. I ended by telling the accused that I had no option but to send him for trial by the High Court on charge of murder.

A month later I conducted another preliminary investigation which went the other way and I ordered the accused to be released. He was a fisherman from one of the villages on Lake Albert and was awakened at night by a noise outside his hut. In previous weeks he had been troubled by hyenas which snatched the fish which were left to dry over a low fire. He assumed the noise was made by a hyena and with spear in hand he crawled out of the hut and looked round. It was a dark night but he saw a slight movement a few yards away. He sprang forward and threw his spear which flew unerringly toward its mark. There came the indistinct sounds of death and he returned to his hut for a torch of flaming reeds. He found that he had killed his grandmother who occupied a hut nearby and who had been obeying a call of nature. The blade of the spear had entered her back and protruded a foot out of her chest.

No judge in the world would convict a man on such evidence. He seemed genuinely saddened by what he had done and admitted that he had been at fault for throwing his spear without first being sure of his target. It had been a moonless night and the canopy of leaves overhead made it even darker. The local chief had given evidence that confirmed his statement that hyenas had been troublesome. I told him that I believed his story and he could go back to his village. As he left the courtroom an impassive African policeman handed him his spear which had been marked as Exhibit A.

It sometimes happens that cases which seem to be all innocence on the surface are the hardest to deal with. One such case in which a young man had been fined for giving a girl a ride on the back of his bicycle was appealed from the Bunyoro Native Court to the District Court and Amory, having looked it over, told me to hear it. He said it seemed straightforward and I was not likely to find any difficulty. 'But be careful with native custom,' he warned, 'and make sure it really is native custom and not something they just invented on the spur of the moment.'

The evidence recorded in the Native Court was that the accused, who had recently acquired a bicycle, had offered to give a young woman a ride to her village about a mile distant because rain was threatening. The girl's father appeared on the scene and accused the young man of 'intending to commit fornication'. He claimed that by pedalling fast and taking the corners at speed the girl was obliged to hold the young man so that she would be powerless to resist his subsequent advances. The court had noted that it was a Raleigh bicycle fitted with a metal grille over the back wheel used for carrying parcels or, in this case, a passenger.

In the native court the decision had been to convict the accused because he had sought to take advantage of the rain and planned to seduce her after she had been thoroughly bounced up and down and her passions roused. In addition, she would appear ridiculous holding on to him, as she was obliged to do if she was to avoid falling. The court answered the rather obvious question as to whether the accused would have done better to leave her standing in the rain by announcing that a wetting would have done her no harm but by making a spectacle of herself the bride-price which the father had a right to expect in due course would be diminished. No honest man, it ruled, would want to marry a girl who had been carried on the back of someone else's bike. The court fined him forty shillings, which represented two weeks' income. It would equate to something in the order of two to four hundred dollars in our money at the present time. The young man appealed to the District Commissioner on the grounds that the girl had accepted his offer of a ride of her own accord and that he had never intended to seduce her.

An obvious defect in the case was that the accused had been charged as though it were a criminal matter when in fact it looked more like a civil dispute between the two parties, the father of the girl and the young man. What's more, by no stretch of the imagination was it a criminal offence to 'intend to seduce a girl'. However, the native courts in Banyoro were often vague as to the distinction between criminal and civil law and Amory took the view that it was better to ensure that substantial justice was done than to waste time on technicalities. Another difficulty was the fact that there were two distinct ingredients, the intent to seduce on the one hand and the loss of bride-price on the other. The lower court had blurred these by fining for wrong intent but doing nothing about the loss of bride-price.

The safest course was to hear the evidence again so this I proceeded to do, having notified the two parties to be present with their witnesses. The young man arrived appropriately wheeling his bicycle. Since native custom was involved I was assisted by two African assessors, Henry Berunga and a senior and respected chief from the Native Government.

The father of the girl made his case first and I shall have to admit that he put on a brave performance. He described in libidinous detail the thoughts and intentions of the young man as he offered his daughter a ride. I interrupted to tell him that he should restrict his words to what he actually saw and heard. It was not his business to make assumptions about another person's state of mind or the intentions which may or may not have impelled him. My words made no difference. He spoke of the breakneck speed of the bicycle which was designed to lessen his daughter's ability to resist sexual advances and of the motion of the wheels over the corrugated road surface intended to make her bounce up and down in a provocative manner. Westerners like myself do not generally talk much about female breasts but our litigant had no inhibitions. He described their motion in some detail and with appropriate gestures.

In support of his case the old man called his wife, daughter and the village chief. The wife and daughter, both of whom were uneducated, had evidently been drilled in what they were to say but they forgot their lines and were unconvincing. The village chief claimed to be an expert in native custom and stated that from earliest times among the Banyoro it had been an offence to carry a woman, other than your wife, on your bicycle. My two assessors mumbled and shook their heads. In earliest times there were no bicycles.

Next I told the accused that we wanted to hear his side of the story. He was a young man of about twenty and he evidently had a few years of education. He said that he had offered the girl a ride with no ulterior motive. When questioned he replied that he was proud of his new bicycle and was perhaps too anxious to show it off. He could not have foreseen that the bride-price might be debased in consequence of his action and if such were the case the old man should have taught his daughter not to accept rides. She could have refused.

Both assessors felt at this point that the old man should be invited to respond to this. Why had not the girl merely refused the ride? he was asked. 'Girls, as everyone knows,' he replied, 'are easily persuaded. They have no minds of their own and must be treated accordingly.'

This case summed up a problem that afflicts third world countries, not merely an isolated little place like Banyoro. A young man with a bit of education and a bicycle and, as it turned out, a regular job as clerk in some co-operative venture was pitted against some illiterate old fellow who had a marriageable daughter. The old man represented the past with all its murky traditions, and he also represented the Banyoro's love of litigation, of stringing accusations together like beads to get what he could out of it. The young man represented the new enlightenment: regular employment, schooling and material possessions.

There was no doubt as to which way I thought the case should go and both my assessors agreed that the young man was not guilty of any offence against native custom. The Native Court had fined him forty shillings for his evil intentions but had not ordered him to pay any compensation to the old man for loss of bride-price, which seemed illogical. If they had believed that the old man had suffered loss then some monetary payment to compensate him would have been in order. Also of interest was the fact that the old man claimed that his daughter possessed no will of her own and could not reject an offer of the sort the young man made. This was tantamount to treating her as an imbecile which, if true, my assessors pointed out, would mean that she was not worth any bride-price at all.

We reversed the decision of the lower court.

Another case at the other end of the social scale involved a Belgian count who was in process of being deported from the Congo. I had supposed, up to that time, that given the sort of reputation the Congo enjoyed internationally one would be deported into it rather than out. However, on Mr Amory's instructions, I drove my Landrover down to the port of Butiaba on Lake Albert to meet the paddle steamer where, in my capacity as magistrate, I signed on the dotted line for the live body of one white male person who had entered the Congo illegally. The fact that he was accompanied ashore by two uniformed Belgian officers, both of whom carried revolvers, and an African sergeant with a machine gun worried me less than the amount of luggage he had, plus the red-headed lady who was described as his travelling companion.

One of the officers explained that the government of the Congo felt quite strongly about illegal immigrants and about this one in particular whom he described as '*indésirable chronique*', which sounds fairly bad. He added that people were generally expelled by the same door they had come in: Uganda in this case. I was handed a sheaf of documents in both French and Flemish and I found the signature of Mr R.L. Dreshfield, Uganda's attorney general, which presumably made the whole thing legal.

The count was not overjoyed at the quality of his reception in Uganda. He and his companion exclaimed that never before had they been driven in such an uncomfortable vehicle, added to which I had omitted to offer them refreshments which, if I presumed to be a gentleman of honour, I was bound to do. There is only just enough space for three people in the front of a Landrover, it is true, and the person in the centre seat has to straddle the gear box. I told them it was not far to Hoima but by the time we arrived it had seemed like a very long way. They complained bitterly and continuously and were not quiet for a moment.

The count was an international scrounger who lived off his wits and played on his title which, I discovered, was the only genuine thing about him. He had never done a day's work in his life, posed variously as a diplomat, war hero, philanthopist and United Nations director general and left a trail of debts and unpaid bills. I was more than relieved to hand him over to a police officer who took him to Kampala. I heard later that he had been held there and charged with an offence which delayed his deportation to Kenya where, as the police have a way of saying, they were anxious to question him about certain matters. He was duly chased out of Kenya after which he was deported to Zanzibar, the Seychelles and finally the Andaman Islands which was the end of the line.

There was not much room in the Africa of those days for white people who didn't behave with reasonable decorum and, looking back after many years, I suppose there was more puritanism than rowdyism in most of us. Only once did I have a white man in my court, a government officer in the Public Works Department. He was resident in Fort Portal about a hundred miles distant and I didn't know him personally so was not ill-at-ease hearing the case. He was charged with being drunk and disorderly, driving through Hoima bazaar at excessive speed and resisting arrest. His vehicle had been impounded because, as Inspector Frisby said, it didn't seem to have any brakes. My predominant recollection of the man was his west of England accent which, combined with a monumental hangover, made him almost unintelligible. I stuck him with a hefty fine and ordered that it be collected over a one-year period by the government pay office.

Amory had told me in his unambiguous way that Uganda was a poor country and fines imposed by the courts were a source of revenue. White people and Asians, if found guilty, should be fined and not sent to prison unless a prison sentence was the only proper punishment.

'Decide,' he had said, 'how long you would have sent the accused to prison if he had been unable to pay a fine. If you settled on sixty days, then fine him sixty days' salary and you are making him work that period for nothing.'

I had a chance to try out Amory's theory not long after but will have to admit that my results were hardly satisfactory. An Indian from the little bazaar at Munteme had been charged with selling drugs which were stolen property. Frisby had heard that the man had some M & B tablets and was dispensing them for one shilling each to any villager who came and paid the money. He dressed two of his Lunyoro-speaking *askaris* as 'villagers' and sent them into the shop. Out came the M & B tablets and the transaction was completed. A whistle from the 'villager' and several police appeared; this time they were in uniform. A search revealed cartons of M & B under the counter and the lot numbers on each box revealed that they had been stolen from a hospital in Kenya.

Many Africans at that time had heard of the miracles attributed to M & B and believed that it would cure them of anything. They would buy a few tablets and then use them for snakebite, malnutrition, jiggers, malaria or whatever. In the hands of a medical doctor the tablets might have done some good but used as they were by the villagers it was a waste.

The Indian had been charged with possession of stolen property to the value of 5,000 shillings and selling prescribed drugs without a pharmacist's licence. He pleaded guilty which I duly noted in the record and then adjourned the case to consider punishment. Amory was out of the District so I was automatically a magistrate with first class powers. On the basis of Amory's ready-reckoner I decided that 5,000 shillings worth of stolen drugs all clearly marked as government property was worth two years in the slammer. Yes, but how much did he earn in a year from his business? What sum would deprive him of two years' work and effort? His shop, I knew, was small and he didn't seem to be doing much business when I had looked in. There was a smell of curry about the place and an old Indian used to sit cross-legged behind the counter meditating. Anyway I wrote down 60,000 shillings which made him burst into tears and go down on his knees babbling about his wife and children starving to death. I told him to pay his fine to the court clerk and adjourned for the day.

An hour later I saw Stephen and asked whether the fine had been paid.

'Oh yes, he paid in cash. But if I may say so you didn't fine him enough. He had over a hundred thousand shillings in his pockets!'

There was no way of upgrading the fine once it had been recorded. If I had felt strongly I could have written to the registrar of the High Court asking that they intervene in the case and use their powers to set aside my decision and enhance the fine 'in view of information not available when sentence was passed'. However, I didn't do so and when I mentioned it to Amory he said only that I should concentrate on becoming a better judge. He paused: '. . . of the bulge in an accused person's pocket.'

Within four or five months of my arrival in Bunyoro I sat my law exams and passed. This led to appointment as a second class magistrate which meant, in effect, that no case was beyond my powers except for murder, manslaughter and rape which had to be heard by the High Court. Amory did little court work himself preferring to concentrate on administrative duties so I was able to take almost the entire caseload, which kept me in court two days a week. If I was absent on safari he would take the plea and remand the case until my return.

The resident magistrate for the Western Province who was stationed at Fort Portal also dropped in about once a month but we rarely had much for him to do. The incumbent during my early days in Hoima was R.J. Martin whom I had known as a schoolboy before the war. He dined with us one evening and I remember him speaking of the Swiss girl to whom he was engaged and whom he planned to marry when he returned home on leave. He had served in the war as a captain in the Grenadier Guards but having survived the war he died a few months later in tragic circumstances.

The fact that we were often able to hear cases immediately after the arrest of an accused person made a great difference to the administration of justice. On dozens of occasions the police inspector came into the office and saluted. (A salute meant trouble. If he didn't salute it was nothing serious.)

'Sir, I have just made an arrest; will you come into court and take a plea?'

Within minutes I would be sitting with a blue court file in front of me and Stephen reading the charge. It might be that the accused had only been arrested an hour previously and, if he pleaded guilty, it was not impossible that he would be in prison an hour later.

One such case involved a clerk in the Treasury office of the Native Government. He began his day by clearing out the main safe and putting the money in a sack which he tied to the carrier of his bicycle. He then set off toward the Kafu river, his destination presumably Kampala. Two or three Native Government police set off in pursuit, also on bicycles, but when the Treasurer (the Chief Acceptor of Bribes) arrived at the office on his motor bike it was a case of superior technology winning the day. The thief was duly arrested a few miles down the road. Inspector Frisby in the police van was a short distance behind and by ten o'clock the man had been charged in my court. Stephen, who knew him well, burst into tears and another interpreter had to be found. I recorded a plea of guilty and that same afternoon the doctor had a long talk with him to determine his mental condition. By the following morning I had enough information to pass sentence.

Another case which was remarkable from a police point of view began when a couple of African police *askaris* were driving from Hoima to Masindi. They came up behind a heavily laden and rather slow vehicle and attempted to pass. One of the *askaris* had sharp eyes and saw that something was dripping from the vehicle and that on contact with the hot exhaust pipe it flamed up. Thinking it was a kerosene leak, which would have been exceedingly dangerous, they pulled ahead and flagged down the vehicle. What they had was a three-ton load of illegally distilled liquor, called *haragi*. Within the hour two accused were in my court pleading guilty. One of the four-gallon cans had been leaking, a fact which cost the owners five years in prison.

Haragi (or *waragi*) was a species of illegal moonshine distilled from banana beer. There was a huge market for it, particularly in the heavily populated area round Kampala. The attorney general was on record as having said that 50% of all violent crime in Uganda was committed under its influence. In small amounts it turned men into violent criminals, in large amounts it caused insanity, blindness and death. The word *haragi* was said to have derived from *arak*, originally the fermented mare's milk of central Asia.

The sad thing about *haragi* is that if made properly by modern methods and allowed to age it is no worse than vodka or gin. In recent years it has been distilled under government licence and sold legally but there is a world of difference between this and the raw variety which caused so much harm.

In the opinion of most of us in those days the solution to the *haragi* problem would have been to legalize it and distill it under licence. The price of an illegal bottle was five shillings, but this took account of the danger faced by the distillers and others who were connected with the trade. If it had not been for the possibility of being caught by the police it would have cost about two shillings. Our reasoning was that if people were prepared to pay five shillings for a hellish and dangerous liquor which might land them in jail they would pay seven shillings quite happily if it were legal and relatively harmless. The illegal distillers would then go out of business and violent crime would be reduced. While they were at it we thought the government should also licence a rum distillery since there was a sugar cane industry in the Eastern Province. We could not imagine how the illegal distillers could stay in business a single day if people were able to buy a bottle of decent booze at reasonable cost.

The argument against it was that the government would lose its tariff on imported liquors because few people would buy Scotch whisky or English gin if they could get something for a third of the cost. Personally I thought this a dubious argument because the government could still have collected a shilling or two for every bottle of locally distilled liquor and the huge market for it in Uganda and the neighbouring territories would have ensured that there was no overall loss of revenue. Anyway, the government did not legalize it, at least not until many years later, and continued to wage a losing war against the illegal variety. Three tons of the stuff, obviously on its way to Kampala and camouflaged by a covering of cow hides, gives an idea of the dimensions of the problem.

The court case files from up-country, other than trivial cases, were reviewed by the High Court and this particular case attracted the only adverse comment I ever received. A judge had noted against my sentence of five years: 'deemed scarcely adequate,' and added his initials and date. The registrar had then written: 'The Kampala magistrates are generally awarding six months for possession of *a single bottle of illicit liquor*. This was *three tons*!'

When the file was received back in the office Amory called me in. In front of him was a blue case file and I could see my own handwriting on it. My curiousity knew no bounds.

'Walter,' he said, 'calculate the price of three tons of *haragi* at six months a bottle.' He didn't smile.

'That's easy, three tons is six thousand pounds. I don't know how much the contents of a bottle weighs, but my guess is that it would not be less than a pound. Off the top of my head I'm going to say three thousand years.'

'Well, if my understanding of these legal people is correct that's the sentence you should have passed. I'm glad you do the court work, not me.'

He pushed the file in my direction.

Village meeting.

Young man outside his house.

A road in Bunyoro.

A road flooded in the rainy season.

Pulling bark off a barkcloth tree.

Matooke – staple food.

The Cotton harvest.

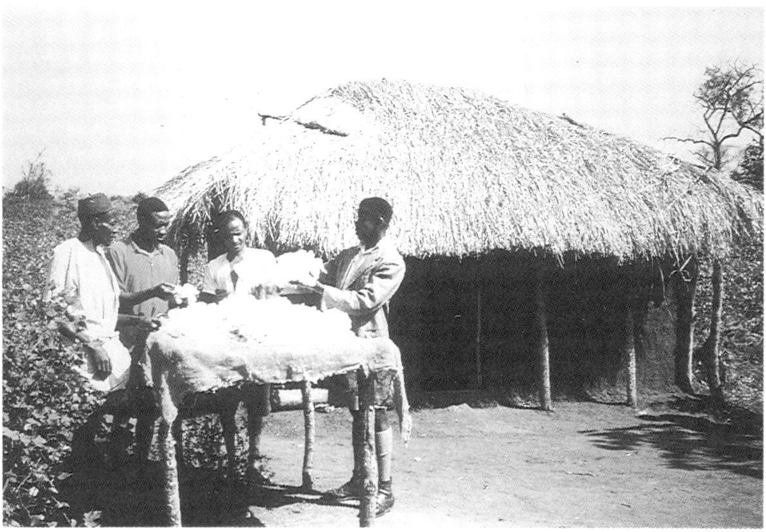

The Agricultural Officer examines the lint.

The flat land at the foot of the escarpment.

Three men with heavy loads of fish begin to climb the escarpment.

Nearing the top.

The market.

Elephant damage in a village.

The culprits are chased away.

Treading out banana beer.

Author and wife.

14

The Missions

There were Protestant and Catholic Missions in Bunyoro which were concerned with both evangelization and education. Primary schooling, that is to say the first six years of school, was under their direction, but there was also a Government Education Officer, Miss King, who oversaw their efforts. Islam had made no inroads and the District was without Moslem schools or mosques.

The Roman Catholic mission had a father superior assisted by two priests and a lay brother, all of whom belonged to the order of White Fathers and all of whom were expatriates: one Dutch, one French Canadian, an Irishman and an Italian. They occupied an imposing complex of buildings a mile or two outside the town whose construction was of sun-dried brick with broad verandahs and a decorative façade. The verandahs were raised four or five feet above the level of the surrounding gardens so that the priests, as they waited for visitors or strolled back and forth, appeared raised, pulpit-like, above the general level of humanity. The mission had a large dining room and a parlour presided over by a life-sized plaster statue of the Virgin Mary who had been caught in the process of open-heart surgery. Each priest and brother had a comfortable and quite spacious room to himself. Nearby was a large primary school and, of course, the parish church.

The White Fathers, in other words, did things properly. They lived in clean and decent surroundings, kept a good table and were waited on by properly attired servants. They had vegetable and flower gardens, the grass was trimmed to discourage mosquitoes and they managed to maintain a good standard of health. A visit to the White Fathers' mission was always a pleasure. They served an excellent lunch of soup, a main course and a dessert which was often accompanied by home-made wine. It was cooked, or at least supervised, by the lay brother who was the mission's jack-of-all-trades.

The White Fathers were resourceful. They grew their own tobacco and rolled cigars which, I always thought, stank like burning camel droppings. They kept a few pigs and a donkey, the latter acting as a sort of wheelbarrow. Their water supply was a marvel of ingenuity, courtesy of the lay brother, and their garden flourished with western vegetables. Most of these grew quite well although some produced unexpected results. Ordinary garden radishes grew as large as tennis balls in the heat and heavy rain but were tasteless so they solved the problem by camouflaging them under a white sauce.

The story was often told of a Dutch missionary in the early days. He could not read English and laid aside the Department of Agriculture's first official pronouncement which was to the effect that cotton could not possibly be grown. Having imported some cotton seed from Egypt he tried it out and it has since become Uganda's chief export crop, responsible for about half the country's wealth.

The overwhelming impression at the Catholic mission was that they were equipped to do the job and were not strapped for funds. This seemed strange in Uganda where so much enterprise was starved of money. It was, after all, a third-world country supported by an economy that was still in its infancy. The government operated on a budget that was so closely controlled that the Canadian public service has always seemed to me wasteful and profligate by comparison.

One day I drove to the mission and noticed a new tip-truck, concrete mixer and other building equipment, all of which was scarce and highly prized in the Uganda of the 1950s. I asked Father Gauthier how he got it.

'You see,' he replied, 'It come from my bruddeur who is Gauthier Construction of Montreal. He gave it to us like a gift, you know.'

'And what are you going to do for him?' I enquired.

'The whole school they gonna pray for him.'

By the way he said it I gathered that his bruddeur needed a few prayers.

The Catholics had, of course, acquired centuries of experience of missionary work. They had an air of quiet professionalism, not starry-eyed, romantic or even adventurous but that of journeymen with a routine job which they performed in accordance with time-honoured formulas. They created the impression of order, continuity and well-tested organization but not much evidence of spiritual zeal. Their patron saint was not the volatile Paul from Tarsus but some lesser saint who possessed the mind and heart of a civil servant.

When speaking of their work among the Banyoro the White Fathers had few delusions. Paganism, they said, was never far beneath the surface and they wondered how long the Church would last when the time came for them to leave. The Banyoro wanted their own priests to replace the White Fathers but there were few Africans at that time who were equipped to undertake the long training, could master Latin and Hebrew and accept the rigorous discipline which the church imposed. They wondered whether a celibate priesthood made any sense in Africa and they seemed, above all, to have prepared their minds for disappointment.

We were impressed by an example of the discipline of the White Fathers. Amory had mentioned casually to the Catholic bishop of the Western Province that one of the three priests had been interfering in local politics. He had threatened to excommunicate any of his flock who failed to vote for the Catholic candidate and had been foolish enough to write it in the parish newsletter. A copy had found its way to Amory's desk and he handed it to the bishop when he saw him a few days later.

'This makes my job so much harder,' Amory had said. 'I hope you'll have a word with him.'

I don't know what Amory expected the bishop to do, probably nothing, but I was not prepared for my next visit to the mission. The priest in question was wearing a gray, ankle-length garment, not the white one which was the badge of his order. He had no shoes or socks, no pectoral cross, and he was serving the food.

If the Catholic Fathers were the solid professionals of the mission business the Protestants were the enthusiastic amateurs. They were zealous and impoverished and the sub-standard conditions in which they lived made them prone to ill-health. We always avoided visiting their mission at lunch time for fear of an invitation. They apologized for their humble circumstances but explained that God approved of poverty and would reward their efforts.

From Acholi, a large District lying to the north, came the incident that summed it up. The mission needed a nurse for the maternity ward of its small hospital and, since there were no qualified Acholi nurses, the Church Missionary Society in England undertook to recruit a suitable candidate. She was duly selected, packed her luggage and embarked for the long voyage round the circumference of Africa. She made friends easily and enjoyed her jaunts ashore with the other passengers and with the ship's officers. The journey took them to Durban, Beira, Dar es Salaam and finally Mombasa where she disembarked, as I had done, a full two months after stepping aboard in England. The railway conveyed her up-country to Kampala where she stayed at a hotel for a few days to await transportation to Acholi in the north of the country.

It must have cost the Church Missionary Society more money than it could afford to get her there and to their dismay the missionaries discovered that she was not quite the type of person whom they had hoped and doubtless prayed for. In a word she was an attractive young woman in her twenties who was not insensitive to the attentions of the unmarried officers. The Police Officer taught her to drive a car, the Agricultural Officer put in a vegetable garden and the Veterinary Officer found her a cat. I forget which of the three was rewarded with the lady's hand, but in a few weeks she was engaged and was married shortly thereafter. As a government officer's wife she might continue to work at the mission for as long as her husband was stationed in that District but as soon as he was ordered on leave or was posted to another District it would all be over as far as the mission was concerned. They had poured a great deal of money down the drain, money that could have been put to better use than by providing a wife for one of the expatriate officers. Home leave is for attending to personal business, getting a wife and all that sort of thing. The Catholics would not have committed the same blunders.

One of the inescapable facts was the simmering resentment between the two missions. The first Catholic missionary to reach Uganda at the turn of the century had been Father Lourdel. McKay, a Protestant, arrived about the same time and set up in business nearby. There was one unholy row after another because both were fanatical, unforgiving and capable of seeing no point of view but their own. The example set by these two men, which came close to involving parts of Buganda in civil war, was a legacy of hardly more than fifty years. Lourdel accused McKay of being an offshoot, breakaway sect of Christianity, a heretic and an apostate. McKay countered with the charge that Lourdel was using questionable methods to attract converts and allowing the end to justify the means. It was a case of both Churches militant with all the familiar animosities and arguments.

One of the things that had surprised me when I first arrived in Hoima was Amory's question after only brief acquaintance:

'Are you a football [soccer] referee?' he had asked.

'Not really,' I replied. 'I have refereed a few games but don't have a certificate.'

'You see,' he went on, 'the Protestant versus Catholic match is coming up and I don't want things to get out of hand. I'll be on the sidelines with Inspector Frisby and some police to keep the spectators from fighting and I want you on the field to control the players. If things get bad you can blow your whistle and use your powers as a magistrate to send players direct from the field to the police cells.'

He made it all sound so simple.

One thing that the missions shared was their knowledge of the local language. This was true all over Uganda where missionaries in close contact with the people became the acknowledged experts in tribal languages and wrote dictionaries, grammars and orthographies and sometimes crowned their efforts by translating the Bible, or parts of it, into the local dialect. This could be the achievement of the missionary's life – the Bible translated into a language that had never before carried those ancient and familiar phrases.

The difficulties were enormous. Some languages had sounds that could not be conveyed by the letters of the standard Italic alphabet.

Neither Lunyoro nor Luganda had this problem because the language possessed few sounds that were much out of the ordinary. Other languages, however, such as Lugbara in the West Nile, required the invention of a whole new set of letters to represent the sound of speech. As an example, '*i-bi*' with a certain intonation meant a leopard, but with another intonation it meant something totally different. One missionary concluded that it required fifty-six letters to accommodate all the sounds, but such a number could not be fitted on an ordinary typewriter.

I asked Stephen about the Lunyoro Bible and whether, for instance, the epistles of Paul and the Johannine gospel were comprehensible to him. My own understanding of Lunyoro never reached the stage of being able to make such a judgement. He replied that most of the Old Testament seemed to make reasonably good sense. The Hebrews as a wandering tribe, the historical and connective passages, the stories of individual warriors and prophets, all this was understandable. The New Testament was another thing. There were so many words that the Lunyoro language did not have, so much abstract thought and esoteric reference that strained it beyond capacity. There were dozens of words for the different kinds of bananas but only one word for wisdom which also had to cover such meanings as cleverness, skill, science, philosophy and much more. The translators had the choice of using English words, in which case it was not a Lunyoro translation; or of inventing words, which was not appropriate; or of trying to give new meaning to old Lunyoro. On balance Stephen was doubtful whether the New Testament was comprehensible to the majority.

The Education Officer in Bunyoro, Miss King, was a mine of information on the education system. She was one of those painstaking, accurate people whose unenviable task was to upgrade the hundred or so schools scattered about the District, many of them bush schools without a qualified teacher or any proper equipment. The performance of teachers themselves had to be assessed and reported, the buildings improved and the school curriculum modernized.

'The first problem we face,' she said, 'concerns their own language, Lunyoro. We teach them to speak in what we suppose to be a grammatical manner, also to read and write it in primary school, but it soon slips away because so little is printed in Lunyoro and there is nothing for them to read. It is the saddest thing to see children who could read when they left school gradually forget what they learned because no books or magazines are available. It is not worth anyone's time to translate news into Lunyoro because the tribe is so small and only about one or two thousand are really literate. You may ask why we don't teach English. If we did there would be no difficulty in finding them books to read but the powers-that-be, supported by the Native Council, have decided that Banyoro children should learn their own language first. They get English in secondary school, which is all very well, but few enter secondary school and even fewer pass through all the classes.

'In my opinion,' she went on, 'English should be started in the second year of primary school and become the language of instruction in secondary school. They would never forget English because there are radio broadcasts every day from Kampala and radios are so cheap that most people can afford one. There is never a shortage of printed matter in English.'

'What about teachers?' I asked. 'The other day in the school at Bugungu I saw a picture of a Red Cross van on the wall and asked what the Red Cross signified. A boy put up his hand but the teacher broke in to say that none of the children would know because he had not yet explained to them about Christianity. I didn't want to make a fool of the teacher in front of the class and allowed the matter to drop. Stephen shook his head in disbelief. The next day we were at the little bush school at Ndandamire and saw no children at all. I asked what they were doing and the teacher said, "helping others who cannot help themselves". Stephen wasn't fooled. He found them putting a new roof on the master's goat house.'

'Typical,' Miss King replied. She went on to say that the problem was that teachers, even those who had been through teacher training college, were so ignorant themselves. Many were quite good instructors in the sense that they were theatrical in their presentation and knew how to keep order, but beyond the bare bones of the curriculum they had nothing to say. They knew little of the world, had never read any books and were locked into village life. Yet the children were wonderfully receptive to learning.

'The really sad thing,' she continued, 'is girls' education. Few girls are to be seen in school and the situation is not improving. The father of a girl is primarily interested in getting a return on his investment and, after all, he has given her a blanket to sleep on, clothes to wear and food to eat since birth. When she is fifteen or sixteen she will marry and the father expects to be repaid by getting a substantial bride-price which will compensate for his past outlay. Much has been said about the custom of bride-price but what it amounts to is that the girl is sold to the highest bidder. In places where they don't have cattle the bride-price consists of sheep, goats, money, clothing and household utensils, not to mention pots of beer and food.

'Young men, however, don't want an educated girl for a wife. An educated girl makes trouble, argues and won't do what she is told. She complains when her husband gets drunk and goes after other women. She may even think she is too good to cultivate the soil and grow food. It follows that girls are kept out of school because the more they are educated the more they deteriorate in value. To add insult to injury, the father would also have to pay for the school uniforms of his daughters and possibly small school fees as well. Even that is not all because while the girl is at school she is not helping her mother so her schooling deprives the father of her contribution as a household servant. To cap it off she is more likely to be seduced or raped on her way to school than if she stays at home. Parents capitalize on this with the claim that it is too dangerous to send a girl to school and that school is where they get pregnant.

'Against all this, girls' education doesn't stand a chance. The few girls who are in school are the daughters of chiefs, schoolteachers or clerks. They expect to marry into their own class and not be beaten for disobedience or laziness.'

A few weeks earlier I had heard a case in the District court in which a man had been charged with beating his wife and breaking two of her ribs. When the charge was read to him he replied, 'I paid for her, why shouldn't I beat her?' He claimed, in other words, that under native custom he was justified in what he did. I explained that mine was the District court and he was charged under the laws of Uganda in which it was an offence to cause grievous harm to another person except in self-defence.

There was a section of law which stated that where a magistrate was confronted by a conflict between native custom and western law he might disregard native custom if it was repugnant to his morality and sense of justice. Not only was this case repugnant to my morality but it seemed to me that we ought to have sufficient faith in our own values that we were prepared to set aside theirs. The accused was not there to teach me native custom; my job was to teach him to respect another human being. Accordingly I sent him to prison but realized there were some magistrates who would have done otherwise.

My own religious upbringing should have given me more sympathy for the Protestant missions and I certainly admired them for their dedication to a life in which they gave everything and received nothing. Well, almost nothing, because a few of the missions practised a form of communism in which they shared their possessions in the way the early Christians were reported to have done in the Acts of the Apostles.

An officer whom I knew later in my service told me that he had been sent out by the Church Missionary Society and had joined a mission where they announced, the moment he arrived, that he was about to be blessed with the privilege of sharing his worldly possessions with others. He was a talented amateur photographer with some expensive equipment and he had not the slightest intention of sharing it with anybody. Without unpacking his luggage he returned to Kampala and joined the Police Department as police photographer.

The strangest of all mission stories came from a former nun whom I met in Canada. She had been brought up in a large Catholic family in Sherbrooke, Quebec, where her father was a minor political figure. One evening on her way home from school she was waylaid and raped by three boys. She was seventeen at the time. There followed discussions between her father, the Church authorities and the family lawyer and in the end they decided that it would do no good to have the boys charged in court. When her baby was born it was taken from her and put up for adoption and she was inducted, against her will, into a religious order. To get her out of the way she was sent to Uganda where she was made to feel as though she were the guilty party and was being punished for her crime.

Her first task on arrival at the mission was to clean the windows and when she had finished she stood back and said, 'Isn't it beautiful?'

'No,' replied the Mother Superior, 'there's a spot *there* and another *there*.'

She had been looking at the white school buildings and green banana plantations but the Mother Superior saw only the spots on the glass.

She said that she had never really been a nun in her heart and always resented the treatment she had received, but it took nineteen years to become a mature person and leave the order. Nineteen years in prison for a crime she did not commit, sentenced by a court consisting of her father, the family lawyer and the Church.

'Now,' she said, 'I have a job in the government with a wonderful view and I never have to worry about the spots on the glass.'

15

Hunting

My first hunting expeditions in Bunyoro were in pursuit of guinea fowl which were abundant in the vicinity of Hoima. They are an attractive, noisy bird about the size of a small chicken with charcoal colouring, white stripes on the neck and dots elsewhere which gives them an art-deco appearance. The head is bereft of feathers and rather vulturine; indeed, one of the half-dozen varieties is called the vulturine guinea fowl. When alarmed they make a cackling noise, with the tempo increasing: 'daaa – da – da – da,' which is distinctive and is why they are sometimes domesticated and kept in place of watchdogs, notably in areas where dogs do not thrive because of tsetse fly. They are as good as any dog at warning of the approach of strangers and do not have to be kept enclosed but can be relied on to remain in the vicinity provided they have been reared in captivity and are fed daily.

No one would claim that the wild guinea fowl is a great game bird because they run more than they fly and when in the air they go straight and not very fast. Aerodynamically they always reminded me of the twin-engined Walrus seaplanes that operated out of the fleet base at Scapa Flow during the war. If a Walrus was too heavily laden to take off it would reduce its weight by unloading a few dozen mail bags and then try again. With crushing irony the sailors called them 'Pusser's Spitfires'. Where guinea fowl were concerned I thought it more sporting to shoot them as they dodged among the cotton plants. At least I missed one or two that way, but once they were in the air I don't know how one could possibly miss.

In the evenings they seemed to prefer open fields but would scurry into the bush and long grass as we approached. This meant miles of walking and quite a bit of running with a double-barrelled twelve-bore in hand, a pocketful of cartridges and a couple of Hassan's men following behind. I used to reckon we would be lucky to travel less than five miles for five birds so it was not a bad way to take some exercise after a day spent in the office or courtroom. The meat of a guinea fowl was like chicken but gamey and tending to be dry; many people thought they were better stewed than roasted.

On the subject of game meat in general it was strongly recommended that it always be thoroughly cooked. Rare or partly cooked meat was unsafe and the North American predilection for roasts and steaks that are pink in the middle was ruled out by the District Medical Officer.

Another game bird found in that area was frankolin, about the size of a partridge. They would rise from the grass as one approached but flew very straight and rarely offered a difficult shot. They were not so common as guinea fowl and were always found singly or in pairs; guinea fowl on the other hand were usually in groups of ten or twenty. The meat of the frankolin was excellent and I would have to say that we kept them for our own table and rarely gave any away.

My first experience of shooting in Africa was one of these late afternoon expeditions in the cotton fields. I see from my diary that it was on 3rd November 1951, and that I took home seven guinea fowl and two frankolin. On the 17th there were seven more guinea fowl and a couple of weeks later ten and two frankolin. That is pretty much how it went month after month. I would stop shooting and head for home at about 6.30 p.m. with the sun nearing the horizon, assuming that by that time my two men had enough to carry. An entry for 11th February 1952, however, shows that I got thirty-one and can only assume that we recruited some local people to help us with so many birds.

The value of these evening jaunts went far beyond merely getting a bit of exercise and knocking over a few birds for the larder. Africans love hunting of any kind and are at their best in such circumstances. The sheer fun of it, the fact that I was getting to know these people and their language and would in any event have become lost in the maze of cotton fields without them, made for an easy relationship. To these two men and the villagers whom we encountered I was not just a distant white administrator but a very ordinary young man in dirty clothes chasing through the fields, getting wet if it rained, cut by the thornbushes and having an exceedingly good time.

One of the reasons I have always loved hunting is because of the unexpected things that happen. One evening a guinea fowl rose from the grass cackling loudly and gave me an easy shot. When it hit the ground it bounced, which meant it was stone dead. A bird that flutters down and makes a non-bounce landing is probably not dead and will run away. I shouted '*enkofu hano*' (guinea fowl here) to the men, reloaded and went after another which had taken refuge in a tree. When I got back carrying the second one the two men had still not found the first. There were plenty of feathers where it had fallen but no bird.

I told them to be absolutely quiet and from thirty or forty yards away we heard a commotion in the grass. Off we went at the run and there was my guinea fowl being pulled along by an industrious family of five mongooses, two full grown and three kittens. Not until one of the men bent down to pick up the bird did they scamper off, obviously having little fear of humans. Their insolence was delightful and I felt inclined to let them keep the guinea fowl as a consolation prize but put aside the idea when I remembered that my two men had a low protein diet and to them a guinea fowl was a rare feast. The mongoose family would have to go and catch their own, which they appeared quite capable of doing.

When I reached home that evening I consulted an old reference book and concluded that they had been the bushy-tailed mongoose (*Cynictis selousi*), not the larger gray variety (*Herpestes caffer*). There are several shapes and sizes of mongoose in Uganda but they are not seen very often. Subsequently I heard dozens of stories about 'dead' guinea fowls simply disappearing. Some of them, of course, were not dead and must have run away; a few others were lost in the grass and a dog would have found them in a moment. A very few others could have been snatched by a mongoose, probably the large gray variety which is big enough to carry the bird and run.

On another occasion one of my two men entered a thick patch of jungle to pick up a bird and trod on a live python. It was relatively small, only about twelve feet and as thick as my leg below the knee and it snapped at the man with its teeth and coiled round his leg. I didn't much like its attitude and killed it. It was getting late and we were some distance from home so I decided to leave it where it was until morning since a dead python is not easy to carry. In fact I wasn't sure if the proper way was to coil it up like a sailor coils a rope, or simply drag it along behind. Anyway, one of the two men returned the following morning but it had been spoiled by predators during the night.

I want to digress for a moment and speak of my boyhood which was spent in a rather wild and mountainous part of the north of England. I was fortunate that my father taught me, from an early age, the safe handling and care of firearms; also the discipline of hunting and the thoughtfulness and good manners that members of a hunting party should extend to each other. He taught me to be observant of nature and considerate towards it, to watch and listen a great deal, to speak hardly at all and to be meticulous. What he never taught me was to shoot straight, only to shoot carefully, because he knew in his wisdom that good shooting was something I could easily teach myself.

In my father's youth, during the first twenty years of this century, a young man who spent his holidays or off-duty hours chasing women was considered a cad and a bounder. On the other hand a man who took his gun in jungle or mountain and pursued game animals, provided he did so with complete sportsmanship and courage, was well regarded. If my father had lived to the present day he would have seen the situation reversed. Womanizers are thought to be very sporting fellows, while sportsmen have now become the cads and bounders. I clearly recall his disappointment in me when I was fifteen or sixteen and went for a perfectly innocent walk with a girl. Equally I remember his unsmiling approval when, in summer, I would get up at five in the morning and be home for breakfast with a couple of rabbits in the bag. He knew that I was shooting them in the farmer's fields round about; we didn't use the word poaching but that's what it amounted to. It was no disgrace in those days for a father to teach his son to be a hunter, outdoorsman and naturalist; it was thought to be an admirable training in discipline and in a subtle way it also taught consideration for others.

When I joined the navy, still in my teens, I found that service in the North Atlantic and Mediterranean in wartime was fairly mild after the training I had received at boarding school and from my father. Navy discipline was nothing that a boy of reasonable education could not accept and I possessed the physical stamina to put up with the kind of life that was imposed on us. I began my navy career as an ordinary seaman on board a battleship and ended as a sort of inefficient, accidental, temporary first lieutenant of a minesweeper. During my two years aboard a destroyer (between the battleship and the minesweeper), I had command of twin Bofors anti-aircraft guns which was a big step-up from the single-shot .22 rifle which had been my constant companion until I joined the navy.

The truth was, therefore, that when I arrived in Uganda in 1951 I had a fairly good grounding in firearms and small game hunting. Shortly after my arrival, before I obtained my game licences, I was tested by the police commander of the Western Province in the safe and proper handling of firearms, was given a marksmanship test by Roy Wyndham and was tested in animal recognition and game laws by the Chief Game Warden of Uganda, Major Bruce Kinloch, who had called in at Hoima.

Bruce Kinloch was in the process of making a tremendous reputation for himself and after a few minutes discussion I was almost sorry that I had not joined the Game Department. His enthusiasm and energy were infectious and his confidence unbounded. He was the only Department head in Uganda at that time who seemed to know exactly what he was doing. He pointed out that Western Uganda contained most of the country's big game, notably elephant, buffalo and hippo, which was why he had posted three of his four European wardens in the Western Province. In Bunyoro, the elephant population was at a reasonable level, but buffalo were far too numerous so he placed no limit on the number that were permitted to be shot on licence. He advised me to go out with Roy Wyndham and see how it was done, then with one of the African game guards.

'Get some practice on buffalo,' he told me. 'They are dangerous and unpredictable. If you are any good you will be in demand to shoot nuisance or rogue buffalo, but before that you must gain some experience. If you can't do it then for God's sake give up altogether. Some people will never be good hunters and no amount of practice is any use.'

My armoury consisted of two Rigby-Mauser rifles plus the double-barrelled twelve-bore given to me by my father. This latter was made by Boss and Co. and was a hammerless ejector, rather on the light side, with twenty-six-inch barrels. For myself I would have been more comfortable with a slightly heavier weapon. It is always said that in the heat of Africa and at an altitude of four thousand feet above sea level a shotgun cartridge develops a slightly increased explosive force. A heavier gun absorbs some of this, gives a longer shot and the pellets are concentrated in a tighter pattern. The Boss was a beautiful gun of exquisite workmanship which I used to good effect for many years but my preference would have been for a little more weight and length.

Rigby-Mauser rifles are famous among big game hunters. I picked up two second-hand weapons before going to Uganda, both quite old but in perfect condition, a .416 big-game rifle and a .350 magnum, which is of medium size. I know all the arguments in favour of a double-barrelled rifle against dangerous game: a slightly shorter weapon which is handier in thick bush and gives two quick shots of devastating power, but I still swear by my Rigby-Mausers. To me the important thing was that the action of both rifles was the same: the sights, safety catch and the operation of the bolt, so I could change from one to the other without ever having to look down or think which one I had in my hand. I might fire two shots at a buffalo with the .416 and without taking my eyes off the target would hand it to my gunbearer and take the magnum from him. He would reload the .416 quietly and we would change again. It was this interchangeability that I valued.

One of my friends in Uganda had four rifles, each one perfect for some specific situation but, hearing him speak, it seemed to me that he never had the right one in his hand at the right moment. Four rifles require two gunbearers fussing around with four different sizes of ammunition, more if hard-nosed and soft-nosed cartridges are both carried, which, combined with the different actions of the weapons, is asking for trouble. Furthermore I could never see the need for a light rifle for shooting the smaller game like wild pig, reedbuck or bushbuck. A Mannlicher .256 or even a light Rigby was all very well but I felt a lot more comfortable with my .350 Magnum, particularly in circumstances where one might run into something dangerous. In the final analysis a hunter's weapons must suit him personally and he must have total confidence in them.

At one point Roy Wyndham loaned me a double-barrelled .500 Express which he wanted to sell. I gave it a try and found that when fired the barrels flew upwards and the two bullets, even when both went off simultaneously, did not stay together. Pulling both triggers of a .500 Express, by the way, is not an exercise to be undertaken lightly. It is best to get a cushion from the sofa and put it between your shoulder and the gun.

Someone else loaned me a rifle with a telescopic sight which I am sure is excellent in mountains or desert where very long shots are needed but in Bunyoro it was useless. I almost trod on a wild pig which seemed in no great hurry to make its exit and when I put up the rifle all I could see was bristles. Through the telescope I couldn't even tell which end of the pig was which so I just let it walk away.

To illustrate the many things that can conceivably go wrong in the bush, I can't resist the story of one of my friends who was travelling in his Landrover along a bush track in the early morning and saw an elephant which he knew had previously been wounded. He jumped out of the vehicle and grabbed his rifle while the elephant turned and seemed to be preparing for a charge. In the confusion between himself and his gunbearer he managed to get a round of ammunition in the left barrel but his fountain pen found its way into the right so that the weapon wouldn't close. He got the elephant eventually but I can't help thinking that his organization was scarcely up to par.

Another, far sadder, story concerned a young man who saw some guinea fowls on the track ahead of him and stopped his car. The vehicle was packed with safari equipment and on top was his shotgun which he pulled towards him by the barrel, intending to fire out of the car window. The trigger caught on something and the gun discharged full in his face, killing him. It was illegal to fire from inside a car and criminally foolish to have a loaded weapon in it, but the truly remarkable thing was that he had served in the army and should have been trained in the safe handling of firearms.

Other incidents come to mind. I was out in the cotton fields one evening with a very inexperienced person whose gun was cradled in such a way that it was pointing directly at me.

'No need to be nervous,' I was told. 'The safety catch is on.'

Failing to persuade the individual to hold the gun any differently I went the other side, to the right, but by that time the outing had been spoiled. It was poor sportmanship and lack of consideration merely to point a loaded gun at another person.

A few days after the Chief Game Warden's visit Roy Wyndham was to carry out one of his normal safaris in the southern part of the Murchison Falls Game Reserve. Amory told me to go with him and pay attention to the problem of game poaching and the measures which Roy and his men were taking to combat it.

'If you are going to sit in court and hear cases against poachers you must know what the poaching situation is like on the ground,' he said.

As an adjunct to the safari it was decided that Roy would shoot a buffalo, assuming we saw any, to show me how it was done. We sat down together and discussed the safari in detail.

The first matter to be decided when planning a safari is who will be on it. The decision was for Roy and myself, his safari servant, who had a driving licence and could handle a Landrover, and two game scouts. Game scouts were employees of the Game Department whose primary task was to put a stop to poaching and illegal methods of hunting. They were armed only for self-defence, not for dealing with dangerous game as were the rather more superior game guards. It was also decided that Roy's Landrover would transport all five of us and that he would be responsible for taking two small tents and the cooking equipment. All I had to take was a bedroll and rifle.

We set out early in the afternoon with Roy at the wheel. From Hoima we took the road northeast to Masindi, then turned on a bush track which led us due north to the boundary of the Murchison Falls Game Reserve, no great distance from where I had been during my Bugungu safari a few weeks before. Within half a mile of the boundary the game scouts knew of a small and rather muddy water supply which was where we made camp for the night. It took no more than a few minutes to put up the two tents, make a fire and get something going for supper.

Roy was a few years older than I and had had a distinguished military career, having fought the Japanese in Malaya and Burma. His uniform bore the purple and silver ribbon of the Military Cross. With the partitioning of India and the ending of the Raj he had been recruited by the Uganda Game Department a few months before these events took place.

Inescapable was the fact that in India Roy had been a member of a small and privileged group which had been well looked after by a whole class of professional servants. It was not that Roy could do nothing for himself, rather that he didn't try, preferring to leave every task, however trifling, to one of his subordinates. On this safari the servant, his 'bearer' as he called him, had been responsible for packing and had come without matches, tea, fly-spray or a lamp. He had, however, included a grotesque mantlepiece clock that looked more like an heirloom than an article one would take in the bush. Roy, as it happened, was a smoker and carried matches in his pocket, but I would have to say I was not well impressed.

In the morning we broke camp early and loaded the equipment in the Landrover. The arrangement was that we would march along the southern boundary of the Reserve, while the Landrover driven by Roy's 'bearer' would return to Masindi, take the main road northwards and meet us at a camp near the Karuma Falls. For us it was a twenty- or twenty-five-mile march, for the Landrover a fifty-mile drive. We assumed that the camp would be ready when we reached it in late afternoon.

We set off in dull, overcast weather. I was carrying my rifle while one of the game scouts had my water bottle and a small cartridge bag. I was wearing khaki shorts and shirt, a jacket and hat. On my feet I had a pair of lightweight boots, also canvas leggings which, in course of time, I came to regard as an absolute necessity. They were proof against thorns, spear grass, snakes and ant bites and were no trouble to put on and take off. I had purchased them at Cogswell and Harrison, the London gunsmiths. The game guards and game scouts wore army puttees which served the same purpose and gave good protection from ankle to knee but were slow to put on and not so comfortable.

The day was a long one. We had taken only a light breakfast and carried nothing for lunch. At midday we simply sat down under a tree for half an hour and watched the animals. There was some evidence of poachers although we did not find traps or snares. It was a long walk in dry, fairly open country where game was in view most of the time. At about five in the evening Roy said we were within a mile of camp and would 'shoot for the pot' from then on. He indicated a low ridge of land which led in a semi-circle into the camp and told me to follow it accompanied by one of the game scouts. He would take a more direct route and would probably be there ahead of me.

I checked my rifle and set off toward the ridge which was visible to the northward. I assumed that splitting up like this, which was not really a very good idea, was Roy's way of testing to see if I knew how to follow simple instructions. I quickened my pace because Roy was a slow walker and for most of the day we had been doing only about two and a half miles an hour. We had been at it for over ten hours. Almost immediately I smelled buffalo and came on their tracks. Roy and his men were out of sight, probably a hundred or two hundred yards away and I whistled but realized that they might not hear. Quite suddenly a bull buffalo stepped out from behind a patch of bush at no great distance and stood staring in my direction. I heard it give a snort and the game scout whispered *'piga'* – 'shoot' in Swahili. I needed no encouragement. The long blue-black barrel was up, the sights came together and I felt a satisfying thump in my right shoulder. Strange to say I didn't hear it go off, only felt it. There was a puff of dust where the bullet struck and the buffalo was lifted off its feet and thrown into the grass.

'*Assante bwana*,' from behind me. (Well done.)

I circled round and walked toward it from its back, not towards its legs, which was a simple precaution in case it was only pretending to be dead. It would have to get to its feet and turn in order to attack and the second or two it takes to turn gives an easy shot to the heart or neck. In this case it wasn't needed because my bullet had broken the neck. This is a very lethal shot on a buffalo because its head and horns are so heavy. It groaned a couple of times, kicked and lay still. Ayuka, the game scout, produced a knife and cut its throat.

Synecerus caffer Sparrman, the big black buffalo of Eastern Africa, is believed to kill more people than all other dangerous game combined, but had proved, in this instance, deceptively simple. This is not the same as the gentle water buffalo of Asia which are domesticated and used for working the rice paddies, but a very savage and intractable animal. Their massive size and the fact that they carry so much meat make them a prime target for African hunters. Leopards and lions may be more dangerous individually but leopards and lions are not seen in hundreds and since they cannot be eaten are likely to be left alone. African methods of hunting with nets and foot traps are only effective against buffalo females and young, the big bulls being more likely to escape with injuries to fight another day. Their cunning and savagery seems to increase with each encounter and a wounded bull can be unbelievably malicious.

My shot had set off a large herd which had been spread out over the area ahead of us. There were three shots from Roy's rifle, so I waited for things to quieten down then walked towards him. He had blundered into the herd and had been obliged to shoot a cow which ran towards him.

The time was about half an hour to sunset so it was decided to cover the two dead buffalo with brush to discourage predators and leave them until morning. For myself, I was looking forward to a hot bath, a meal and a dry bed for the night. 'Bath' is not quite the word but I could have done very well with a plastic wash basin of water which I would have sloshed over myself with a washcloth and felt better for it. However, my hopes were confounded because when we reached the campsite there was no sign of the Landrover. The camp was a large tamarind tree which had previously been used for camping judging by the ashes and the stones set round them. Tamarind means 'Indian date' which name is doubly at fault because it is not Indian nor is it a date. There were no fresh Landrover tracks and if any further irritation was needed a light rain began to fall.

I unloaded my rifle and told Roy that I wasn't impressed. He lit a cigarette and despatched one of his game scouts to backtrack to the buffalo and cut a few pounds of meat to be roasted for supper and the other one eastwards to the main road to see if the Landover was waiting there. The first became lost in the dark and did not reappear until morning. The second, Ayuka, heard elephants ahead of him on the track and turned back, which I thought very sensible. Roy and I collected wood and lit a fire. There was nothing to do but sit on a log protected only slightly from the rain by the tamarind tree and keep the fire going. Neither of us felt much like conversation.

At about nine o'clock I got up to see if I could find a dry patch under the tree where I could lie on the ground and get some sleep but as I did so I caught sight of two pairs of eyes twinkling in the firelight from a nearby bush. I put down my rifle, circled round behind the bush and moved cautiously towards it by which time I could hear chirping and knew that they were frankolin. The rain, of course, was my ally; the noise made in the leaves round them and on their feathers drowned out whatever noise I was making and their preoccupation with the fire prevented them from seeing me. I worked my way under the branch which was about seven feet from the ground then simply grabbed the pair of them with my hands.

I would have loved to see the look on Ayuka's face as I handed him one of the birds which was still alive and chirping nervously, as well it might have done. This was something that a white man, for all his cleverness and technology, was not supposed to know how to do. It was the primitive instinct of the hunter at work, influenced by the fact that we hadn't eaten all day. We plucked and gutted them in short order and Ayuka roasted them over the fire. We shared the meat between the three of us.

This incident, much as I would have liked to forget it, produced unintended results. The Banyoro usually invented nicknames for their officers but the officers themselves were never told what they were. The Lunyoro language helped because there were many levels of meaning attaching to quite simple words so that they could say one thing and mean another. My nickname was bestowed upon me in consequence of this incident. Stephen would never tell me what it was in Lunyoro but said that it could be translated into English as 'the sharp-eyed hunter' or something like it. Another clue came from the Mukama who referred to it about a week later and asked me to confirm that the story was true. When I admitted that it was, he beamed and said: 'So you know how to hunt just like a Munyoro.' Even Amory was intrigued and his very first words were: 'They're saying Roy couldn't organize a piss-up in a brewery and you caught your supper with your bare hands.' News had a way of getting round.

To return to the safari, however, I did manage to get some sleep that night in a dry spot under the tree. For breakfast we sucked the tamarind fruit which has a flavour like old English acid drops, a memory of childhood. We then walked to the road where Roy hitched a ride in an Indian's lorry to Masindi to make enquiries there. Next the Landrover appeared, coming from the north, which was the wrong direction. The driver had missed the turning and gone on to the Nile ferry at Atura where he noticed that one of the tires was almost flat. He couldn't find the jack, had to walk three miles to borrow one, changed the tire, returned the jack, reloaded the car because the spare tire is not accessible when the vehicle is loaded . . . and so it went on. Before returning to the buffalo, however, we recruited some men from a road labourers' camp to help skin and cut them up. On the promise of some meat they volunteered eagerly.

This was my first experience of watching Africans at work on a dead buffalo and I thought they managed well. It would have been easier if Roy had kept a tackle in the car so that the carcass could have been hoisted up by its back legs from a tree branch. As it was they had to do the whole thing on the ground, which was slower and more painstaking.

I learned one other lesson which was that a Landrover can easily tow a dead buffalo. We first drove to where the cow had fallen, found a short length of rope and tied its horns to the towing bar. I put the car in four-wheel drive and pulled it to where the bull was lying two or three hundred yards distant. The idea was that I could watch the whole proceedings and, as Ayuka pointed out, the men couldn't steal chunks of meat by hiding them in the grass. However, realizing how easy it was to tow the cow, I tied the bull buffalo behind as well and drove back to the tamarind tree with both of them. The bull could not have weighed less than three-quarters of a ton, the cow somewhat less and I think it was at that moment that I began to appreciate just what a Landrover could do.

The rest of the safari was uneventful. The road labourers went to work butchering the two buffalo while Ayuka and I unloaded the Landrover and collected armfuls of clean grass in which to pack the meat. We kept four back legs, tongues and back meat, but not the ribs which we cut off so as to take up less space. We had seven or eight hundred pounds of meat, and the rest, necks, heads, spare ribs and skins, we gave to the men who had done the work. Meanwhile the safari servant redeemed himself by preparing breakfast after which we repacked the Landrover and headed for the main road. Halfway to Masindi we met Roy who had again managed to get a ride in an Indian's lorry. I was about to ask him if he had found anything to eat in Masindi but the smell of curry which surrounded him like a cloud answered my question. We were back in Hoima by early afternoon.

My next buffalo bore out the Chief Game Warden's predictions with uncanny accuracy. He had spoken about complaints of rogue buffalo and, surely enough, when on safari in Buhaguzi county a few weeks later a *gombolola* chief reported a buffalo in a banana garden. The owner had come out of his house in the early morning and, confronted by the animal, had taken refuge in a tree. He shouted to his family to stay inside, but his son, a plucky boy of about ten, ran off to get help. The nearest game guard was at the other end of the county and it might have been hours or even days before he could be summoned. With a subtle blend of flattery and good humour the chief put it to me that I could scarcely refuse to go to the aid of the poor fellow and his family.

It was a Saturday and being mid-afternoon we had finished our work. I walked back to the rest camp to change into old clothes and get my rifle which, as usual, was chained and padlocked behind the seats of the Landrover. Stephen said he would follow at a distance.

'You realize,' he said, 'that what the chief told you was probably only half true.'

This was borne out when we reached the banana garden. There were tracks of a buffalo in the soft earth but no sign of their owner.

The *gombolola* chief had supplied me with a tracker whom he described as a capable man. His name was Yozefati, which I suspected was the local rendition of Jehoshaphat, onetime king of Judah. He was talkative, unobservant and liked nothing better than to order others around. I wished that Ayuka had been there. We followed the buffalo tracks for about a mile from the banana garden into thick jungle where we could only see a few yards in any direction. Yozefati was five yards ahead of me carrying a spear. We came to a small tree where the buffalo had evidently been resting for much of the day. The grass was flattened and there were droppings nearby. I bent down to feel if the ground was still warm but as I did so I distinctly heard it moving through the bush, not ahead of us, but off to one side. It was the classic manoeuvre of the buffalo that knows it is being hunted and works its way round so that the tables are turned and the hunter becomes the hunted.

A few yards back I had seen an open pathway or 'ride' between the trees leading at right angles from the direction of the tracks that we had been following. If the buffalo were to cross it I would get a shot, so back I went at a run, scattering three or four of the camp followers who were on the path. The buffalo was more than halfway over as I reached the place, ground to a halt and put up my rifle. I couldn't really see the neck so I guessed at where the heart was and snatched at the trigger. Again that satisfying thump into the shoulder but this time I got a slight concussion because I had not planted my feet firmly as I fired. However I heard the bullet strike and the buffalo, no more than the length of a tennis court away, crashed into the bush.

If I had been an experienced hunter I would probably have sent Yozefati home. He was too much of an enthusiast, too anxious to show off his prowess and he lacked the meticulous care of a real tracker. I tried to get him to wait and let the buffalo's wound stiffen so that it would lie down and perhaps have difficulty getting up, but no, off he went following heavy blood which was obviously coming from the heart. We went for a quarter of a mile, Yozefati ahead following the blood, myself fairly close behind him with my rifle in both hands pointed upwards to the left. The bush was thick and visibility no more than a few yards. Quite suddenly, thirty yards ahead of us, the buffalo got up from the grass and started its charge. It was obviously sick and I should have had all the time I needed to put two shots into its chest. What Yozefati ought to have done was drop to the ground and roll or crawl out of my way but he did nothing of the sort; he threw his spear at it. Then he turned and came straight back towards me which prevented me from shooting.

My predominant recollection of the next half minute was of trying to finish off the buffalo without shooting Yozefati. It knocked him down with the end of its nose and he crawled away in the grass. Its massive rump was toward me as it tried to scoop him up and toss him. It was no earthly use shooting at its backside and its head and neck were down in the grass where Yozefati was. Much better let Yozefati take his chances with the buffalo than risk a ricochet off its skull or horn. I ran round a ten foot high ant-hill and found Yozefati draped over its neck so I tried to get into better position but tripped over a fallen tree and lost my own footing. When I had collected myself Yozefati was making another attempt to crawl away but the buffalo was standing over him. If I had shot it at that moment the entire ton-weight of the animal would have come down on him so I held my fire. Seconds later he crawled out between its back legs and stood up, again getting between the buffalo and me.

The buffalo staggered away into the bush but circled and returned a second or two later with renewed malice. Thinking to climb the ant-hill and get a better view of the situation I met Yozefati coming up from the other side but somehow we resolved the question of ownership of the ant-hill and I got to the top. The buffalo was standing quite still about ten yards away behind a bush and my shot broke its neck. The recoil, however, knocked me clean off the ant-hill and into the grass.

Looking back, it is hard not to laugh at the whole episode. Yozefati was uninjured, indeed, he scarcely had a scratch and his bravado remained intact. He was the worst tracker I had ever had in the bush and his folly could have cost him his life. Luckily the buffalo had been seriously hit by the first shot which had passed close behind the heart. The men gathered round and Yozefati treated them to a blow-by-blow description of his experience. One of them asked if he could have the 'eggshell'. I stared at him uncomprehending and then realized what he meant. There is no word for 'empty cartridge case' so they call it an 'eggshell' and he wanted to find it and wear it as a charm. I told him where to search and he located it in the grass.

With villages all around more than a hundred men had heard the shots and came with their knives. The *gombolola* chief and his two policemen appeared so I asked him to take charge and see to the equitable distribution of the meat. The only parts that I wanted were the tongue and two fillets, these being smaller on a buffalo than on a beef animal but equally tasty. I had no plans to return to Hoima for several days so it would have been pointless to take more than I needed for my own cooking pot.

This buffalo's behaviour, even to a person of my limited experience, had been unusual, although it is difficult to say what is or is not unusual in so temperamental an animal. However, it was a lone bull which should have known better than to be in someone's banana garden at first light. Furthermore, having encountered the owner and chased him up a tree its movements from then onwards seemed uncharacteristic. It travelled a relatively short distance and rested for several hours until we came along, when it immediately tried to turn the tables on us by moving round behind us.

The answer was plain the moment we examined it. A front foot had been caught in a trap because the part above the hoof was swollen and filled with pus. In addition there were two old wounds that looked suspiciously as though they had been caused by spears. This buffalo clearly had a history which they had not mentioned to me and Stephen had been right when he said that I could expect to hear about half the truth. The local people, the chief included, must have known more than they said and should have warned me.

Yosefati was worse than useless because a good tracker would have noticed the peculiarities of its footprints in the soft earth and given me better information. In favourable conditions a tracker can read animals' footprints, rather as an expert can tell much from a specimen of handwriting. Finally, Yosefati's inability to get out of my field of fire and let me shoot was even worse; he seemed to be courting disaster. For myself, I was learning fast and at that early stage in my career I took one lesson to heart: namely, that in the African bush the real danger is from people, not animals. A truly competent hunter is equipped to deal with animals but he is not equipped to deal with fools.

About two years later Roy Wyndham was killed, not by the lion which attacked him and threw him down, but by another hunter who shot him in the back. Roy was a courageous man and an excellent companion, but I did not think of him as a first-rate hunter, a view that was shared by others. Roy had been escorting a visitor, a senior officer in the NATO forces, and the lion, wounded, had retreated into a patch of thick bush. As Roy prepared to go in the lion charged. There had been no plan and the other hunter was behind Roy, not to one side where he should have been and they had not waited for the lion's wounds to stiffen. Worst of all, Roy did not hear the lion's charge and did not even get a shot at it. The other hunter, at a distance behind, saw the lion before Roy did. If the lion had merely knocked Roy down and tried to bite him Roy could have defended himself for a few seconds until the other man got into position for a safe shot. He would have suffered a mauling which, however, is a good deal better than being shot in the back.

16

Game Guard Kiiza

When, in mid-year, Roy left the District he was not replaced by another game warden and his duties were shared between Amory, myself and Game Guard Kiiza. Kiiza means that he was born after twins; his tribal name was Mbulamukolo. Although uneducated and with not a word of English, he was by far the best game guard and hunter with whom I have ever been out in the bush. When the Chief Game Warden introduced the rank of head game guard Kiiza was among the first to be promoted to the higher level. Years before, my father had taught me the basic discipline of handling firearms and good sportmanship; it was Kiiza, however, who taught me the fine points of hunting and game control. More than that, it was always thoroughly enjoyable being with him because he was supremely observant and had a wonderful sense of humour.

With the large numbers of buffalo in Bunyoro our favourite quarry were the old bulls that had been expelled from the herds. They usually live solitary lives although sometimes we came across two together. They were old, ill-tempered and dangerous, particularly in pairs because they had formed a bond and always came to each other's defence. Many hunters have noted that an old buffalo is sometimes to be seen following the herd a mile or so distant and have assumed that they are lookouts whose job is to warn of approaching danger. Kiiza thought this was nonsense; they had been kicked out of the herd by the younger and more aggressive bulls but continued to tag along having not accustomed themselves to a solitary life. After some weeks or months they would leave the herd altogether. Kiiza's contention was that these solitary bulls contributed nothing to the breeding of the herd and were far more dangerous than the herd itself, particularly to Africans who were out collecting honey in the forest, or picking up firewood. It follows that when we wanted meat these were the ones we went after so that the breeding herds were left to carry on undisturbed. On more than one occasion we followed the tracks of a herd and when we knew they were about half a mile ahead Kiiza would circle and search out an old male which had been expelled.

On one occasion an African woman was killed by a buffalo near her village so Kiiza and I drove there the following morning. I remember vividly the uncharacteristic silence of the twenty or thirty villagers who gathered as we loaded our rifles. A man came to show us the place where the body had been found. The buffalo had tossed her with its horns, stamped on her with its feet then rolled on her. The Medical Assistant said there was not a bone in her body that had not been broken. As we set off Kiiza told me to station myself twenty yards on his left.

We followed carefully for about an hour and probably covered no more than half a mile. A small bird seemed to be acting strangely and we both knew that we were close. A moment later the buffalo burst out of a thicket and was on the point of charging Kiiza but saw me as my rifle went up. It looked my way and hesitated. I was in the perfect position, slightly up the slope of the hill with a clear shot of only fifteen or twenty yards. I felt my rifle go off but the buffalo stayed on its feet and it was not until the second shot that it sank down.

It was the biggest buffalo I had ever seen and must have weighed a ton and a half. It was covered with old wounds and when the villagers came to cut it up they found two lead slugs, besides the three bullets we had fired. I wondered how such an enormous creature had been forced out of the herd and concluded that the other bulls must have ganged up on it. Out of respect for the old woman who had been killed we took no meat for ourselves. This was a pitifully small gesture but the only one I could think of in the circumstances. Its horns were still smeared with blood.

The lesson to be learned from this incident was the value of not being one behind the other but a few yards apart so that if one of us could not get a clear shot the other could. The second lesson, of course, is to pay close attention to what the birds are telling you.

One type of hunter whom I am wary of is the one who fancies himself as a marksman and takes long or difficult shots that are more likely to wound than kill. The whole point is to get close for the first shot, as close as possible so that you really can't miss.

One day Kiiza and I were out with one of the Kampala magistrates, Chris Olding, who had asked if he could accompany us. We saw a lone buffalo in a clearing with his head down in the grass. There was a strong wind and he was heading into it; all grazing animals feed into the wind so that the succulent grass tips are blown into their mouths. There were about a hundred men following us and Kiiza told them to sit down and keep out of the way. Chris came walking a few feet behind us.

What we were doing was showing off to the audience seated in the grass and treating the whole thing as a bit of a skylark. Kiiza knew that the buffalo was so engrossed in its feeding and heading so consistently into the wind that we could walk right up behind it, which is what we did. Side by side and with no attempt at concealment we walked through the grass toward its backside. At ten yards or thereabouts Kiiza stopped and I did the same. I pushed my safety catch across, Kiiza coughed like a leopard which made it jump around and face us and I fired at its neck. The massive head went down and that was the end of it, a more humane end than it would have met with in a modern slaughterhouse. We measured the distance from where my feet had been to the tip of the buffalo's nose: eight and a half yards. Chris only had one comment: 'You make it look so damned easy.'

Only on one occasion can I recall trying a fancy shot. I was ahead of Kiiza walking through fairly open country when I saw a slight movement in deep shade about sixty yards ahead. I sank to the ground and Kiiza and another man behind me did the same. The main body of camp followers were some distance behind and Kiiza motioned them to get down. Africans are very good at this; they simply disappear in the grass. Next I crawled forward to an ant-hill and took a long look through the binoculars. It was a bull buffalo lying in the shade partly hidden by leaves and what I had seen was the flick of its tail. The head was away from me but there was enough neck exposed for a lethal shot. I put the binoculars down and took my rifle from Kiiza but couldn't distinguish the black buffalo against the equally dark background.

We rarely spoke to each other in the bush, preferring to communicate by hand signal, but this time we allowed ourselves a few whispered words. The buffalo, Kiiza explained, had chosen its resting place with care. There was thick bush behind it and a papyrus swamp so it only had to get to its feet and take two steps and we would lose our chance. It was no use making it stand up, nor was it any use trying to crawl closer because the ground was bare and open. I studied it again with the binoculars which had a high magnification, then with the naked eye, but wasn't satisfied that I could see exactly where to put the shot.

Kiiza had meanwhile rolled away a few yards to the left and beckoned me to follow. When I reached him his plan became clear; he had found the spot where two stems of dry grass crossed in an exact line with the buffalo's neck. Provided I was in the right place I had only to aim at the two stems which were about fifteen yards ahead of me and if my aim was right the shot would be lethal. I took my time, studied it through the binoculars; then rested the rifle, gave the binoculars to Kiiza and while he kept them to his eyes to warn me if the buffalo moved I took aim on the crossed grass stems and pulled the trigger. It worked perfectly and a very old buffalo died on the spot. This technique is known in the army as an 'aiming mark' and is sometimes used for spraying machine gun fire at night, but I had never thought of it as a possibility by day for a single shot.

To demonstrate how badly things can go wrong in the bush, my worst experience occurred when Kiiza was away on some other duty and only the young Ayuka was available. I had been asked by the Chief Game Warden to arrange a one-day hunting safari for a visitor whose passion in life was to shoot a big buffalo. Hearing him speak, which he did much of the time, one had the impression that he had shot every game animal in the world except buffalo. He was physically a big man, which he needed to be to handle the firearm which he had. It was an old, single-barrel .577 with a side action, so that only one shot could be fired after which the gun had to be opened and reloaded. It had been manufactured during the reign of King Edward VII and while it doubtless packed a tremendous punch, hunting had changed since then, the animals knew they were being hunted and were more dangerous. Besides, it was much too heavy and would have taken a very exceptional man to fire from the shoulder without resting it. My Rigby .416 looked like a toy by comparison. It reminded me of the anti-tank rifles supplied to us during the war for shooting at floating mines.

We drove to Biseruka in the Landrover and after about an hour came on the fresh tracks of a lone buffalo. I told the visitor I could not be sure it had a good pair of horns but that it was big in the body, judging by its footprints. The meat, I explained, would all be used and nothing wasted. It had been raining overnight and the ground was still wet so that a chartered accountant could have followed the tracks. I went ahead, followed by the visitor and after him game scout Ayuka carrying the visitor's rifle. My 'regulars' from Biseruka were well back.

It was the 'regulars' who saw the buffalo first. The tracks crossed a small re-entrant valley filled with bush and while the three of us were making our way through the thicket in the floor of the valley the buffalo walked up the other side in full view. As we emerged from the bush a whistle made me turn and a shirt being waved left me in no doubt as to the situation.

I told the visitor we were not going to rush forward because the wind was in our favour and the buffalo would now be searching for a place to lie during the heat of the day. It already showed signs of meandering around rather than travelling straight which indicated that it was ready for its siesta. We went on slowly and the footprints showed that it was not aware of our presence. It was walking, not running and taking a nibble of grass here and there. Another small re-entrant valley lay ahead of us with a patch of dense brush at the lowest point.

'He may be in there,' I said. 'I'll go through the bush and try to drive him out at a walk. You go round the left and take your shot when you see him.'

I pointed to a small tree. 'That would be your best place, behind that tree.'

It worked perfectly and the buffalo co-operated. The thicket was dense but I could smell it a few yards ahead of me. It moved and I saw a branch tremble. A few more steps and I was in the stream bed at which point there was a crash of branches and I heard it move out. A few seconds later came a shot and the thump of the bullet striking.

I was in the wrong place because if the buffalo was only wounded it might return to the thicket where I would have been at a disadvantage. I retraced my steps and went round the outside and found Ayuka and the visitor still under the tree. Ayuka said that the buffalo had run out but stopped suddenly and turned giving an easy shot at less than fifty yards. The bullet had struck but the buffalo ran off.

We went forward to where it had stood and I could see the skid marks in the earth as it tried to keep its footing when the bullet hit. If the visitor had used a proper rifle he would have had a second shot as it turned away. There was much red, frothy blood from the lungs which suggested that the shot had been too far back to be instantly fatal.

We continued to follow the tracks in the same order, myself ahead, the visitor now carrying his rifle, Ayuka behind. The country was open and grassy and we had only gone a short distance when I saw the curl of one of its horns in the grass ahead of me. I could not see its head or any of its body although it was quite close, so I put up my left hand which brought the visitor and Ayuka to a stop behind me. I felt confident because in the space of time that the buffalo would take to get to its feet and face me I would have an easy shot. I whispered to the visitor to take half a dozen steps to the left but he put up his rifle and fired over my left shoulder, the muzzle being only a few inches from my ear.

It was like being hit with a hammer on the side of the head and I was thrown down in the grass, my rifle underneath me. For a few seconds I must have been unconscious because when I pulled myself together the buffalo was standing staring at us about twenty yards away and Ayuka was calmly cleaning the mud out of the muzzle of my rifle. He had noticed that as I fell it had plunged into the wet ground so he took out the bolt and was using a long stem of hard grass to clean the barrel. His training had taught him that a bit of mud in the muzzle of a heavy rifle is dangerous and that when fired it can burst the weapon. The visitor was somewhere in the background in a very agitated state.

Ayuka pulled me into a sitting position, gave me a drink from the water bottle and put the rifle back in my hands. The buffalo had seen all it wanted to see and unbelievably it simply ambled away. We waited for the Biseruka contingent to catch up and I took something to eat and had another drink of water. Half an hour later, feeling somewhat restored although totally deaf in my left ear, I followed up again with Ayuka and finished it off.

To this day I have no idea why that buffalo didn't charge and if it had done so Ayuka and I would have been helpless. Ayuka's calmness prompted me to write a note to the Chief Game Warden in which I commented favourably on his conduct. Later he showed me the knife that the visitor had taken off his belt and given him; in those days it would have cost about ten dollars, more like sixty now, and was as practical as it was beautiful. It restored the man in Ayuka's eyes if not in mine.

I never met him again but my hearing was back to normal within a week. The only funny thing about the whole episode was that the second shot fired by the visitor missed the buffalo completely so in fact the shot caused me more damage than it did to the thing he was aiming at. If the man had done what I said and moved a few steps to the left we would have been perfectly safe and of course it is the first rule of sportsmanship that you don't shoot at what you can't see. I won't even guess what prompted him to fire over my shoulder and the truth is I never subsequently asked. I suppose, in retrospect, I should have looked round to see what he was doing and how he was reacting, having already noted that his nerves were on edge, but my attention was focused on that bit of horn projecting above the grass. I didn't think that anyone could do anything so foolish as to fire before getting well clear of another person. It was poetic justice that the horns of the buffalo were broken and ill-matched and worth nothing as a trophy.

The question was often asked as to why some hunters always seem to get into difficulties and are charged by animals when to others it is a rare occurrence. Part of the answer can be attributed to mere carelessness or stupidity, but there is something else at work, the fact that animals seem to pick on certain people. Kiiza said that good hunters were rarely charged and that young, novice game guards went through a period of getting into all sorts of trouble because they didn't understand the minds of the animals. This seemed to be as good an explanation as any, although there were plenty of other rather weird theories to account for this phenomenon. For myself, I concluded that the reason why some people got chased around like a matador in a bullring was immaterial, the main thing was not to share the bullring with them. I heard one sporty individual say that he had had five narrow escapes out of six safaris so I made a mental note never to go hunting with him.

Kiiza certainly had an instinctive knowledge of the animals' moods and what they were likely to do next. One afternoon we were told that a herd of elephants had moved out of the Bugoma forest, which was their normal range, and were feeding in some banana gardens not far from Munteme bazaar. When we got there we discovered that the herd was actually visible from the road. The local *gombolola* chief was waiting with a large crowd and asked us, very reasonably, to drive them back into the forest. Kiiza's response was surprising if not downright hilarious; he walked right up to them through the banana trees, shouted mild insults and threw chunks of mud. Like naughty children they grabbed a last mouthful of young banana leaf and with much complaining gathered themselves and made off.

'We must get them running faster,' Kiiza shouted, so together we trotted after them and stepped up the abuse. There were over a hundred in the herd and put together they probably weighed five hundred tons which proves, as I later said to Jean, the power of a few well-directed insults.

On the way home Kiiza said that the elephants knew they were in the wrong and would not make trouble. However, he warned that you could not always deal with elephants that way and once in a while you had to shoot. This was borne out a few months later when another game guard, a Sudanese, was attempting to drive elephants out of cultivated land near a little place called Busingiro. An old cow elephant turned on him so he shot it, after which two younger bulls came at him and he shot both. Within seconds two more attacked and by the time the herd made off he had five dead elephants in a circle round him. He said that throughout the encounter he had scarcely changed the position of his feet, he had simply stood out in the open and shot them as they came.

The Game Department naturally deplored the killing of large numbers of elephants and some ingenious alternatives were tried. In one experiment army 'thunderflashes' were used, a sort of grenade used for training purposes which goes off with a brilliant flash and a frightful bang but does no harm. To begin with they worked well but the elephants soon learned they were harmless and discovered how to tread on them while they were still fizzing and put them out.

Another story that did the rounds in Bunyoro was about an elephant that deliberately set a house on fire. It was told to us by the Mukama who vouched for its authenticity. A cultivator heard noises at night and opened the door of his house to find an elephant standing in his yard. He took a burning stick from the fire and threw it at the elephant's feet but the elephant picked it up carefully in its trunk and lodged it in the grass roof of the man's house.

I had one run-in with an elephant which was pure farce. Kiiza and I were driving a herd out of cultivated land which involved crossing a wet valley bottom where the elephants had spent some time before climbing up the slope into the banana gardens. As was so often the case in Bunyoro, the hillside was cultivated but not the valley floor, which was swampy and had been left under bush and grass. The large feet of the elephants had churned the valley floor into a sea of mud which I sank into up to my ankles as I ploughed across it with the elephants streaming up the hill on the other side. I sloshed round a bit of thicket and came to an abrupt halt on being confronted by a cow elephant with a very young calf; I would have guessed it to be less than a week old. The cow turned and faced me and pushed the calf under its belly.

Two things occurred to me, first that the calf was so young it had not been able to get through the mud which was why the two of them had been left behind. Secondly it was well known that a cow elephant with a newborn calf has a 'sister' or 'auntie' elephant in attendance whose arrival at that moment could have complicated matters. I was rooted to the spot in mud a foot deep and while I would have been quite content to retire gracefully I simply could not go backwards through that sea of mud; forwards, yes, but not backwards.

It is a cardinal rule that you never turn your back on a dangerous animal so I could do nothing but stand there with the elephant less than ten yards away towering over me. The baby elephant was all curiosity and peered out between its mother's front legs. I pushed the safety catch of my rifle across and decided that if the cow took one step towards me I would have to shoot. My point of aim would be six inches below the second wrinkle on its forehead. For about half a minute we stood glaring at each other, then the elephant put its trunk down, searched around and blew some dirty water in my direction. To be honest it didn't hit me, although I think the gesture was a moral victory for the elephant. With that it turned, all the while keeping the baby under its belly, and flounced off. When I told Kiiza about it he thought it a great joke.

The amount of damage that a herd of elephants can do in cultivated land has to be seen to be believed. Not merely do they have four feet as big as manhole covers and weigh up to six tons apiece, not merely do they stuff hundreds of pounds of green food into their bellies on a daily basis but they also seem to take pleasure in sheer destruction. They will push a tree down, take a few leaves and go on to the next, and in a banana garden they will uproot every single plant and eat very little. They are particularly fond of sugar cane and potato vines, although they will never touch tobacco plants. A herd of elephants can be an unmitigated disaster for cultivators and whole villages can be wiped out overnight. There is always a danger to human life if a herd should stampede through a village.

My story would not be complete if I didn't record the incident of Kiiza and the warthogs. It was one of our Tonya and Kaiso weekends and we left the Landrover, as usual, at the top of the escarpment and spent the night camped by Lake Albert. On Sunday afternoon, as we came back across the flats, the sky opened and there occurred what the meteorologists call precipitation; it was as though the rain was trying to obliterate the earth. We struggled through the downpour towards the foot of the escarpment, Kiiza and myself in the lead and about twenty Biseruka regulars strung out behind with loads on their heads. To complicate matters we had arrested some Congolese poachers who had crossed the lake in a canoe. We came on them quite by chance with their spears, nets and other paraphernalia as they sheltered under a tree waiting for the rain to stop. They had already killed a number of animals so there was a lot of meat to carry. I had no alternative but to arrest them and make them carry the 'exhibits' except for spears and knives which Kiiza took.

Kiiza and I were rather ahead of the others so we stood and waited for them because I didn't want us to be strung out as we climbed. If the whole group were together we could keep a better eye on the prisoners and could go to the assistance of anyone who got into difficulties on the slippery path. Everyone had a heavy load; Kiiza had what were essentially weapons, I was weighted down with two rifles and all the small things like binoculars, water bottles and cartridge bags. We stood talking quietly as the men approached, the grass up to our thighs.

Suddenly I heard a slushing noise from beneath Kiiza's feet and for a moment had no idea what it was. A few seconds later a huge warthog emerged from a hole which neither of us had seen, ran round in a circle, then made off. It was followed by a second full-grown animal and four smaller ones, each of which I would have guessed to be fifty pounds in weight. The younger ones were confused and one of them bumped into Kiiza hitting him at knee level from behind. On the slippery ground and with a heavy load he collapsed with one leg on top of it and the other leg down the hole. The piglets ran round in confusion making yapping noises but finally galloped off after their parents.

Kiiza was physically a big man and his reputation as a fearless hunter was second to none. To see him sprawled on the ground, levelled by a yapping warthog piglet was too much for the Biseruka regulars who dropped their loads and with rain streaming down their faces they collapsed in laughter. Here was the respected Mbulamukolo Kiiza, the superlative hunter, winner of a thousand encounters against elephant, buffalo, hippo, lion and leopard not to mention poachers, laid low on a rainy afternoon by a warthog. Even the Congolese poachers thought it was funny and of course Kiiza himself, once he had overcome his confusion, laughed as much as anyone.

I realized then that the slushing noise I had heard were the warthogs trying to scramble out of their hole which was filling with rain. Perhaps they heard our voices, or smelled us, or perhaps it was just the rainwater running into their large underground den that set them off, but the fact is that they decided to leave precisely as we stood there. It surprised me, in retrospect, that I had not smelled them although rain tends to obliterate odours by carrying them down into the ground. Elephants normally have an astonishing sense of smell but are helpless in heavy rain and one can walk right up to them. The clatter of the rain on their bodies and in particular their huge ears also means they can't hear anything.

I don't know how influenced I was by the warthog incident and the rain, but when we reached Biseruka I held a brief conference with the *gombolola* chief and we decided to release our prisoners. As I remember there were six of them. I gave them the choice of going before another magistrate in Hoima – obviously I would be disqualified from hearing the case – or of accepting my punishment on the spot. I said that their spears, snares and meat would be confiscated but that they could return to their canoe which they had hidden in the reeds and go straight home across the lake. The loss of their spears and nets was a heavy blow but they would certainly have lost them if they had gone to court and would probably have collected a prison sentence as well. I told them that I took into account the fact that they had carried heavy loads up the mountain and had not tried to run away. Kiiza, however, insisted that their knives be returned because a man was helpless without his knife. They had evidently expected something a good deal worse because they went on their knees and thanked me. The *gombolola* chief told them not to come back unless they came peacefully to sell their fish.

I look back with some apprehension at the swift and perhaps youthful decisions made in those days in the name of justice. And what a scene it must have made, myself as judge, the *gombolola* chief, the accused and some onlookers standing in the *gombolola* hall like drowned rats. Except that my face was white it would be hard to know who was who. However, 'plea bargaining' is not unknown in civilized countries and I think we reached a reasonable compromise.

The Chief Game Warden of Uganda, Major Kinloch, had a small zoo at Entebbe where captured animals and birds from up-country were forwarded. For obvious reasons the animals caught were usually young. He would keep them until there was a demand from one of the great zoological gardens of the world and they would then be despatched by air and an emotion-filled half column about it would appear in the *Uganda Argus*. If the animal was small and cuddly there would be a cute photo of a pretty stewardess holding it at the foot of the aircraft steps. The girl would have a nervous smile on her face which said, between clenched teeth: 'Don't piss on my clean uniform you little . . .' Most young animals, by a sort of unwritten law, whether they were leopards, buffalos or warthogs, would be named after the District Commissioner's wife of the District where they came from.

My first contribution to the zoo began as an ornithological disaster but subsequently redeemed itself. One morning our gardener, Heneriko, peered round my office door with a huge eagle under his arm.

'Sir,' he said, 'The *mem sahib* [Jean] told me to bring you *empungu* [eagle] because she doesn't know what to do with it.'

'Very well,' I said, 'where did you get it?'

With his free hand he made the motions of a Junkers 87 dive bomber and explained that it flew into the chicken wire.

'The chickens were confused,' he said.

I called an office messenger who produced a large cardboard box and cut a hole in the top the size of a tea cup. The eagle was placed inside with its head out the hole. I liked its air of old-world nobility; a sort of melancholy disapproval. The box was then tied up with government red tape and a label attached: '*Empungu*. Deliver to Bwana Chief Game Warden, Entebbe.' The office messengers were proud of their handwriting and liked to show it off on such occasions.

In a country where everyone knew everyone else's business it was not difficult to find someone travelling to Entebbe that day. A telephone call alerted Bruce Kinloch as to what was in store for him and later in the afternoon he returned the call to say that it had arrived. All was courtesy and compliment: 'We like our eagle; magnificent specimen; wonderful opportunity for the experts; owe you a debt of gratitude,' and so on.

I told Jean at supper that the operation had been a success and we were well on the way to making a name for ourselves in the rarefied atmosphere of ornithology. She had meanwhile looked up 'eagles' in the old Lydekker reference book and was unsure which one it was. It could scarcely be the fighting eagle, *Spizaetus bellicosus* but what about *coronatus* or even *occipitalis.*

'He had a nice gentle look about him,' she declared. 'I think he was *occipitalis.* Just possibly he'll turn out to be a separate sub-species, wouldn't that be marvellous?'

'*Spizaetus occipitalis Bazleyensi*,' I suggested.

We finished our supper on cloud nine of ornithological speculation.

The following morning I had no sooner reached the office than a call came from Entebbe. It was Bruce Kinloch.

'You know what your bloody eagle did last night, it ate the other birds including my painted quail. Why the hell do you send these damn things to me? I had to let it go.'

Yesterday it had been his eagle, the Chief Game Warden's, today, a painted quail later, it was mine. Oh well, I thought, that solves one question, it was *bellicosus*, not *occipitalis.*

Weeks passed and we assumed that *Spizaetus bellicosus Bazleyensi* would fly back into the African sky, soar upwards on the thermals and disappear from sight and memory. It did no such thing. It chose a tree on the Entebbe golf course and set about constructing a large, untidy nest and by that time it had found a mate. We never discovered whether ours was the male or female, but whichever it was it redeemed itself when a famous American ornithologist built a tower near the tree and took pictures that were absolutely spectacular. A rumour, false I might add, was being spread by penny-pinching, golf-playing Scotsmen to the effect that *S. bellicosus* occasionally swooped down on their golf balls and stole them.

Anyway *bellicosus* became a topic of dinner party conversation which was only one step away from a tourist attraction. The two majestic birds were a fixture of the golf course, they screamed mightily and the ornithological glory they generated was quite properly shared by Bruce Kinloch, whose inspiration it had been to feed one of them a painted quail, and the American genius who captured them on film.

17

Water Supplies

It is difficult to think of any single factor which affects a third-world country so closely as the provision of water. An abundant supply of clean potable water is the first essential for a healthy community and it requires no expert knowledge of medicine to name those deadly diseases that are caused by contaminated water. In many African countries the mere drawing of water from existing springs or wells is an all-day task, nearly always relegated to the women. One of the most pathetic sights was to see lines of them, water pots on their heads, walking for miles down the village paths to collect a gallon or two of insipid water for their families and themselves; a waste of time and effort and a danger to health which mocked the ingenuity of the modern world.

The government of Uganda, parsimonious in many other respects, was at least willing to spend money on clean water supplies in the form of bore-holes. These are holes a couple of inches in diameter drilled by machine into the water table below ground. A simple hand pump at the surface brings up the water and to draw it the villager only has to place his pot on a concrete platform and operate the handle with the classic up-and-down motion. Such a pump requires little in the way of maintenance and operates for years with no more than a dab of grease on the moving parts.

The arm of government responsible for drilling bore-holes was the Department of Geological Survey, water supplies being a branch of its more glamorous function which was to locate and exploit the mineral wealth of the country. The Department had half a dozen expatriate geologists who searched for minerals that could be mined and exported for the benefit of the economy. The copper mines at Kilembe in the Ruwenzori mountains were a case in point, also the lime deposits at Tororo which gave rise to Uganda's cement industry. The geologist who stumbled on the Tororo deposits, Cyril Williams, told us that the proven value of his find was in excess of a hundred million pounds and that he discovered it before he had been two weeks in the country. In ten subsequent years of searching he had found nothing of value, which seems to confer a new wealth of meaning on the saying about beginners having all the luck.

Water drilling cannot have carried the same panache to a geologist as the possibility of discovering a clay pipe bearing diamonds or a seam of gold buried in white quartzite, or even the lesser finds such as tantalite, columbite or tin, but water affected people as nothing else did. There were some parts of the country where satisfactory water supplies already existed such as when springs were found emerging from the hillsides. An iron pipe, some cement and a few hours' work was all that was needed to make a muddy pool clean and safe for humans. In such places the geologists had no need to locate bore-holes. Where there were no natural supplies, however, they studied the ground and decided where each hole should be drilled to have the best chance of success. At that point they turned over the work to the drilling crews, a hard-bitten bunch who trundled their machines from one site to the next. They generally took from seven to fourteen days to drill a hole, depending on the hardness of the subsoil and the depth of the water table.

Our borehole driller in Bunyoro was Erik Andersen, a large Viking of a man who was assisted by about ten Africans. He lived in a trailer a few yards from where the rig was hammering day and night. His men had a sort of collapsible Nissen hut nearby. At weekends he would drive to Hoima to pick up supplies, mail and such spare parts as were needed for the drilling rig, and he would usually spend Saturday night in the Rest House. There being no club, one of the Europeans would invite him to supper or to any party that seemed to be taking shape. Beyond anything Erik enjoyed a party.

Erik's story was touched with good fortune and bad. He was born in Esbjerg, a small seaside town on the west coast of Denmark, and when the German army invaded in the early months of the war he joined the local resistance. It was not long before his group was betrayed and one night, knowing they were being hunted, he and a friend escaped from the house where they had been hiding and ran down to the harbour. His uncle owned a small fishing boat and Erik knew where he could find oars, rowlocks and tiller. As they pulled away into the fog some Germans drove down the jetty and fired at them. It was after midnight and the fog was heavy as the two rowed into the North Sea. They had no compass, food nor water. The east coast of England: Newcastle, Sunderland and Scarborough were over four hundred miles to the west. They heard E-boats searching but the fog saved their lives and after two days they were picked up by a British destroyer.

At this point one might have expected them to volunteer for the Royal Navy but they enlisted in a famous British regiment, the Northumberland Fusiliers. In those desperate and anxious times able-bodied men were accepted almost without question. Erik survived the war and emerged as a sergeant with a distinctly north of England accent. He was demobilized and returned to Esbjerg to find that his childhood girlfriend had married a German and gone to live in Germany. He returned to England and answered an advertisement for water drillers to work in Uganda. He admitted that he didn't know the whereabouts of Uganda and had not even heard the name before.

Erik was lonely in the bush and he liked nothing better than a visit from any of the Europeans who happened to find themselves in the vicinity of his drilling rig. He was immensely hospitable and enjoyed cooking a meal and serving it with cans of cold Danish beer. Amory had allowed him to license a shotgun and rifle so he and his men were well supplied with meat: guinea fowls, bushbuck or wild pig.

Quite by accident we discovered that Erik had played soccer in his youth and was willing to try out as a referee. In the event he became good at it; those pale blue eyes missing nothing on the field. He interfered little if the game was cleanly played but he would tolerate no foul play and seemed to have a knack for making the players realize that they couldn't get away with it. In no time he became the

District's official referee and was in demand for all the important games. Drillers are not normally high on the social scale but refereeing did much to get him accepted by all races and the best part of it was that he never received a penny for his work. In Bunyoro there was no fund from which he could possibly be paid but, as he explained, he would not have accepted money. As a white man living in an African country this was a service for which he sought only the respect which it brought. One day I asked him, after a game, what he thought of the Acholi District team. 'They the ones in green shirts or red?' he wanted to know.

Erik's life, however, contained an overwhelming question mark, a problem for which none of us had an answer. Before coming to Bunyoro he had worked in the neighbouring district of Toro where he had found an African girl, taken her with him and refused to pay her father a bride-price. The Batoro women of a certain clan had a reputation for their beauty, their cool skin and competence as lovers. It was a tradition that they serve as the concubines of great chiefs and their lovemaking had been taught to them as a profession. Amelia was one of these women and for my part I shall have to say that until I met her I was sceptical that any African could possess the type of beauty that a westerner can find truly attractive. She was conspicuously Nilo-Hamitic with features that were far more European than negroid; her skin was copper-coloured and her dress and bearing expressed refinement. Her education, however, was non-existent and her only language was her tribal Lutoro and a smattering of Swahili.

Erik was deeply in love with Amelia and wanted to marry her but the obstacles were formidable. She was technically a Catholic, he a Lutheran. Father Gauthier refused to marry them on the grounds that Erik would not undertake to raise the children as Catholics. The Protestant mission would not marry them since she was African and no bride-price had been paid. This only left the civil ceremony which Amory was empowered to conduct and very reasonably he asked Erik about the future. What would they do when the country became independent? Would they live in Uganda, neighbouring Kenya or Europe? Or somewhere totally different like Canada or Australia?

Amory could not refuse to marry them if both appeared sane, were over twenty-one and could produce proof of age. Erik had his army discharge certificate but Amelia, who was probably nineteen or twenty, had nothing to offer because she had never been registered in the *gombolola* chief's birth register, or so it was stated by the District Commissioner of Toro. For Amory to have married them without proof that she was over twenty-one would have required the father's permission which he would not give unless he received a bride-price. It seemed that the old boy knew he was onto a good thing and was asking fifty head of cattle. Erik's reply was short and to the point; Amelia was worth fifty head of cattle but he was damned if he would lower himself to the level of buying the woman he loved.

The only alternative scenario was unattractive to both parties. So long as Erik paid Amelia on a weekly basis and pretended she was a domestic servant they would both be beyond the reach of law or native custom. This meant that Amelia would not have the status of a married woman, which would have made it embarrassing for them to travel together outside Uganda. The kind of hotels normally frequented by white people would create difficulties and aside from that she would not benefit from any pension or other payments if he were to die. However, from Amory's point of view this was how the matter stood and it was the fiction that he would have to put forward if there were any official enquiries.

It might sound as though everyone was making more fuss than was needed but it must be remembered that we lived in a rigid, government-orientated society. The standards expected of white people, most of whom were subject to government discipline, were Victorian in their rectitude and bear no comparison with the barnyard attitudes toward sexual morality that are prevalent today. As an example, a young officer in his first tour of duty who had an affair with a married woman was promptly thrown out of the country. Another, a departmental director whom we knew quite well, was likewise told to leave because of his rather messy home life. The governor had no wish to see Uganda's orderly march toward independence jolted by minor scandal and squalid behaviour from those who were supposed to be leading that march. The white community, therefore, few in number but conspicuous, was expected to set an example.

Even in the matter of appearances the white community was not beyond reproach. On one occasion a senior officer visited an up-country station and found the Assistant District Commissioner working in his office in green trousers and a flowered shirt. He was formally rebuked and a circular sent to all up-country Districts demanding that rigid dress standards be applied.

The Africans were observant of any lapses in the conduct of their white overlords and quick to criticize what they perceived to be the reprehensible customs that Europeans had brought to Africa in their baggage train. In Buganda the Native Council passed a by-law to the effect that European-style dancing, that is to say when two persons of opposite sex hold each other and move in time to the music, was gravely immoral and to be discontinued on pain of a substantial fine. This practice, according to the Council, encouraged couples to fornicate after dancing, to the detriment of marriage and family life. They were nothing if not straightforward about it. This by-law, which was binding on Africans within the three districts of Buganda and affected about a million and a half people, received very wide publicity and even appeared in some Canadian papers.

The opinion of editorial writers and columnists outside Africa was unanimous that it was medieval to make dancing a punishable offence and that the by-law was ill-considered and probably unenforceable. The governor, they concluded, should require the Council to reconsider. We in Uganda, however, felt differently. Dancing, depending on who is doing it and why they are doing it is not strictly moral. Ask any sailor why he goes to a dance and if he's honest he'll tell you he's there to find a girl. The Council, we thought, could scarcely be faulted for its views about dancing, particularly as conducted in the dance halls and brothels in Kampala's outskirts, and if they wanted a by-law on the subject our best course was to let them have it. In the event the by-law stood and other Districts followed Buganda's lead and passed similar legislation.

The Immoral Dancing By-law, as it came to be known, illustrates the puritanical side of some African official thinking. If European dancing were to provoke such an outburst of indignation then Erik's action in appropriating a local girl was not likely to be accepted without protest. As a white man, an expatriate, Erik was not subject to native custom which included the payment of bride-price, nor was he subject to any native by-law nor the authority of any chief. Only the District Commissioner and the Uganda courts were empowered to touch him and of course he had done nothing to offend Uganda law. Even so, native custom was not to be lightly set aside. It was admittedly in a state of change and there were divergencies of opinion as to just what it pronounced on any specific subject, but it was still the law for millions of Africans.

As an aside, government policy discouraged any move by District Commissioners or their staffs to write down, codify and tidy up native custom. This was because native custom was changing and, presumably, improving, by casting off inhuman practices and adapting to the needs of the modern world. If native custom were codified there was a danger that copies would find their way into the hands of chiefs who would apply its provisions rigidly in their courts. Cast in stone there could be no change, and progress would come to a standstill. The course adopted, therefore, was that the humane and reasonable aspects of native custom were to be encouraged and applauded, such as the one requiring all able-bodied men to assist in local emergencies. When it came to the deplorable ones such as the treatment of women as incompetent and inferior, the policy became suddenly elastic to the point of encouraging amendment.

Amory adopted a policy that he described as masterly inactivity, in his words: 'Do nothing and do it well.' His comments had a ring of exasperation in them. 'Dammit, the old bastard gave her no education except lovemaking so why does he complain when she finds a big strong fellow like Erik and tries it out? If you ask me she looks more fun than those thin-lipped women at the mission.

'By the way,' he went on, 'Erik is within six weeks of finishing his current list of boreholes so we need a fresh programme. You can look after it.'

He passed me a bulging government file and sat back.

'There's no better way to learn the ins and outs of a District than setting up a borehole programme. They all clamour for a borehole outside their own front doors, particularly the chiefs and more influential council members. You'll make lots of enemies because most of them have to be refused. And by the way, when the geologist marks a tree and writes in his notes that the hole is to be fifty yards to the east of the tree, the chief usually cuts it down and marks another one near his house. That's why we had ten dry wells in the current programme. We realize now that Erik didn't drill in the right places. You'll just have to find a better way of doing it.'

This was the kind of problem that tests the ingenuity of an administrator. We were to be allowed fifty boreholes which would be located in places where they were most needed. Were they needed in the dry and sparsely settled areas in the north of the District, or in the more heavily populated parts round Hoima? Should we have a rule that no hole would be dug within a mile of any borehole already in existence, or of any other satisfactory water supply, or two miles, or three? What would we do if there was no road and the borehole machine couldn't approach the site? It seemed that whatever decisions were reached they would invite exception and whatever assumptions made would provoke dissent yet one could not fail to sympathize with the people for feeling so strongly and making the task difficult.

The first step was to mark on a map the existing water supplies. I had hoped to be able to place a copy of this map in the hands of the District Council and the five *saza* chiefs but Stephen dissuaded me on the basis that it would confuse more than enlighten. Reading and understanding a map is something that a western-educated person takes for granted, particularly if he has been in a military service, but is not something that would be taught in the local mission schools. Instead, I approached the chairman of the Bunyoro District Council and asked for some decisions to be made and guidelines set out.

It was decided that each of the five *sazas* should have ten boreholes, and that each *saza* council should establish the locations which were not to be less than a mile from any existing water supply. The Council members could, if they wished, accompany the geologist to each site and watch him at work. Once selected, a site was to be marked by a stake hammered in the ground which was not to be moved on pain of a heavy fine. The local people were encouraged to take an interest in the proceedings and be sure in their own minds where each hole had been located so that any attempts to meddle with it would be met with protest. My job was to accompany the geologist, mark each site on the map and ensure that approach roads were adequate for the drilling rig. I would give a copy of the completed map to Erik and work out with him the sequence to be followed. The dry northern areas of the District would be done during the rainy season when the village roads in the south were impassable. During the dry season he could move south.

While working on the borehole programme I discovered from Stephen that the Banyoro did not understand the idea of distance in the way we understand it. They think of five miles more in terms of the fatigue induced by the journey than of any fixed measurement so that their minds would be influenced by the load they were carrying, whether it was up or down hill and whether or not they had bicycles. The effort required to get there, in other words, was an ingredient of the notion of distance, which accounted for the erratic estimates they made. It also explained their response when I asked how far it was to a certain place: 'Do you have a bicycle?' Stephen, of course, was wise enough never to ask; 'How far is it from the main road to the borehole?' but instead: 'How many paces?'

We westerners possess a vestige of this way of thinking. We might say: 'It's not far but it's a tiring two-hour walk,' with the emphasis placed on the fatigue induced and the time required, without mention of actual distance. For every time we say: 'Kampala is a hundred and twenty-eight miles,' we might put it differently: 'Kampala is a three-hour drive on a poor road, but it's not too bad if you start early.' Our minds, like those of the Banyoro, have a tendency to emphasize the fatigue factor and the effort required to get there.

An interesting part of the borehole programme was watching the geologist at work. He had a reputation for being able to pinpoint underground water and avoid rock layers and in one District he was said to have scored ninety-four 'live' wells out of a hundred although he admitted that one or two had produced salt water, which he could not have anticipated. The water table in Uganda was generally deep, he explained, often between two and three hundred feet so that digging wells by hand was out of the question. In some places he would walk around for an hour or more studying the slope of the land, the soil and the map. In other places he would walk directly to the spot, stick his heel in the ground and say 'there!' He scorned the use of divining rods because he said he could do just as well without. However, he showed me how to use them and I found, to my amazement, that I got results. I have to admit that it gave me much childish pleasure to walk behind him saying 'Whoops' every time the rods jumped. Some of the others tried, including Stephen, but the rods remained obstinately unmoved.

In one or two places my rods did not respond and the geologist said that the chances of finding water in that locality were so poor that it was not worth drilling. One could only express sympathy with the local people and then call the chief and his council members for an impromptu meeting. It usually meant searching the area for a more promising site but this led to delays and the geologist had equally important work to do in other Districts.

With the new programme of fifty sites agreed on Erik decided to have a party and he asked Jean if he could use our house. He drove to Kampala and returned with a huge supply of beer and he must have cleared every grocery store of the ingredients that can be used in open-faced Danish sandwiches. There was also a buffalo meat stew cooking outside in a huge oil drum. Erik had invited all the government officers, the missionaries, the Asians from the bazaar and about fifty Africans, including the Mukama. As I looked round I thought to myself that the only really celebrated person who was not there was Mulisi Alideki. Amelia was beautifully dressed in an Indian saree and I made a point of introducing her to the Mukama, who was very pleasant.

It always amazed me how well these interracial parties used to go, due in large part to the wonderful manners of the Banyoro and their obvious pleasure at being entertained. Also, like sailors on a crowded mess deck, they were accustomed to confined spaces and had learned to move carefully. Our own two servants looked after the beer and Erik's men were in charge of the food. All seemed under control; Amory was surrounded by Africans while he held forth on one of his pet subjects; the pious young doctor and the missionaries were in a corner together; Inspector Frisby was drawing on his huge fund of anecdotes to keep his listeners amused.

At about 9:30, when all the guests had eaten, Aberi asked Erik rather formally if he could distribute the remaining food, which is one of the most charming of African customs. In a land where food spoils rapidly and where the vast majority of people have no refrigerators it would be senseless to store leftovers so they are finished off by servants, bystanders or anyone who happens to be passing. When Africans first come in contact with white people they are appalled at their miserliness. A white family will eat what they can of a meal and are so stingy that anything they can't eat is put away for another time. To the open-handed and hospitable Banyoro this appears cheap beyond belief.

I never knew how the Erik and Amelia story ended. When Erik finished the programme of fifty boreholes just over a year later he was posted to Mubende District and after that to the Eastern Province, where we lost track of him. Our sympathies were with Amelia because she had been introduced to the western world but without education had not really been accepted by it. She had been born and raised in a mud hut where her father would have arranged her marriage on payment of a bride-price. Her husband would then have taken the place of her father. Erik, a kind but lonely man, picks her up and they live together in his ten-by-twelve-foot house trailer as though they were man and wife. She meets people, learns to cook and sew and wears beautiful clothes. She could never return to her village which would be like a prison after the life she had lived with Erik. Yet, saddest of all, having trodden the threshold of the western world her future in it was by no means secure.

As usual, Amory had the last word. 'There may be countries in the world like yours, Canada, and mine, England, where lovers are tolerated provided they are young lovers and provided the whole silly business doesn't go on too long. But there are plenty of other countries where love is a form of lunacy; bad for business, unpredictable and it undermines parental authority. Here there has been no tradition of courtly love, no comprehension of its spritual base and they don't even have a word for it.' He shook his head. 'Making love to the sound of the borehole machine. God help us!'

18

The Witch Doctor

I have been a light sleeper as far back as I can remember. During the war a sailor would only tap once on the metal side of my bunk and say: 'Ten minutes to your watch,' and a moment later I would be pulling on my seaboots and reaching for binoculars and cap. For some of my brother officers it was not so easy, their sleep taking them into deep waters from which they emerged grudgingly to the world above. The officer with whom I shared a cabin was of this kind and the rattle of a sailor's knife on the metal headboard returned him only very slowly to the land of the living.

One night, my family supposedly secure in that strange and rather ghostly little house where we lived, I became suddenly aware of an unfamiliar noise. It was as though something was flowing across the floor, a sound like the rustle of leaves or the whispering of rushes by some unhurried stretch of river. It was not alarming, almost the reverse, but I sat up and looked round the room which was faintly illuminated by moonlight falling on the mosquito net. A moment passed and then I saw it, a single ant on the white net and almost immediately there came a whimper from the dog. The sound I had heard was the movement of an army of ants across the floor.

In the next few seconds I grabbed the baby, woke Jean and we ran from the house. Ants swarmed over our ankles and legs, stinging us with the sensation of hot needles. The dog, still only a puppy, howled with dismay. Frederick was put on the front seat of the Landrover and we took off our pyjamas, shook them and brushed the ants off our bodies. By the lights of the car we could see the intruders in their thousands forming a river across the garden, up the verandah steps and into the house. We sat in the car and talked while Frederick slept on the seat between us. An hour later the ants seemed to have gone so we simply went back to bed. There didn't seem any point in waking anyone else at that hour.

I don't think that either of us was particularly alarmed. One often heard of ants going on the march and Roy Wyndham had said that they would not only eat food left lying about but would also make a clean sweep of all the pests in the house, cockroaches in particular. Nobody seemed to know where they came from or where they went but it was generally agreed that dogs were vulnerable and would die if unable to escape.

In the morning I awoke to the sound of Aberi sweeping the floor. We exchanged the usual courtesies but he appeared upset and kept his eyes averted.

'*Dudu nyingi*,' he said. (Lots of ants.)

'They woke us and we had to go outside,' I said. 'Perhaps they were attracted by food.' I knew this wasn't true because the food was in jars but I was trying to sound unconcerned.

Aberi shook his head. '*Shauri ya Mungu*,' he mumbled. (God only knows.) He went on sweeping the dead ants and was obviously worried.

After breakfast I walked across the grass to the office and Stephen came in immediately. He leaned forward and laid a hand lightly on the desk.

'Sir,' he said, 'It's being said that they've hired the local witch doctor to put a curse on you. I know that white people don't believe in witchcraft but I thought I ought to inform you.'

I must have looked at him in total astonishment.

'What sort of curse?'

'I don't really know but they are saying it is a very great curse. It has to do with Mulisi Alideki.'

I leaned back in my chair and looked out the window. What does one do about a curse, I wondered. Do the missionaries have an antidote or is there a government policy and a set of guidelines? The only thing I was sure of was that I was not going to tell Jean and have her worry about it and I certainly wasn't going to say anything to

Mr Amory who would laugh at the whole thing. So Mulisi Alideki was behind it, I said to myself.

I turned to the papers on my desk but was interrupted almost immediately when two Asians from the bazaar, Muljibhai and Patel, knocked on the door.

'Come in and sit down,' I said, but they seemed agitated and remained standing.

'Hyenas there have been in bazaar,' Muljibhai began.

'This is not good,' from Patel.

'Women are awakened from sleep and much frightened,' in that sing-song voice which made it sound as though he had learned his English from a Welshman.

'Hyena is dirty animal; it is eating excrement,' Muljibhai persisted.

'Township rubbish dump is perhaps attractive to hyena,' from his side-kick.

'There isn't any excrement in the area of the township rubbish dump,' I retorted, 'We burn rubbish on a daily basis. I'll go there and see for myself.'

'Kindly thanking,' from Muljibhai, and with their hands held together they bowed and left.

Later in the morning Hassan came in to report. We drove together to the township rubbish dump and I explained what the Indians had told me. His reply was not altogether supportive of their statements. He used a mixture of Swahili, Lunyoro and Luganda languages and what came through was that they didn't know a hyena from a pussy cat.

We found two township employees sorting garbage which had been collected that morning. They threw paper, wood and wet garbage on a low fire and kept cans and bottles to one side. A wizened old man in filthy clothes was sitting under a tree, oblivious to the smoky fire. Hassan pointed his military cane at him. 'He expects to get an empty bottle,' he said.

I got on well with Hassan and always enjoyed his company. He was a Nubian by tribe, his homeland being fifteen hundred miles to the north in the deserts where the river Nile makes its spectacular loop before entering Egypt. In the later years of the Roman empire some legions were said to have contained a number of Nubians, which must have surprised our British forefathers when they saw them. They were a warrior race, very black and courageous beyond belief. Hassan's father had been an *askari* in one of the early expeditions and when the expedition leader died he simply stayed where he was, in Bunyoro, married a wife and faded into the countryside. In 1914, Hassan, then a boy of twenty, responded to the call of the bugle and rose to the rank of sergeant before the war was over. On his return the District Commissioner made him township headman, a position he had held ever since. He wore an old khaki uniform and went about his duties with that exaggerated ferocity which afflicts the military. On his chest were the faded medal ribbons of the war to end all wars and his yard-long cane was his constant companion. He barked out his orders in parade-ground style but his bark was worse than his bite and the workmen seemed to get on well with him.

Hassan knew everyone's business and took pleasure in displaying his grasp of wordly matters. He waved his cane towards the pile of bottles and cans.

'An ordinary tin sells for one cent but a beer can for two cents because the quality is better and they last longer as drinking cups. Jars with screw caps are usually ten cents and are used for sugar, tea or rice. Four-gallon kerosene tins sell for fifty cents. Some white people don't know the value of the things they throw away. Indians,' he added, 'are more careful.

'Imagine,' he went on, 'a local Munyoro who has a few chickens and an avocado pear tree or an orange tree. He will sell an egg or an avocado for one cent and then buy cans or a jar that may last him for years. He believes he has made a magnificent bargain. How difficult, the man thinks, to construct a tin can and how easy to take fruit from the tree.'

I listened to him with bemused attention as we inspected the place but it was clean and there was nothing that would attract a hyena. The smoke was unpleasant so I went back to the Landrover and with my hand on the door handle turned to Hassan. He was waving his cane and telling the two men what they already knew, namely to wash bottles and cans and bring them to the store. The foreign words for 'bottle' and 'can' sounded out of place in the soft, rather delicate

Lunyoro language. Next he said something about sharing the meat of a buffalo that had been shot by a game guard. They were to go with their *pangas* (knives) and help cut it up.

'*Ndio*,' they said, 'Mmmm . . . Mmmm . . .' (Yes.)

I opened the car door and my blood froze. Coiled on the driver's seat was a snake, a black mamba, with its head raised and its fiery red eyes looking straight at me. It drew its head back and struck so I simply stepped backwards and slammed the door across its body. The forward thrust of the strike had carried it downwards and the head and about two feet of body were trapped outside the car, the remainder of its length inside.

'Hassan!' I shouted, '*Ijja hano*!' (Come here.)

Hassan came running and between us we held the car door so that the snake was caught between the lower edge of the door and the body of the car. Hassan struck at the writhing head with his cane and after ten or twenty blows the movement stopped and the two labourers pulled it out. Suddenly I remembered the old man under the tree and realized he had gone.

'That old man,' I said, 'you know who he is? We are going to the police station and get him arrested. Now, put the snake on the fire and burn it.'

'But sir,' Hassan pleaded, 'these men can remove the skin and it would be worth several shillings. The Indians will take it down-country and sell it.'

'No, burn it! I want it to burn.'

I was frightened and angry and I needed revenge. Some deep instinct demanded that I witness its utter destruction. They pulled it across the fire still convulsing slowly in its death agonies and I stood for a few minutes and became calmer. The snake was six feet long and as thick as Hassan's arm. It was black with faint white flecks and appeared the very embodiment of evil.

At the office I worked until midday and then climbed the hill the short distance to my house. A drink at lunchtime was not my habit but seemed to be in order on such a day. I hated and feared snakes, as most people do, and had been badly shaken by the morning's events. Uganda as a whole was famous for its snakes and Bunyoro had its fair share, but to find a black mamba in your car was unheard of. I wondered whether Roy Wyndham would be able to shed any light on it. As game warden of the District he was supposed to be the expert on all forms of wildlife.

That afternoon Inspector Frisby came to the office with the news that Hassan had accompanied a couple of his police *askaris* to the house of the old man. He had made a half-hearted attempt to run off into the bush but the young *askaris* caught him in moments. They handcuffed him and made a routine search of his mud-walled hut with its grass roof and dirty, unswept yard. They had found articles which, in their opinion, related to the practice of witchcraft. These articles, such as dried human fingers, unbilical cords and so on had been gathered up and brought to the police station as exhibits.

Frisby explained that Uganda law did not prohibit the practice of witchcraft because it was impossible to define what such practice really was or when it had taken place. However, witchcraft involved the witch doctor in certain articles, easily recognized by the native authorities, and it was the possession of such articles that constituted the offence. All the police had to do for a viable case was prove that the offending articles had been in the possession of the accused person.

Inspector Frisby knew about the curse that had been laid on me personally and treated it rather lightly. He said I could have a police guard if I wanted but with the prime suspect behind bars he didn't see what good it would do. If the witch doctor was separated from the tools of his trade he would presumably be rendered harmless.

The only thing that Frisby had not figured out was which court should hear the case. Both the District Court and the Native Court had jurisdiction but there were difficulties either way. If the Mulisi Alideki group was behind it, as he suspected, then the Native Court might be intimidated, besides which their powers of punishment were limited to two years imprisonment. If he put it in the District Court the case would have to be heard by the resident magistrate from Fort Portal, a well-intentioned young lawyer who, however, knew little of Bunyoro or its problems. It would certainly be his first witchcraft case and there was no telling what his reaction would be. He might just laugh at the whole thing.

Later that afternoon a note came from the Mukama to say that the weather appeared fine and he would enjoy a game of tennis. I got hold of Amory and Henry Berunga to make up a men's four and had the tennis court swept and made ready. A few minutes before five I walked to the court to find the three tennis boys waiting. Taking the press off my racquet I left it on the spectators' seats under a giant eucalyptus tree. Amory had mentioned that these trees had been brought from Australia many years before and had done well in the rich soil and heavy rainfall of Uganda's Western Province. They towered over the indigenous trees and their foliage provided good shade, but for some unexplained reason the wood had a tendency to brittleness and in a strong wind the branches would break off and crash to the ground. However, my mind was on something else.

'There is something I want to show you,' I said to the tennis boys in halting Lunyoro. 'When you throw the ball to the person who is serving, do it like this.'

The three of them smiled politely but I could see that they had not understood.

'Come and I'll show you.'

They ran onto the court while I picked up a can of tennis balls and ran after them. As I reached the court I saw one of the boys screw up his face and raise his hands in horror and simultaneously there was a splitting sound from the tree behind me. I spun round as the branch was about halfway to the ground, an enormous branch, thicker than a man's body and thirty feet in length. It shook the ground and a cloud of dust rose round it. The spectators' seats had caught the full impact of its fall and were shattered. The wooden press from my racquet was obliterated.

The Mukama arrived and we surveyed the damage. If it had happened a few minutes later there might have been people sitting and watching the game and it was hard to see how they could have escaped death. What made it worse was that it was a quiet evening without a breath of wind. There was no reason for that branch to have fallen and I found myself in the grip of a cold, irrational rage toward the witch doctor. I wanted to go and kill him, not so much for trying to kill me, but for endangering everyone else in the process. The Mukama could have been reading my mind. 'I hope this is nothing to do with the witch doctor. If it is, he must be punished severely.'

One mistake I had never made during my time in Bunyoro was to underestimate the Mukama. He was weak in some ways and reluctant to relinquish the old customs of his tribe but he knew everything that was going on from one end of his kingdom to the other. Every event that occurred, every incident from a quarrel to a house burning he always heard about. Information must have poured in to his office, always by word of mouth, never written, and it seems in retrospect that he and his forefathers maintained their influence and ruled this people by always being forewarned. It did not come as a surprise that he knew about the witch doctor's arrest; indeed I assumed that he knew more than he said. The fact that the man was a witch doctor was common knowledge and that he had assembled the tools of his trade and was practising must also have been known to the Mukama. It was typical that he had not used his influence to put a stop to it and had simply allowed it to run its course. He lived, I thought, too comfortably with paganism.

The astonishing thing was the fact that both the Mukama and I had attributed the fallen tree branch to the witch doctor. It seemed to me that branches don't drop off trees on quiet evenings unless there is some malevolent influence at work. Nor, for that matter, did snakes take up residence in the front of one's car or ants parade in thousands through your house in the middle of the night. But the fact that all this had happened in a single day, added to Stephen's warning, made my mind reach out in only one direction. The Mukama evidently thought the same.

It was not until much later that I realized that by attributing the sordid events of that day to the witch doctor, in effect crediting him with the power to perform at the level of the miraculous, I had placed myself in the same company as the Mukama and the Banyoro generally. If I believed in the witch doctor's powers I was little different from them; I had fallen into their way of thinking and my mind was as primitive as theirs. In the matter of the snake I was in little doubt that the witch doctor had put it there. I heard later that snakes were not part of his usual arsenal of gadgets but this was the obvious explanation and it would have to do. The moment I had said this, however, I was committed to the presumption that the witch doctor was attempting to inflict evil on me and that he wanted me to realize what he was doing. To put a snake in someone's car is an unfriendly gesture, mischievous to say the least, and it meant that he became the prime suspect and, what is more, he fully intended it so.

The tree branch was the easiest to explain away. The witch doctor was in a barred cell and it could have been mere coincidence. Amory had said that these trees were dangerous. Thereafter I had all Hoima's eucalyptus trees cut down and replaced with muvule trees.

There remained, however, the ants. The witch doctor had a reputation for being able to manipulate ants and he boasted of it at his trial. It was no secret to the local people that this was one of his parlour tricks. My guess is that he dropped food in their path to make them go the way he wanted: sugar perhaps. This is not altogether convincing because our house was surrounded by cut grass for at least a hundred yards in every direction. There were no ants or ant-hills nearby and one might have had to go a long distance to find ants in such numbers. We are saying that he found a huge colony of ants somewhere in the surrounding jungle, got them to wake up in the middle of the night and then led them on a sort of feeding migration to the steps of my house. Perhaps this is not as unreasonable as it may sound because when I had first entered the house, months earlier, there had indeed been an ant-hill some six feet high in the living room.

Such explanations are all very well but the man was also a confessed witch doctor of considerable reputation and he had been caught red-handed by Frisby's *askaris*. The tools of his trade, in Frisby's phrase, were found on his workbench. The Mukama and people of Bunyoro were convinced that he had been responsible and at that time I would have agreed with them, not so much because my reason told me so but because of the way I felt. All that day I had a sensation of gloom and oppression, of something hanging over me. I was mildly relieved when I saw the snake burn and smelled it burning, like an ancient god that had to be propitiated with sacrifice, but when the tree branch came down my mood changed and I was so enraged against him I could at that moment have beaten him to death with my hands. There could have been people sitting under that tree:

women, children, white or African, and they would have died. My anger seemed to have a cleansing effect and thereafter I returned to normal. The witch doctor had failed, he was behind bars and separated from the filthy objects he used to attain his purposes. The oppressiveness of the day lifted and the world returned to normal because I felt instinctively that he had expended his ammunition, had no tricks left. I saw the witch doctor as a hired assassin, a devil in human shape.

I heard many witch doctor stories during subsequent years in Africa and just as many theories to explain them. Occasionally medical officers tried to work with them and there was a modernistic view that they acted like psychiatrists and their powers could be harnessed to help patients who needed this kind of treatment. I feel very dubious about this because my limited but poignant experience tells me that they are uneducated people who trade in evil. To pretend that they can be reformed is building on sand. In some of them there may be a component of medicine and medical specialization but in the Bunyoro variety their operations leaned more toward primitive religion, not medicine. They inflicted harm on people and one never heard stories of where they did the slightest good.

One of Frisby's *askaris* claimed he had been bewitched. He sickened and was unable to do his work although the medical officer could find nothing wrong with him. Frisby sent him back to his village in a hopeless and demoralized condition where he died a few days later.

The case of the witch doctor who went after me was finally laid to rest in the courtroom in Hoima. In front of a large crowd he was charged with possession of the articles used in witchcraft. He was informed of the seriousness of the charge and told that he might have a lawyer to assist him, but he preferred to plead guilty and to boast of his accomplishments before the resident magistrate, Robert Martin. It had been arranged that Martin would sit with two African assessors who would advise him on native custom as it related to witchcraft. The individuals selected were the Keeper of the Royal Tombs and the headmaster of Hoima's largest school.

Martin said afterwards that in spite of the guilty plea it was not an easy case. Nothing in his legal training had prepared him for it but he felt instinctively that the accused's statements should be disregarded and not placed to his disadvantage. The law could not compel him to have a lawyer but if he had had one he might have been saved from the consequences of his own recklessness. The question in Martin's mind was whether he should pay the penalty of his own ignorant admission of guilt which went beyond a mere guilty plea. The two assessors were unhampered by such legal scruples and showed impatience at the delicacy of Martin's reasoning. They wanted him to receive the maximum sentence, which was ten years, because he not only admitted possessing the articles of witchcraft but also of having the power to kill people by their use. He had gone further, claiming to have used these, or articles like them, in some of his more spectacular jobs.

Martin sentenced him to five years to the disappointment of the two assessors. He told Inspector Frisby to keep the exhibits in a place of safety in case of an appeal but at this point Frisby made a fuss on the grounds that the exhibits were foul and objectionable and should be burned. Frisby's view prevailed and the articles of witchcraft, like the snake, went up in smoke.

19

Fisheries

A young couple whom we used to see regularly in Hoima was the Fisheries Officer, Don Rhodes, and his wife who lived three hundred miles to the south at a place called Kichwamba. Their house was perched at the top of the escarpment overlooking Lakes Edward and George. The Ruwenzori mountains rose, snow-peaked, less than thirty miles away and it was generally agreed that the views from their house were the most beautiful in Uganda. As Fisheries Officer his task was to develop fisheries in the three great lakes, Albert, Edward and George, license the fishermen, conserve the fish stocks and ensure compliance with fishing regulations. In co-operation with local administrators in the four western Districts he was also concerned with the marketing of fish.

The species of fish that was the mainstay of the Uganda lakes at that time was called *ngege* by the local people, a variety of tilapia. They are excellent for the table being fast-maturing and about a pound in weight. Their flavour was that of a Dover sole, the meat firm but delicate. The two varieties found in Uganda were the *Nilotica*, from the Nile, and the *Zillii*, a weed-eater which was distinguished by a black spot on the side of its head. Another variety, *Galileensi*, was found in Lake Galilee, three thousand miles to the north but still essentially in the Rift valley. At each fishing village there were uniformed African inspectors who counted the catch and enforced local regulations.

In Bunyoro we had half a dozen fishing villages on Lake Albert and their catch of fish amounted to hundreds of tons a year. The problem we faced was simply one of transportation. To carry fish across the plain and up the escarpment in that searing heat and then market them in the population centres round Hoima, all this without ice, taxed the ingenuity of Fisheries Officer and District Commissioner alike. Yet the Banyoro people lacked protein in their diet and if a family could get even one fish meal a week its health and resistance to disease would be improved. The doctor thought it was of vital importance to put fish on sale in the village markets at twenty cents each, twenty cents of an East African shilling, not of a North American dollar. Five fish, in other words, would cost a shilling, which was roughly equal to an American quarter. Smoked fish were not as popular as fresh but they were marketed all the same.

One problem we did not have in Bunyoro was a reluctance to eat fish based on tribal custom. In some other parts of Uganda the people claimed that fish were not good for them, making them sterile or causing disease. Such claims could, in time, be countered with argument or example but what could not be prevailed against was the bland statement that eating fish was contrary to tribal custom. How does one argue with someone about native custom or prove that the custom was futile? It would be like trying to promote cannibalism among westerners. There can be no negotiation with tribal custom any more than there can be negotiation with religious dogma or with any other deeply-held belief. The fact that tribal custom varies between one tribe and another is to no avail. Tribes are different, they will tell you, because people are different; what is law to one is not law to another.

Anthropologists are supposed to be knowledgeable about these things and have suggested a simple explanation for fish-reluctance among some African tribes. The tribal land, let us say, did not include a lake or river so there was no experience of eating fish from early times. A hunting party might stray beyond its usual territory and come to a lake where they found fish floating on the surface. Hunger forces them to eat what they would not otherwise have eaten and they become sick. The event leaves an indelible print on the tribal consciousness and henceforth it is tribal custom not to eat fish.

The Mukama operated under dietary rules that were different from those of his people, and custom forbade him to eat fish or eggs simply because he was the Mukama. At a reception given by the governor a waiter came forward with a tray on which were small open sandwiches spread with caviar.

'What is that black stuff?' he enquired.

'Sir,' I replied rather pompously, 'it's a disgraceful Russian combination of fish and eggs. If I may presume to say so, both are contrary to your dietary customs.'

'In this instance,' he replied, 'your understanding of native custom is incorrect. It is said, is it not, that two wrongs make a right?'

The Fisheries Officer and his wife passed through Hoima about once a month. They would stay overnight at the Rest House, dine with Jean and myself and hold discussions with Amory before driving on to Butiaba and the fishing villages. Discussions were typically about the tonnage of fish caught, a bull hippo which had sunk a canoe, crocodiles tearing the nets and all the other problems which afflicted equatorial fisheries.

It would be remiss of me at this point if I failed to speak of the Fisheries Officer's wife and yet I confess that I have forgotten her name. She was a remarkable person who was a pleasure to entertain because she had not only found a situation in life that suited her to perfection but had also found words to describe her encounter with the world. Such people who can love their fellow men, their work and the world in which they live are the very elect of human society.

The circumstances in which the two of them met are worthy of a latter-day opera. Her husband, at that time a quiet and rather shy bachelor, had driven to Entebbe airport to meet the Imperial Airways flying boat. On board there was supposed to be a fisheries expert from the Colonial Office in London. He was to have taken the man to the Lake Hotel for the night and then spent a week showing him Uganda's fisheries which were more developed than those of most other African countries.

As he drove down the airport road he saw the Sunderland flying boat sweep over the walls of forest and turn into the wind for its landing on Lake Victoria. He entered the airport lounge and the passengers came streaming in, tired, thankful for the pause and ready for a drink. Any one of them could be a fisheries expert, he thought to himself, so he approached a flight attendant and asked if she had a passenger list. It turned out that Sir Somebody Something had cancelled his flight and his name was not on the list. He was on the point of leaving but his eyes caught those of the flight attendant which seemed to be inviting him to stay. A little awkwardly he suggested they sit down and have tea.

As a flight attendant in Imperial Airways she had learned how to approach people and talk to them. In those days aircraft were slower, passengers fewer and flying was still something of a novelty. There was time to sit with the passengers and she had met all types, from the quiet, uncomplicated ones like her husband, the boastful loudmouths who were often frightened underneath it all, to the rich and bored who made vulgar passes at her. With this man, she thought, she would have half an hour and two cups of tea, then a swift goodbye, but their eyes met many times while he told her, a little self-consciously, of his life in Uganda. Then an officer went to the public address sytem and switched it on. To both of them it was a sad sound and they waited painfully for the words of departure.

'We've got a slight problem,' he began. 'It seems that when we landed on the lake a few moments ago we struck an obstacle which made a hole in the fuselage.' The remaining words were indistinct to both of them and she put her hand across the table towards his. The officer was still talking, but they were not listening. 'Apologize for the delay . . . passengers for Salisbury, Johannesburg and Capetown . . . Captain Hamilton hopes that repairs . . .' It was all too good to be true.

That evening they dined together at the Lake Hotel. They spoke of their families and of themselves and of how the war had affected their lives which was the ultimate topic of conversation in those post-war years. He had led an infantry platoon across the charred and exhausted face of Europe from Normandy to the river Elbe and then returned to Cambridge to finish his science degree. She had gone into the Women's Auxilliary Air Force as soon as they would take her but the war ended and she had been demobilized. Next she took a one-year course in nursing and joined Imperial Airways. She had been some months on the African run but had not seen much of the continent except from the air. He spoke of safari to the western lakes and upon the fast flowing Nile, of more leisurely cruises on Lake Victoria, its challenges and dangers. She was in another world, a world about which she could not have dreamed. Afterwards, under the equatorial stars, they spoke of more intimate things; their feelings for each other and their hopes for the future.

The following morning they met again briefly in the hotel lobby and he gave her a letter that was not to be opened until the aircraft was at ten thousand feet. He watched as the flying boat roared into the clear morning air and turned southwards. 'Go on, Captain Hamilton,' he found himself saying, 'Fly your plane to the ends of the earth but for God's sake bring her back.' They were to meet again on the return flight and a fortnight later she would step off the plane with the other passengers to become his wife.

He confided in Reggie, his best friend, Reggie the Spitfire pilot, who had flown in the battle of Britain. And as so often happens in the outposts of empire the story got round and no one could do enough. The Governor of Uganda granted a special marriage licence, picked up the bride from the hotel in his Rolls Royce and gave her away in marriage. The flowers she carried were rare orchids grown in Entebbe's renowned botanical gardens. They were married by the local curate after which the Archbishop of the Upper Nile bestowed the Church's blessing.

'What happened?' I asked. 'What was it that changed the water into wine?'

'I am not very religious,' she replied, 'more of a romantic and idealist, and my husband the same. Of course it was love at first sight because I think we fulfilled each other's most cherished expectations, but it was more than that. I had met other men in my life and two or three had proposed marriage but they offered me the wrong things. My husband on the other hand offered me a house at the top of a beautiful escarpment and on the grass in front the crested cranes would form a circle and dance their mysterious dance. No one else had promised me that. And then there was a real king on a leopard throne surrounded by his people, poor and in need of food; five thousand waiting for the miracle that good organization and hard work would bring. Nor had anyone else offered to take me up the

Mountains of the Moon or to open fish and list their stomach contents or to nurse the injuries of a woman who had been dragged into the water by a crocodile.'

She paused and no one spoke.

'When we flew the Nile route I sat by a window from Khartoum to Entebbe because most of the passengers slept at that time. Beyond the green of the Nile was the brown desert which stretched away to infinity. The harsh beauty of the desert has always fascinated me and I wanted, for some strange reason, to pitch my tent in the desert and lie down to sleep and learn the wisdom of its silence and feel its ascetic pain. I wanted to smell its dustiness and experience its extremes of heat and cold, to stand on a patch of sand that perhaps no man or woman had stood upon since the creation of the earth. I can't explain myself better than to say that I am an earth person, obsessed by its beauty and conscious of its agony.

'Then we would fly over the green foothills of Equatoria and the mood would change. Gray monolithic rocks reared up like cathedrals from the tops of the hills, sentinels pondering the very emptiness of the land and the absence of humanity. We would soar over Uganda and I could sometimes see Lake Albert to the westward, surrounded by mountains. I looked down at the forests and the green fields of cultivation and wondered what sort of people lived there and whether their dark faces were turned towards us.

'I had never asked for more than I have now: a husband, a house to live in and friends who will listen to me and not think me strange. As I say, I am an earth person, tied to the earth by love and fascination. One day we sail on Lake Edward or Lake George to visit the fishing villages and we are buffeted by waves and drenched by the monsoon rains, the next we are driving the red murram roads through miles of jungle dotted with banana gardens. At the villages we are surrounded by people, talking, laughing and smelling of fish. We are helping those people and thousands of others who buy their fish. What more could anyone want?

'And the ten-thousand-feet letter,' she added as an afterthought, 'I shall keep it for the whole of my life.'

20

The Kafu Bridge

In May of 1952 the rainy season, instead of tapering off, seemed to intensify. Day after day the clouds rolled in and rain beat down on the ancient kingdom of Bunyoro turning roads into quagmires and making human life miserable. The people could get little work done in their fields so they sat under the endlessly dripping thatch watching the downpour while the tide of greenery crept to the very doors of their houses. The large plantain bananas kept them fed but the rest of their gardens were left neglected, choked with weeds and overrun by animals that sensed that sugarcane, potato vines and yams were theirs for the taking. Hassan pointed to the tracks of bush-pig which had been gorging themselves on the unaccustomed luxury of avocado pears a few yards from our house.

During the first two weeks of May I had gone on a standard safari in Bugahya County in the south of the District. Two days had been spent in each of the five *gombololas* and two more at the county headquarters at the end. I was getting used to the work of safari by this time, the novelty was wearing off and I had become more perceptive to the nuances of the Banyoro and their problems. The rains made it tiring and produced a strange effect on the people themselves, making them stoic and hard to reach. It might have been argued that all safari work could have been postponed until the dry season when there was more activity in the countryside, more to be seen and the mood of the Banyoro less withdrawn, but that would have been to give in to the elements and miss that portion of their lives which was lived under difficult conditions. It would have been like trying to know and understand Canada without experiencing the blatant fact of the Canadian winter. Accordingly I concentrated less on walking through villages and gardens and more on studying the court records and tax returns and talking with the chiefs about their work.

During this safari I conceived the idea of bringing the chiefs into Hoima for regular training courses. It had been assumed for years that a local Munyoro of character and education would take naturally to the work of being a chief. He would begin as a *muruka*, or village chief, with a few hundred families under his jurisdiction. Paid a modest salary by the Bunyoro Native Government he wore no uniform and carried no identification yet he was the agent of progress and fountainhead of law and order for his people. If he did well he would be chosen from among the eight or ten *muruka* chiefs in his *gombolola* for special duties. He might be called upon to act for the *gombolola* chief during the latter's absences or to sit and hear disputes or witness the payment of bride-prices. Gradually his work would be noticed, not only by his *gombolola* chief but by his *saza* chief, and he might expect promotion to a vacant *gombolola*, one of the twenty-eight in Bunyoro's five counties.

It was for these *muruka* chiefs, the subalterns of the native government system, that training would have been particularly valuable. In wartime we had seen the part played by training in the military services, from teaching young men to become air pilots to brief courses lasting only a few days on some new gadget like radar or asdic. Training, as opposed to lengthy apprenticeship, had been amazingly effective, especially when conducted with flair and ingenuity, and it did not seem unreasonable to apply the same principles to the training of junior chiefs. They had, after all, a varied portfolio of duties ranging from the administration of justice to such matters as soil erosion and public health. Furthermore, the Department of Community Development seemed the ideal department to take over the training task.

It would be wrong to pretend that the idea of chiefs training courses, or training for any other group of employees, had not occurred to others, and equally wrong if I had not foreseen that it would take time to get anything done in Bunyoro. I would be told that there was no suitable accommodation for the trainees, no money to build a hostel, no teachers and that on-the-job-training was just as effective.

'The idea is quite good and we might include something in the next estimates, but don't expect quick results,' was the response I expected. 'In the meantime you might care to find out what the other Districts have done along those lines.' Yes, it was all very predictable: faint praise, then bury it in paper and endless argument.

All safaris are hard work and those undertaken during the rainy season particularly so. It was impossible to stay dry, even in my old navy oilskin coat, and all my clothes smelled of smoke after being dried over wood fires. However it was one of those safaris where nothing had gone wrong and I had spoken to a lot of people and filled my small government notebook with comments, problems and ideas. Back in Hoima these notes would form the basis of a comprehensive tour report which Amory would read and pass on with his comments to the Provincial Commissioner in Fort Portal and the Chief Secretary in Entebbe. It was not unknown for interesting tour reports to reach the Governor's desk. I suppose, in addition, I was looking forward to a couple of weeks at home in our little house at the foot of the hill, a weekend trip to Kampala, a small dinner party and perhaps by then the rain would have tapered off.

Mr Amory, however, had other ideas. As I returned my safari equipment to the store he told me to prepare for another outing, this time to the bridge over the Kafu river at a place called Kibangya. We looked at the map on the wall of his office. From the town of Masindi about thirty-five miles north-east of Hoima a road had been built eastwards across the Kafu river and into Mengo District. It was flat, swampy land with little habitation as far as Nakasongola where the road turned due south and led to Kampala. This was to become one of the main trunk roads of Uganda under the charge of the Department of Public Works, not a mere District road under the care of the Native Government. For years there had been a ferry over the river at Kibangya, a pontoon onto which you drove your car and which was then shunted across the few yards of water by a system of wires and pulleys. This was being changed into a bridge with concrete abutments and a steel frame that would be strong enough to carry the largest vehicle. The framework had been used in wartime as a temporary bridge over the river Thames in London and had been dismantled at war's end.

Amory was warming to his subject. During the dry season Public Works had built the concrete abutments and begun the work of setting up the steel girders but they had been caught by the rains and had to stop when the water overflowed the banks and threatened their camp. The beams had been strained and did not fit properly and as the rains continued they had no option but to abandon the project and return to Kampala. It was then that the unexpected had happened and a great mass of floating papyrus had broken loose and smashed into the bridge forcing it to the edge of the concrete abutments. One more such blow and the whole structure, a hundred feet in length and forty feet high, would topple over. The abutments, as anyone could guess, had been built too low.

The Kafu river was not really a river but a swamp over much of its length. In the north it flowed toward the Nile and in the south toward Lake Albert but in the central part, which included Kibangya, the flow, if there was any, depended on rainfall and wind direction. At the moment it was going northwards at about one mile an hour but with typical perversity might change and conceivably the papyrus would clear itself.

'What am I supposed to do?' I asked. 'From what you say this sounds like a Public Works Department fiasco; nothing to do with us.'

'This is an emergency,' Amory retorted, 'and we are closest to it. Have you never heard of marching toward the sound of the guns? If we leave it any longer the bridge will be pushed off the abutments by the vegetation piling up against it. A channel must be cleared to let the water through. The local *gombolola* chief was here yesterday and said that there was a solid wall of papyrus jammed under the bridge which had the effect of flooding the land for half a mile in all directions. Your job is to cut away the papyrus and let the water drain. This will save the bridge.'

'Cut a channel through hundreds of tons of wet papyrus?' I asked incredulously. 'What with?'

Amory was determined to be patient with me.

'All you have to do is employ some men locally, pull out the weed on the upstream side and throw it downstream and let the current carry it away. The *gombolola* chief says he has a number of tax defaulters and, as you know, or ought to know, they can remit their taxes by doing public work. However you choose to do it, that bridge has got to be cleared, do you understand?'

'Very well, but you have not explained to me how I transport an army of tax defaulters from dry land to the bridge through a mile of flood water. Nor have you explained what I am supposed to do if the bridge topples while the men are at work. Stephen told me that Banyoro rarely know how to swim because the presence of crocodiles in shallow water means they don't learn when they are young. If, as you say, the bridge is in danger of collapsing then the best thing might be to close the road and leave the whole thing until the dry season.'

Amory glared at me. 'The trouble with you navy chaps is that you're not tough enough. You wear all sorts of medal ribbons on your uniform but when it comes to a job of work you don't have what it takes. Many young officers would jump at a chance like this. Oh well, I shall have to inform the Chief Secretary and an adverse report will doubtless be placed on your file. I was hoping to be able to tell him that you had been there yourself and done everything possible to save the situation.'

So that was it! He didn't care about that silly bridge which Public Works had built out of war surplus materials and built too low. No, he merely wanted to be able to report to the Chief Secretary that the effort had been made. Sending me to the Kafu was a gesture, a paragraph at the end of an official report saying that he had done everything in his power. Success or failure was not the point.

'I don't see how this can possibly work,' I said, 'but if you want me to go, I'll go.'

On arriving home I made fun of the whole thing.

'My middle name is Horatio and I shall be saving a bridge with a small army of tax defaulters,' I announced. 'The fact that Public Works have made a fiasco means that we must have a fiasco of our own because one fiasco deserves another.'

If Amory had stated the case differently I would not have taken exception. If he had said: 'Go and see what can be done; you are free to take action if you think it will do any good,' it would have been different. He was quick to criticize headquarters when directives took no account of local conditions. 'Local decisions must be made at a local level' was one of his pet phrases. 'The man on the spot is the only one who really knows what to do.' Yet Amory was not on the spot, he was fifty miles away and had heard about the problem from the *gombolola* chief.

Quite possibly, I said to myself, I am making too much of this. I had not even unpacked after my last safari, hadn't had a bath or a decent meal and rain had been falling all afternoon, which made it more depressing. Perhaps I was being unreasonable, but then again Amory had not exactly been reasonable either.

Amory had not served in the war but he loved to use the vocabulary of war, which always irritated me. He was all for launching campaigns, conducting operations on a broad front, carrying the offensive into someone else's territory, bombarding people with ideas and becoming firmly entrenched when under fire. To someone who had been at war and witnessed death and destruction at first hand his words sounded ill-chosen in peace time. Words relating to war and conflict have, it is true, infiltrated legal jargon because the courtroom is adversarial by nature. One talks of attacking a witness or preparing a defence but it seems unfortunate that those same bloodstained words have taken over the business of ordinary administration. The vocabulary of artisans, craftsmen and builders would have served better. I have often wondered why the peace movement has failed to espouse the vocabulary of peace and reject the vocabulary of war.

The following morning I repacked the Landrover and set out for the Kafu river. Stephen's presence would have been an unnecessary luxury because the *gombolola* chief spoke English and when dealing with the men I could stumble along in Lunyoro. I took Georgi, as usual, to look after the camp and cook my meals. There was a small Rest House at Kibangya consisting of a single room with grass roof, cow dung and ant-hill floor and mud-and-wattle walls. It was better than having to use a tent.

On the way there I couldn't shake off the feeling that something was about to go wrong, that there was a primal fault with the safari. I was also worried at the fact that Amory and I had had a fairly substantial row the day before. He had threatened me with disciplinary action and for my part I had not been particularly co-operative, which was no way to behave toward a senior District Commissioner during one's first tour of service.

We took the road to Masindi, then turned eastwards and followed the muddy track across a flat, featureless landscape to Kibangya. Sebastiano Mukoto, the *gombolola* chief, was at his headquarters and, leaving Georgi and the safari equipment at the Rest House, we went to inspect the situation, which involved wading over half a mile in waist-deep water. The bridge structure was bowed like a handsaw, the bend being most visible when looking at it end to end, but not so obvious when seen from the side. It dominated the landscape, an unfinished bridge of steel girders surrounded by miles of swirling water. Clambering up the structure itself we found that rats and snakes had taken refuge from the flood by doing just what we were doing, climbing the girders and looking down on the whole sorry affair.

The first thing that struck me was that the bridge was in considerable danger of going off the abutments just as Sebastiano had reported. It was resting on the edge of the concrete and an increase in the pressure from the papyrus either from wind or current would topple it onto its side on the downstream side. If there were men working on it when that happened some of them, if not all, would be drowned. Another island of papyrus floating down and hammering the first one would do the trick.

Papyrus, from which we get the word paper, is the predominant vegetation throughout the length of the Nile from Lake Victoria almost to the Mediterranean. It is a sedge plant that occupies the shallows for miles on both banks finding its way into swamps and tributaries to the point where a sizeable proportion of the country is covered by it. The green stems stand to a height of ten or fifteen feet and are about the thickness of a man's wrist, topped with a circle of delicate fronds. These fronds figured in the art of ancient Egypt and seem to have caught the ancient imagination as an ornamental device. Pleasant appearing, almost attractive from the surface of the water upwards, below the surface it is an unremitting nightmare of tangled and impenetrable roots. Even the hippo and crocodile shun it, seeming to prefer open water, although they at least can move about in a papyrus swamp. For a man, however, the mass of roots does not carry his weight and he can neither walk nor swim. The early explorers found it an impassable barrier and it is noteworthy that they ferried themselves across the Nile at places like Wadelai where the banks were steep and the papyrus limited to a few feet.

Further north it was not uncommon for papyrus islands to break away during the rainy season and float down the Nile. We asked ourselves the question as to how deep the mass of roots extended and the answer seemed to be about six feet. Much later in my career in Uganda when I was serving in the West Nile District an island of papyrus about a mile in length broke free and, borne by the swift current, engulfed a group of fishermen in their canoes. They were never seen or heard from again even though we sent an aircraft to search. Their fate must have been one of unmitigated horror; they could not paddle their canoes through the papyrus, nor walk through it, nor swim.

Early the following morning, 19th May, Sebastiano Mukoto appeared at the Rest House at the head of about forty men whose taxes were in default. I looked them over and would describe them as an unlikely bunch, but then men with the physique of Olympic swimmers were not to be found at Kibangya. I assured myself that they were volunteers and knew what they were letting themselves in for.

We didn't have a flag but we pushed off from what was more or less dry land in the ancient ferry which had seen service for so many years. It was a comedown from a fleet destroyer but we were set upon government business and we reached the bridge after half an hour of shouting, splashing and general confusion. Another half hour was spent chasing the snakes and rats; the snakes were pushed into the river but rats were of the edible variety and, having been struck with a stick on the upper girders of the bridge, fell into the hands of the men lower down.

I then called the meeting to order and with Sebastiano's help showed the men how to pull up handfuls of papyrus from upstream and throw it downstream. At the end of an hour we had moved about a ton and there remained only a few thousand more and the job would be finished. The weed was dirty, smelly and difficult to handle and if we had had twice the number of men it would have made no difference because there was only limited space for them to work. Using an African style hoe they hacked at the sodden mass, cut off a section about the size of a bushel basket and dragged it to the other side of the bridge. It was hard work, inefficient by any standards and we were obviously getting nowhere.

The only real accomplishment on that first day was that I composed a song in Lunyoro to the tune 'Way Down upon the Swanee River'. The word for papyrus is '*ebisagazi*' which was hard to fit in, although the tax defaulters were not harsh critics of my work.

At about one in the afternoon, under a very hot sun but with rain threatening, I decided we had all remitted our taxes for that day and paddled back to dry land. Before leaving the bridge I made scratches on the concrete abutments to show the exact position of the steel structure. If it moved even a fraction of an inch overnight I would see it the following morning.

We worked for four more days. At Sebastiano's suggestion one of the men brought a drum and played from a topmost girder. It was reminiscent of the fiddlers who perched on the rotating capstan drums in Nelson's day and played while the men toiled at the capstan bars. On the fifth day, 23rd May, I checked my scratches on the cement and discovered that the bridge had shifted about an inch and the small opening we had cut in the papyrus, representing about twenty tons of vegetation, had closed overnight. At that point I ordered everyone back to dry land and told them that their taxes had been remitted in full. Feeling rather groggy I went back to the Rest House and we packed for the return to Hoima.

During the remainder of the day I became steadily more ill and demented. I seemed to have lost my comprehension of time and space and I must have driven my Landrover those fifty miles more by instinct than by any rational process. Georgi was almost paralyzed with fear at my appearance but somehow we got home and I stumbled into the house. My wife put me to bed and Georgi went to find the doctor.

As a child I had suffered from migraine headaches, indeed my childhood had been blighted by them, but then I had left home and gone to sea and never had another. In the intervening years I seemed merely to have grown out of them and left them with the other things that St. Paul said were the relics of childhood. Now, here I was again, not exactly with a migraine headache but with the same sense of doom, the raging turmoil of body and mind. I passed in and out of consciousness and saw visions of my youth and of the war. Again I was riding my bicycle on familiar pathways and heard the plain and desolate North Country accents of speech. Then I was in a bombed church in Italy, stained glass lying about the floor among the saints and martyrs who had come down from their niches in the walls. A bird flew in through a hole in the roof but it carried no olive branch. The scene changed and I was back on the Kafu bridge with the foul smelling papyrus, the snakes and the rats.

The Swanee River; the tax defaulters had sung it tunelessly; I suppose they had never learned to sing the things we choir boys took for granted, the Te Deum, the Benedictus, the Nunc Dimittis. 'Lord, now lettest Thou Thy servant depart in peace.' Surely, I thought, it has not come to that. I hoped that those poor tax defaulters in their dark huts were not suffering as I was.

As evening approached my mind cleared and I recognized Jean holding our young son, now almost a year old. The doctor was there asking me questions which I could not answer and Amory was stammering some sort of an apology. Behind was Aberi whose grief was written on his face. He had become a fixture in our lives, always in attendance, quiet, methodical and taken for granted. He gave me something to drink and I heard voices saying that they would leave me where I was because the hospital in Kampala had no iron lung. Iron lung? What on earth was that?

The night that followed was the most terrifying I ever spent. Some intuition told me that I mustn't sleep but hold on for dear life and fight every yard of the way. Pain and nausea washed over me and a feeling that something was draining away but I put it from my mind and returned to the memories of rolling seas, gray ships and gray horizons.

'Is the ship in station, sub-lieutenant?'

It was the captain's voice but I couldn't find the gyroscopic compass or the rangefinder and I couldn't answer. The sharp bows of the destroyer rose and fell, slicing through the larger waves, disdainfully passing over the smaller ones and there was the persistent sound of the asdic, the eternal sameness of its note probing the depths for enemy submarines.

Strangely clear in my mind was the recollection of an August night in the Mediterranean when we had steamed from Malta round the heel of Italy and into the Adriatic. The Yugoslav partisans had funnelled a contingent of escaped prisoners to a little fishing village under the very noses of the Germans. We crept in and went alongside and hundreds of weary, tattered men emerged from the darkness and came over the rails. With hardly a word spoken we picked our way out, turned southwards and thundered over the dark sea. Not until the brown hills of Malta rose ahead of us in the early afternoon did the captain relax battle stations; we had been at our guns for thirty hours. The log book on the bridge jolted me to the recollection that it was 7th August, my nineteenth birthday. I looked at the men sprawled on the torpedo tubes and round the guns, men of perhaps twenty nationalities united in their desire to fight against Nazi Germany. I decided then and there that it was the best birthday I would ever have.

Finally some shreds of tattered light came through the window and fell on the doctor who slept uneasily in the other bed. One of the talkative black and white crows started ranting from a treetop and finally Aberi came in having, as I discovered later, sat up all night in the kitchen. The familiar sounds of morning, the baby waking up, the fire being started, teacups rattling somewhere in the background – all came through like the music of the world's first day. The doctor roused himself, looked me over, tried my pulse and stuck a thermometer in my mouth. As he left the room I knew from the look on his face that he was going to tell Jean that I had passed through the valley of the shadow.

During the next week or two I recovered my health. I sat under the jacaranda tree in our garden and watched the hoopoe birds like miniature gladiators performing their antics. All was outlined in radiance for I was now seeking to redress the balance of evil so that my song had changed from the Nunc Dimittis to the Te Deum Laudamus: 'Thou, Lord, we praise.' Hassan came and sat beside me and talked of trivial matters but I knew he and all the others were holding something back. Finally Jean told me the truth and I had never seen her so deeply distraught.

A polio epidemic had passed through Hoima and what I must have had was not malaria but the dread virus of polio. Inspector Frisby was dead. They had tried to get him to Kampala but he died on the road with his young wife beside him. Robert Martin, the resident magistrate, had passed through Hoima, heard some cases and contracted the disease. He died a day or two later in Fort Portal hospital on 26th May. Rachael Thorpe had lost part of the use of her arms but her affliction was slight. The Amorys, the doctor, the Community Development lady and Roy Wyndham had been unaffected. Nor had any of the Africans or Indians in Hoima been touched. This variety of polio seemed only to affect young white people in their twenties and early thirties and it reserved its most terrifying onslaught for those who were physically fatigued.

The rains eased off and a semblance of normality returned. Word had spread that Hoima Rest House had been the centre of the epidemic and for about a year no one from down country would use it. A police inspector was appointed to replace Frisby but when he learned that he had been booked into the Rest House for his first night he refused the appointment and was dismissed from the Service. Bunyoro had an unhappy reputation at the best of times and the happenings of May 1952 seemed only to confirm everybody's worst suspicions. It seemed to be the District where nothing was right: a murderous game guard who terrorized the countryside and a polio epidemic which devastated the small white community. When we drove to Kampala for a few hours of shopping the people who knew we were from Bunyoro viewed us with pity and amazement.

One could not help feeling sorry for Amory. He had not chosen to be District Commissioner in Bunyoro any more than a naval captain would choose to command a ship with a curse on it. The records showed that no District Commissioner who had served in Bunyoro had ever emerged well from the ordeal; few, if any, had been promoted and none had made a great name for himself. Bunyoro reeked of failure and wasted effort and its progress was pathetically slow when matched against other Districts. For myself, a newcomer to the Service, this was not necessarily a disadvantage because a lot can be learned from setbacks and failures. I did not expect to be in the District more than a couple of years, three at most, and I would not be held responsible for the District's misadventures unless, of course, I did something exceptionally foolish. If, in my first three years, I were to pass my law and language exams and learn the business of District administration then I should, theoretically, have avoided Bunyoro's malevolent influence. Later I was to find out how different it was to work in a truly progressive District.

To step ahead in time, the Kafu bridge was completed by the Uganda Public Works Department late in 1952. When the water subsided the papyrus was burned and the remaining vegetation cut into sections and dragged out by machine. Two hundred men and a huge amount of equipment worked at it for three months under the supervision of an engineer who lived on the site. Meanwhile the bridge itself was dismantled and the steel girders straightened piece by piece. The abutments were then raised by several feet and the bridge rebuilt across that hundred-foot gap where I and a few dozen tax defaulters had laboured so pointlessly when the river had been in flood.

I visited the site while the work was in progress. The river was a mere trickle by that time and the area round it had been transformed from a lake into a buzzing community of old army huts, clanking machines, native beer shops and loose women. It had the flavour of those western railway towns that spring up overnight and disappear when the work is done.

My suggestions for a training centre in Hoima were well received by the Mukama and the Native Government. What they particularly liked was the idea of a hostel under their control with accommodation for about forty people and meeting rooms which could be used for training courses and for native government functions of all kinds. Those who were on duty, such as chiefs, would be accommodated free, those who merely wanted to use it as a motel would pay a small amount for their food and accommodation. Indeed, they wondered how they had ever managed without it and no sooner had it been built than plans were drawn up to expand its facilities. It came to be known as Hoima Hoteli and it turned out that most other Districts in Uganda had something similar.

One other thing came out of the polio epidemic that killed Martin and Frisby. Frisby's place was taken by Inspector Ian Donald and almost immediately he and I became good friends as did our wives and even our two small sons. Donald had common sense, energy and good humour and in no time he had earned the respect of all. He was also an outdoorsman and owned a shotgun. I showed him all the good places to go for guinea fowl and frankolin.

21

Football Match

Martin Mukidi was an official of the Bunyoro Native Government who included 'Sports' in his portfolio of duties, which brought us together fairly regularly. His English was excellent and when he came into my office Stephen didn't bother to accompany him.

'Sir,' he said with a worried look, 'Mr Amory has put the goalkeeper in prison.'

'In prison,' I repeated, 'what on earth for?'

'Theft. Six months. He's the only good goalkeeper we have. With the match coming up . . .'

Yes, I knew all about the match against Acholi to be played on Saturday afternoon, only two days away. The Acholi were hunters and athletes of the first order and theirs was one of the best teams in Uganda. The two of us walked down the hall to Mr Amory's office.

'I can't believe he's a good goalkeeper,' Amory said. 'He stole so much from Hassanali's shop that he had to steal a wheelbarrow from the township store to carry it away. Then he sang lewd songs and woke up the bazaar. And you're telling me that such a badly organized thief is a first-rate goalkeeper?'

'The best we have,' Martin said. 'Without him we're lost.'

'Well, strange as it may seem,' Amory mused, 'a magistrate can put a goalkeeper in prison but he can't order him out until the sentence expires. Only the Commissioner of Prisons in Kampala or the High Court can do that. Your best chance is to send a telegram to the Commissioner asking for a three-hour release on compassionate grounds.' He turned to me. 'Walter, prepare a telegram for my signature.'

Back we went to my office and I began to write, 'Commissioner of Prisons, Kampala. Most urgent. Approval for three-hours' leave requested for prisoner number 429827 . . . What's his name?'

'Coming-going,' replied Martin.

'Coming-going, what sort of a name is that?'

'Well,' said Martin, 'he used to work in the township labour force and when he did something stupid the District Commissioner said to Hassan: "This man doesn't know if he's coming or going." After that Hassan called him Coming-going and now everyone does.'

With a name like Coming-going the Commissioner of Prisons wasn't likely to be sympathetic. Some aged and humourless turnkey with a bit of gold on his hat would put Coming-going in the same category as Jack the Ripper. Bad luck, I thought, now I shall have to make a really convincing case. I picked up my pen again.

'Saturday nineteenth urgent compassionate grounds stop. Both District Commissioner and committing magistrate recommend approval equally stop.'

Of course they approve equally, I said to myself. Amory was both.

'During period of his deincarceration' (I liked that word, it made it sound more important than it was) 'he will be subject to close and continuous surveillance.' Well, the spectators watch the goalkeeper pretty closely, don't they?

'And restricted to a small and well defined area' – the goal.

Amory signed it without reading it, thank God, and an office messenger took it to the post office. Martin Mukidi seemed a lot happier.

Soccer, or European football, was the predominant game in Uganda at that time, its advantage being that it could be played with little fuss and relatively little equipment. Every *saza* had a football pitch as did most of the larger schools, all that was needed being a level patch of ground suitably marked, goal posts and a ball. The goalposts were made of green wood cut from the forest and often the uprights, having been stuck a foot or two in the ground, would take root and sprout leaves.

The Africans would always play in their bare feet which were much harder than our feet although slippery on a wet field. Being accustomed to carrying loads on their heads they took very naturally to heading the ball and seemed more adept at this aspect of the game than non-African players. To say that the game was popular in Uganda is an understatement, and many of the players were good by almost any standards.

I have always thought of soccer as a participating sport, not a spectator sport, and in this respect I think it falls behind North American football which is the best spectator sport in the world. The American variety is a war-game, highly organized, harder to follow and characterized by a blend of subtlety and violence. I maintain that you can never really understand a game that you have not played yourself and I still have difficulty, after twenty years, with some of its peculiarities. However, I am a convert to North American football, America's favourite game, and I much prefer watching it to watching soccer. The American game has something in common with the Roman arena and indeed the players wear helmets and other armour. The fact that there is a small army of officials on the field speaks for itself. The point is that the violence takes place on the field and not in the stands as it so often does with soccer.

Hoima's football ground was located conveniently between the District Commissioner's office, the police station and the Bunyoro Native Council buildings. There were no stands and spectators simply crowded round the field as best they could. Many took up their positions on the roofs of buses. That morning Hassan had told some men to mark the lines with whitewash, fit nets to the goals and tidy up generally.

The Acholi team arrived by bus and were met by Martin Mukidi. They were taller than our men with darker skin and very consistent features. Also consistent were their names which all sounded practically the same; Okot, Odong, Olam, Odweng . . . Amory looked them over and asked if arrangements had been made to give them lunch. I told him that Martin had it in hand.

'Good,' he said. 'I hope he gives them a very big lunch and all the beer they can drink. And if it doesn't quite agree with them . . .' he trailed off.

The Commissioner of Prisons had proved himself reasonable, even statesmanlike by approving Coming-going's temporary release. Coming-going, wearing distinctively coloured shorts and shirt, was accompanied on the field by a prison warden. An elderly chief whom

I knew remarked that it was clever of Mr Amory to have put Coming-going in prison. 'This way,' he said, 'he will get good football practice in the prison yard with the other inmates. Besides, he will receive nourishing food, better than he is used to, and will not be drinking beer all the time. And of course the warden will make sure he arrives in time for the game.'

I was a bit shocked and sprang to Amory's defence.

'He was put in prison for theft, not football practice. Mr Amory had no idea he was the goalkeeper. Besides, he's had two previous convictions for the same type of offence.'

The chief gave me a knowing look and turned to other subjects.

'Football is all right for young men nowadays but in my youth we used to steal women and cattle from the Acholi. Times have changed,' he sighed, 'and not always for the better.'

I had not previously thought of prison as a place to keep wayward goalkeepers but I knew that the prison diet was excellent by the standards of the District as a whole and the prison was often referred to as Kingi Georgi's Hoteli. It was said that the Banyoro felt only slight shame at being put inside and little sense of punishment or even inconvenience. Before my arrival in the district Amory had a case that told the whole story. A working party of ten prisoners had gone out to repair a road accompanied by an armed warden. Hearing sounds of drumming and music from a nearby house the warden propped his firearm against a tree to remind his charges of his continuing authority and went to join the party. He drank a lot of banana beer and became drunk so the prisoners sat down in the shade to decide what they should do. Sweet reason prevailed. They arrested the warden, took his rifle and keys and escorted him back to the prison where they locked him and themselves up for the night.

'I asked the High Court to reduce their sentences,' Amory concluded, 'which wasn't very logical since they all seemed happy where they were. They told me that the warden was a disgrace to the prison and they were determined to preserve its good name.'

A week or two earlier I myself had received a letter of application from someone in the District for the job of prison warden. It read: 'You should make me a prison warden quickly because I know the work having been a prisoner for the past year.'

At five o'clock the Mukama arrived in his official car with his personal flag flying. An impromptu band struck up the Banyoro national anthem. He went on the field to shake hands with both teams accompanied by the Swatter of Flies and the Handkerchief and then took his place next to Amory on the sideline.

The first five minutes were disastrous for Bunyoro with Acholi scoring two unanswered goals. Our players always seemed to be in the wrong place or moving the wrong way or just not fully alert, but they settled down and gradually began to improve while Acholi, feeling confident, slacked off and allowed us to get an easy goal just before half-time.

When the whistle blew for the second half the Acholi came out fighting and Coming-going made some brilliant saves. At times the Acholi were crowded round his net shooting from every angle but somehow he saved them. The prison warden behind the net was becoming frantic, waving his red fez in the air and shouting advice. Suddenly the Banyoro forwards broke away, took the ball the length of the field and scored again and when Erik blew the final whistle the score was still two goals each. We all thought that we were lucky to have held them to a tie and that Coming-going had saved the day. In truth the Acholi were a better team.

The players were cheered off the field and gathered round the Mukama and Amory. A whispered word and Stephen was at the Mukama's side, also a serious-looking Acholi who had accompanied the visiting team. The Mukama spoke a few words and Stephen translated into English and the Acholi into his own language, a throaty but musical sound, a little like the plucking of violin strings.

It has never ceased to amaze me how bad North Americans are at making brief impromptu speeches and how good Africans are, at least in their own language. The Mukama spoke easily and without faltering. He thanked the Acholi team for coming and praised them for their performance. 'You are not strangers here,' he said. 'Some of the police who are posted to this District . . .' Amory shot him a nervous glance because the man whom Mulisi Alideki had killed had been an Acholi but the Mukama caught the glance and avoided adding 'game guards.' He also had pleasant words for his own team and the referee, and ended by asking Hassanali to provide each team with a crate of *ekide* at his expense. *Ekide* is the Luganda word for a bell but everyone knew that it meant beer because it was brewed at Port Bell, near Kampala and carried the logo of a bell on the label. Port Bell was named after Sir Hesketh Bell, an early governor.

A crate of Bell beer in those days contained twenty-five large bottles which I always recall as being heavy to carry and difficult to get in and out of the trunk of a car. The crates were made of muvule wood and were not light even when they were empty. Anyway, a crate of twenty-five for each team was generous.

The Mukama drove away and Amory and I turned to go.

'Isn't it bloody wonderful,' Amory said. 'Fifty years ago they'd have been cutting Acholi throats and stealing their cattle.'

'And women,' I prompted.

'And now they're playing football and drinking beer together,' he went on. 'You've got to admit that things have changed for the better.'

'Except when something goes badly wrong and one of them has a gun in his hand.'

'Yes,' Amory spoke slowly, 'he let the side down, didn't he? By the way, Walter, will you see that Coming-going gets back to his proper accommodation after he's had his bottle of beer and tomorrow I want you to write another of your telegrams, you do it rather well. This time it'll be the High Court to ask them to knock three months off his sentence on the grounds of . . .' he hesitated.

'Conscientious attention to his duties in the most trying circumstances,' I suggested.

'Yes, something like that.'

22

Buruli *Saza*

It was time for a full-scale tour of Buruli *saza* in the north-east of the District and Amory told me to concentrate my efforts on the improvement of agricultural production. Specifically he wanted to see a doubling of the acreage of land under cotton and the renewal of all village famine reserves. Until that time the cassava plant had served as the main famine reserve, a food so lacking in nutrition and flavour that when I told Kazimir I would like to try some he made excuses, one of them being that it was bound to make me sick. In the western world cassava is used in the production of starch, Robin Starch, for instance, and may also find its way in small amounts into certain foods. The Belgians in the Congo called it manioc which is close to its generic name, *manihot*, by which it is known in South America where it came from originally.

In Kazimir's words even the wild pigs wouldn't eat cassava so I didn't feel badly about trying to persuade the people of Buruli to plant sorghum instead. Sorghum is a magnificent, grain-bearing grass which is highly nutritious. Its seed was often purple in colour, clustered at the head of the plant. When the grain was harvested the leaves were fed to the sheep and goats and the bare stems thrown on the ground as a mulch. The grain was cooked and eaten rather in the manner of couscous, although it possessed a more distinctive flavour. In recent years the health experts have taken it up with enthusiasm.

Anyway, the people of Buruli seemed to respond to the idea of sorghum as a famine reserve but an increase in cotton acreage met with more resistance. Buruli was flat and featureless and cotton grew as well there as anywhere in the District but there was only muted response to my pleading for increased land under cultivation.

Until that time a fact of every administrative safari had been the tax exemption parade. In each *gombolola* those who claimed to be too old or too sick to pay taxes were interviewed by the touring officer. Some would receive permanent exemption on grounds of age and inability to work, others were exempted for one year only, usually because of sickness. It was a dismal spectacle when forty or fifty men in each *gombolola* came forward to plead their cases. The *muruka* chiefs would be in attendance and their advice was invaluable. Sometimes they would simply shake their heads and say: 'He does no work, is very poor and is content to die.' At other times they would say: 'He has a big garden, three wives, two of them pregnant, many sheep and goats and a marriageable daughter for whom he will get a bride-price. He can pay taxes for another ten years.'

The Banyoro's predilection for putting on a good act was nowhere more evident than at these parades. The suppliants would have dressed for the part in the filthiest clothes or animal skins, they leaned on sticks or crutches, walked painfully and groaned at every step. Only the chiefs knew whether or not it was genuine and whether it was any real hardship to pay the thirty shillings (seven dollars or thereabouts) which was the same for all. What made it so difficult was that permanent tax exemption was taken to be a certificate of retirement from all employment and once a man had it in his hand he would go home and do nothing for the remainder of his life. When the war ended some District Commissioners awarded permanent exemption to returned soldiers even though they were sound in body and mind. Many of these men retired from work and from life also and sat around doing nothing. It was a fatal gift.

Only men paid taxes, never women. One person presented himself or herself at my table claiming that he or she had been judged to be a man by the *muruka* chief and his or her tax demanded, but he or she announced that in fact she was a woman. On the basis of his or her facial appearance and voice I would have been inclined to agree with the *muruka* chief. I noticed that Stephen was in difficulties because the Lunyoro language does not distinguish between he and she; 'he went' and 'she went' would be exactly the same, but he sorted it out and discovered that the person wanted me to examine the primary evidence for myself. I declined on the grounds that I was not medically trained and that if she was indeed a woman it was inappropriate that I should make such an examination. Instead I sent him or her to Masindi Hospital with a note addressed to the doctor. It was the only case of its kind I ever encountered and when I told Amory he said that if he had been present his curiosity would have got the better of him.

During my Buruli safari the whole business of tax exemption was being delegated to the Native Government. The *gombolola* chief and his council were to conduct the interviews and reach a decision, after which a right of appeal lay to the *saza* chief from anyone who felt aggrieved at having been refused. In some *gombololas* there was an immediate and clearly unjustified increase in the numbers awarded and we came across one instance where the owner of a new motor bicycle had been exempted. It did not seem reasonable that if he could afford a luxury costing him ten thousand shillings he could not also pay thirty shillings tax.

My notebook for this safari contained the usual range of observations and comments. A new road was needed in one place, a cotton store somewhere else, repairs to a culvert, and so on. Late one evening I was returning to the *gombolola* rest house when a full-grown leopard sprang from the bush at the roadside, stared at me for a few seconds, his eyes shining in the headlights, then disappeared in the blackness of the tall grass. Also on that safari a tragedy occurred when a Peugeot car driven by an Indian struck a buffalo. Both occupants of the car were killed and the vehicle was a total wreck. I would not have believed that collision with a buffalo, even at high speed, could have done so much damage. The day following I went with a game guard to find the buffalo and put it out of its misery if it were not already dead. We located tracks on the roadway and the place of impact was obvious from the shattered glass but the buffalo had entered a swamp and we never found it.

The town of Masindi had fallen on hard times by the early 1950s. As an economy measure during the war the Western and Northern Provinces of Uganda had been combined into a single administrative unit with headquarters at Masindi. With the post-war return to normality, however, Fort Portal in Toro District became headquarters of the Western Province and Gulu in Acholi the headquarters for the North. Our Provincial Commissioner had already moved to Fort Portal together with his staff: agriculture, veterinary, medical and others, leaving many empty houses. To make Masindi even more of a ghost town the East African Railways and Harbours had also closed its operations there because Masindi had been the jumping-off place for the 'Nile Route' northwards to Egypt. With the arrival of the Sunderland flying boats few were inclined to take the time or trouble to go by paddle steamer.

One of our friends had done so before the war and told us that Uganda to Cairo was twenty-two days travelling by train, road, steamer and, for a short distance, on foot. He said that it was a memorable experience but one that he would not wish to repeat. Some officers travelled the Nile Route on their way to Uganda from Europe with their newly married wives, reasoning that if the marriage could survive such a trip it could survive anything. Masindi had been an overnight stop on this route and consequently had quite a good hotel. Passengers from down-country would disembark from the steamer at Masindi port on the Nile, drive the thirty miles to Masindi town, spend the night and then go on in the morning to Butiaba where they would catch another steamer for the long run down to the cataracts. The purpose of the Masindi detour was merely to circumvent the Murchison Falls.

The Nile route to Egypt was a reminder that Africa was the last continent to be opened to western man because it is essentially a tableland. The rivers like the Nile, the Zambesi and the Orinoco would have been an admirable means for explorers to reach the interior had it not been for the falls where these rivers plunge off the tableland. There was always talk of the Romans or Phoenicians having ventured as far as Uganda although the evidence was non-existent, but if the Nile had been navigable for its full length the story would have been different.

To one of our friends, the game warden of the Northern Province, the paddle steamer represented a vision of unattainable luxury and abundance. He had been on a long and exhausting safari in Acholi and was camped at Wadelai where the Nile narrows to about a hundred yards. In the old days this had been one of the few places where travellers could be ferried across the Nile because there were no papyrus swamps and in consequence Wadelai is marked on all the old maps although in fact there is nothing there. His supplies of food were exhausted, even tea and coffee, because he had run into some stranded tourists and had given them all his food. As he looked across the river and contemplated two biscuits and a chunk of smelly game meat, the paddle steamer, a blaze of light, came round a corner of the river. As it drew close he could hear laughter on the upper deck, see the steward serving cold drinks and smell the food cooking. It was all so damnably unjust, he said, and he even prayed for it to run aground, but the water was obviously a quarter of a mile deep and he was left in misery.

The brewing of banana beer was carried on in Buruli as elsewhere in the District. A cultivator would collect up to a dozen full bunches of the special beer bananas, called *mbidde*, and allow them to rot on the ground. This represents something like a thousand pounds of fruit and the smell was overwhelming but not unpleasant. The next move was to obtain a two-shilling beer-brewing permit from the *gombolola* chief's office after which he would return home and make his preparations for the big event. Some cultivators possessed a beer 'canoe' which was a hollowed-out tree trunk, others merely dug a hole in the ground and lined it with layers of banana leaves so that it would retain the liquid. The bananas were then cut from the stems, thrown in the trench with water and clean grass and trodden out by foot. It was a slippery job and the joke one commonly heard was about someone falling headlong in his own beer. The better organized brewers had a pole stretched across the trench at shoulder height so that the person (or two people) had something to hold while they worked. At this point the women usually came on the scene, their job being to scoop the beer out of the trench and into large gourds which might hold two or three gallons each, sometimes ten or twenty of them from a single brew.

The reasoning behind the brewing of so much beer at one time was that a two-shilling permit had to be obtained whatever the quantity.

After a few days of maturing the beer was ready to be drunk and the cultivator would recoup his expenses by charging his guests for what they consumed. The drinking vessel was a gourd which would hold a little more than a pint and cost ten cents. Most people liked to drink it through a straw. According to Stephen, one could drink at least a gallon of beer for a shilling.

Having watched beer being trodden out by unwashed feet I never felt much inclined to sample it. The doctor in Masindi, however, who had been in the country for many years, said that it could be purified and made palatable for Europeans. When he had first come to the country banana beer was about the only drink he could afford and he acquired a taste for it. He described it as slightly sweet, banana-flavoured and with an alcohol content of about three per cent. He also thought it had some nutritive value and acted as an aid to the digestion. The Protestant missionaries had condemned it as the work of the devil but the good doctor said that if that were the case he sided with the devil and thought it did more good than harm.

From the administrator's point of view banana beer generally caused only mild drunkenness and was not a social problem of any consequence. It was not unlike the 'wine coolers' or light beers which are sold in North America at the present time and the revenue gained from the sale of two-shilling brewing permits augmented the finances of the Native Government.

Where banana beer had been brewed the sweet smell lingered for days afterwards, clinging to the leaves that had been used and attracting clouds of butterflies. A thousand or more might congregate, presumably mistaking the smell for some sort of flower and they would slowly flap their wings as though in time to music.

I always noted down the stories that local people told about the wildlife and in Buruli I came across one that was very perplexing. They said that there was an animal in the bush about the size of a hyena that would steal chickens during the day by a most unusual method. It lay on its back near the place where chickens were scratching and covered itself with leaves or grass leaving only the anus exposed. The anus opened wide and contained some internal component which resembled a worm or edible grub. The chicken would peck at it and the anus clamp shut over the chicken's head. The animal would then run off with the chicken flapping hysterically. The telling of it always provoked mirth. Many Africans claimed to have seen it happen and some of them, *muruka* chiefs, game guards and schoolmasters, could have been mistaken in some way but I would not have accused them of being deliberately untruthful.

The thing that surprised me was to hear the same story years later in Madi in the far north of Uganda. Not only are the Madi a long distance from the Banyoro but they speak a totally different language and it seems remarkable that the same error of perception, if that is what it was, could have occurred. I was left not knowing what animal they were referring to, although it could have been a large mongoose, but no one had a name for it and there seemed to be no confirmation from any authoritative source. Amory had never heard of it and thought it was some sort of joke. The only thing I was sure about was that they had seen something, were trying to tell the truth but may not have observed it accurately.

There are, of course, strange creatures in Uganda and one that we saw and heard frequently was the nightjar. These birds used to rest on the warm dusty roads at night and rise at the approach of a car, their eyes luminescent in the headlights. Their peculiarity lay in the elongation of some primary wing quills which gave the bird the appearance of towing a feather attached to a length of string behind each wing. The bird was much hampered in its flight by these appendages and we were left wondering what function they could possibly serve. Our old Lydekker reference book described them as pennant-winged nightjars (*Macrodipteryx vexillarius*) 'distinguished by the great length of the seventh, eighth and especially the ninth primary quills of the wing which are white and appear to attain their extreme development only from October to January, and then solely in the males.' Their call was distinctive and rather mournful.

The nightjars preyed on a species of moth which protected themselves in a unique manner. When the nightjar threatened, a group of moths would assemble on a leaf in a circle with their heads inwards and the wings round the circumference like the petals of a flower. The naturalists said that they were, in fact, mimicking a flower and that the nightjars were taken in by the deception and flew past. What the naturalists could not explain was how the moths came to mimic a flower that did not exist in nature. How could they mimic something they had never seen?

A unit of the Tsetse Control Department was operating in Buruli at that time and I visited their camp and spoke to the man in charge. The function of the Department was to eliminate all the game animals from a specific area so that the tsetse fly, which fed on the blood of game animals, would also be eliminated and cattle reintroduced. A team of hunters marched through the bush and systematically killed every living creature. The meat and skins were sold down-country to pay for their operations.

The Tsetse Control Department was altogether separate from the Game Department and the spectacle that presented itself was of one department of government attempting to preserve the game while another was busy destroying it. The Game Department was, of course, outraged by the slaughter and was supported by just about every naturalist and nature lover in the world. They pointed out with justification that game clearance had never been proved effective and was scientifically unsound because the tsetse flies could also subsist on small rodents, lizards and birds. The decision to undertake game clearance had been reached too rapidly and without sufficient discussion. Alternative methods of tsetse control such as discriminative bush clearance (chopping down and burning those types of bush to which the flies were attracted) and spraying, particularly along watercourses, had not been given a fair trial.

The Tsetse Control Department claimed that game clearance operations had met with some success in other parts of Africa. They pointed to the fact that tsetse flies tended to occur in 'belts', which were quite narrow and well defined so that one can pass suddenly from an area thick with flies to one where they are absent. Their game clearance operations were localized and confined as far as possible to these belts so that the damage they were doing to the game was limited and specific. The Game Department's reply was that a belt could be cleared and within days or weeks game would re-enter from surrounding areas. In fact the Tsetse Control Department shot out vast areas of country with questionable results as far as the elimination of tsetse fly was concerned.

Tsetse flies themselves are about the size of ordinary house flies but brown in colour and when at rest the wings fold across each other. Their bite stings like a pin-prick which hurts more than that of a mosquito but less than a horse fly. To prevent motor vehicles from carrying flies from infested to non-infested areas one would quite often be confronted by 'fly posts' on the roads manned by one or two of the Department's staff. They asked drivers and passengers to get out of their cars which they searched with small butterfly nets and also sprayed underneath the vehicle, particularly inside the mud-guards. Any flies they caught in their nets were consigned to glass jars so that they could be examined later by the experts or just left to prove to other travellers that the danger of carrying flies was not hypothetical. A single tsetse fly carried in one's car or even in one's clothes might bite the family dog when you reached home and one bite would kill. The trypanosome carried by the fly is harmless to the game animals and doesn't seem to affect humans, at least I never felt any ill-effects from tsetse bites. Domestic animals, however, particularly cattle and dogs, are very vulnerable. Sheep and goats seem to have an easier time of it although they are by no means immune.

Back in Hoima a few days later Jean and I prepared to move into the Wyndhams' house. Roy was due for home leave and the Chief Game Warden had told him that on his return to Uganda he would be posted to Ankole District. We looked round his house which was a big improvement over our old one, larger, airy and with a bigger garden. If Jean looked forward to moving into the house I was thrilled at the prospect of performing some of the game warden's duties. It meant, for instance, that I could get out into the bush with Kiiza or other Game Department staff and feel that not only was I having an interesting time but doing something useful into the bargain.

I am not sure how the idea originated but at this point I decided to make the Tonya-Kaiso flatland on the shores of Lake Albert into a 'hobby area' and visit as often as possible. It had all the requirements for making it interesting and challenging: two fishing villages which could only be approached on foot from Biseruka and were much in need of improvements; a plain teeming with game animals; a thriving fishing industry. The best way to reach it was by leaving the

Landrover at Biseruka and walking down the escarpment with as little equipment and as few people as possible. Taking the government launch from Butiaba was not a good idea because the expense could not be justified on a monthly basis and the walk down the escarpment and across the plain was part of the challenge.

Jean pointed out that this would in fact be my third work-related hobby. My first had been Hoima itself. I frequently toured the station with Hassan, planted three hundred muvule trees which we obtained from the forestry research establishment, and attempted with trees and flowers to make Hoima the most beautiful up-country station in Uganda. During the war I had seen some of the great beauty spots of the east, Kuala Lumpur in Malaya, Nuwara Eliya and Kandy in Sri Lanka and Ootacamund in the Nilgiri hills of Southern India so I had a picture in my mind of what I was trying to accomplish.

My second 'hobby' had been the training of *muruka* chiefs which had become something of a passion in my life. It made no sense that these junior chiefs, who were individually responsible for anywhere between two hundred and six hundred families, should have no indoctrination into their work and no formal training. Uppermost in my mind was the thought that they could do so much good if they were well trained, so much damage if they were not. In addition, the course would spot the really talented performers at an early stage while the unsatisfactory ones would drop out of the system. I wanted to organize two-week courses of instruction in Hoima for twenty trainees to be practical, interesting and demanding. A course in which the students merely get lectured at by so-called experts was less appealing than a see-and-do curriculum where they would be confronted by real life conflicts and expected to solve real problems. I was so anxious to get something started and so full of ideas that I was probably a nuisance to both Amory and the Native Government.

Tonya and Kaiso was my third hobby. I could take a game guard or game scout and set out in the Landrover when the office closed at midday on Saturday and be at Biseruka in less than an hour. There was no difficulty finding half a dozen young men to act as porters, even at short notice, because to them it was a brief overnight adventure and a chance at some meat. We would go down the escarpment and walk across the flats to either Tonya or Kaiso and camp for the night. Georgi would then cook supper for the whole party, a meal that one would not expect to find described in a French cookbook and which is still known in the family as 'safari stew'. He followed the biblical injunction of not letting the left hand know what the right hand was doing.

There was no *muruka* chief at Tonya or Kaiso since the numbers of people did not justify it but the *gombolola* chief at Biseruka was persuaded to appoint an unpaid headman for each village whose sole perquisite was a free supper whenever I was there. He would call a meeting of the villagers in the morning and for an hour we would sit under a tree and discuss the problems they faced and the improvements which might be made.

It was typical of the Banyoro that decisions did not get made by individuals but by the group as a whole. One Saturday evening I reached Tonya to find the entire village working on improvements to their houses and was told that Kaiso was doing the same. I had urged this many times and now the wheels were in motion and all was bustle and activity. The Banyoro were capable of rousing themselves in this manner but only after much discussion and the final decision had to be unanimous.

Georgi would meanwhile pack the safari and dole out any remaining food and by ten or eleven on Sunday morning we would start back toward the escarpment in a wide circle across the plain. Sometimes I would shoot a game animal, a warthog for example, because these rather prehistoric looking creatures were not limited on a resident's game licence. On one of my visits I shot a large male kongoni (*Alcelaphus cokei*) which had been caught round the neck by a wire snare and was pulling a two-hundred-pound log behind it. There was no possible chance that it could do other than die in agony. By the time we reached the escarpment and began to climb upwards towards Biseruka the half dozen porters were probably carrying loads of meat; Georgi and the game guard would have the camp equipment and some fresh fish while I had the rifles, ammunition pouches, water bottles, knives and, if we had found wire snares, I might have them as well. In other words we were well loaded and the sight of the Landrover parked under a tree was welcome when we reached the top.

During the time I was in Bunyoro game poaching was much reduced in the Tonya-Kaiso area and the two villages themselves made a number of improvements. I visited every five or six weeks on the average and learned from the experience. Much of our administration was extensive in the sense that we were dealing with thousands of people, as had been the case in Buruli county. Here was something different, an intensive effort focused on two villages containing fewer than a hundred people. The interesting thing was the amount of patience required, the fact that nothing was accepted without weeks of debate and that a majority vote was not enough to bring about a change; it was only when all the villagers were convinced that an idea would translate into action. This was all the more surprising because there were no old people at Tonya and Kaiso, no natural bastion of entrenched conservatism. The inhabitants were young men who had homes and families in the Biseruka area and regarded Tonya or Kaiso as a fishing camp, the fish being their cash crop. They came down the escarpment with their requirements for a week's stay, caught fish and smoked them, then went back up with a huge load. It was, therefore, a transient population, but not one that should have been difficult to convince. In fact it was a year before the standard of house-building had improved, the hygienic arrangements made better and before all were using mosquito nets at night. Such results were scarcely cost-effective but were worthwhile in human terms.

It was a subject of discussion in Uganda at that time as to whether wives ought to accompany their husbands on safari. There were a few instances of childless couples where the wife did so and while her husband carried out his duties she was with the *gombolola* chief's wife giving lessons in cooking or child care to the local women. Other wives painted in oils or studied the language, some visited local schools or medical dispensaries or simply tried to help the women in the villages. Their childless condition, however, was a disadvantage and few stuck it for any length of time. All their efforts were, of course, unpaid and many found the task physically and mentally exhausting.

For married women with children safari was rare and no one would have advised it except during the dry season and in areas that were known to be healthy. Even so, the amount of equipment needed, the move every two days and the dangers to small children made it difficult for the wife and at times thoroughly unpleasant. Only once did Jean try a full safari and two incidents which occurred stand out in my mind.

We had borrowed a large, old-fashioned government tent, the size of a garage, and it took our servants, the *gombolola askaris* and a few bystanders an hour or more to get it erected in those *gombololas* where there was no rest house. One morning very early it came on to rain so I put on my old navy oilskin and a pair of gym shoes and went round slacking off the ropes so that the pegs would not be pulled out of the ground by the contraction of ropes as they became wet. The rain increased, sheets of pink lightning rent the sky and the thunder sounded like the main armament of a battleship. The wind was obviously trying to blow the large, ungainly tent into the next county.

Armed with a huge mallet and a flashlight I laid about me like a madman driving the pegs deeper in the ground and replacing those that were torn out. I shouted to Jean to get the children in the car and at that moment a wild gust tore out all the pegs along one side and the tent flapped like the sail of a windjammer. The trouble was that the ground was so wet by this time that the pegs wouldn't hold but in half an hour I had a fresh lot hammered in and the wind began to slack off. I assumed that Jean had got the children organized and was applauding my efforts to keep the whole thing from blowing away. An hour later, as dawn came up, the wind died and the rain changed to drizzle. Things were finally under some sort of control although I was soaked to the skin, covered with mud and moderately exhausted. I threw down my mallet and stumbled back inside.

'Good heavens,' Jean said when she woke up, 'what on earth have you been doing?'

'Didn't you hear anything?'

'Hear what?'

We moved to another *gombolola* where there was a small rest house recently re-floored with the traditional mix of cow dung and anthill. Our family had by this time been blessed by the appearance of a daughter, Caroline, whose beauty was marred by only one defect, the absence of any hair on her head. It was a hot day and in all the confusion of unpacking Caroline crawled away and found a pile of cool, sweet-smelling cow dung and ant-hill which she piled on her head. I cannot guess what arcane motive had impelled her, or what primitive Aesculapian wisdom was hers, but the inescapable fact was that from that day forward her hair began to grow.

23

Mulisi's Capture

In June of 1952 a meeting took place in Amory's office between Amory himself, Inspector Donald, Roy Wyndham, who was almost ready to leave the District, and myself. Donald began by reporting that Mulisi Alideki was becoming increasingly bold and outspoken and that this could lead to his downfall. He was telling people that he had created the disease which killed Frisby and Martin and was about to inflict even worse punishment on the white community in Hoima; Donald and I were on his hit-list as prime targets although Amory for some reason would not be killed until later. His plan was to turn Bunyoro into a self-governing country with its own army of which he was to be the commander. The lost territories would be retaken by force of arms while money was to be printed in great quantity so that all would become rich. His two sons were to be made *saza* chiefs of the counties in Mubende District, Buyaga and Bugangaizi, after they had been wrested from the hated Baganda.

Donald said that he had inherited a group of informers from Frisby but having been in Bunyoro for only a month he didn't know who could be trusted. The chiefs at the *gombolola* and *muruka* levels were useless and he was building up a file itemizing their collaboration with Mulisi. One of them, a *gombolola* chief, had recently invited Mulisi into his house for a supper party. He also knew that Mulisi had ridden his bicycle through Hoima bazaar late one evening but had not been recognized. In Donald's words, one black face on a dark night looks much like another. His two sons, one of whom was very 'Muchwezi', that is to say fair-skinned, made no attempt to hide themselves and were seen openly in the area round Hoima. They could not be charged as accessories because Mulisi himself was still at large.

Mulisi was operating in five *gombololas* to the south and west of Hoima where buffalo and hippo were plentiful. He knew where the game was to be found and was shooting about three animals a week. He seemed to have no difficulty obtaining black market ammunition and Donald admitted that no progress had been made in cutting off his supplies. There was some indication that the *haragi* merchants, dealers in illegal liquor, were also in the ammunition trade but this was in the nature of speculation.

It was Roy Wyndham's turn to speak and he pointed out that the pockets of dense bush and elephant grass which existed in every *gombolola* gave Mulisi an instant refuge, just as the jungle was the refuge of game animals, bushbuck, pig and buffalo. He could be in someone's hut, eating, transacting business or just resting and the jungle was only a few steps distant where no one would follow him as long as he had a rifle in his hand. It was known that he kept on the move and that his two sons and one or two other young men were his scouts and lookouts.

Roy Wyndham wondered whether there was enough information to plot his movements on a map. Did he move clockwise or anti-clockwise or in a completely random manner? Were his movements governed by the seasons, the rain and the condition of the rivers? It had often been noted by game wardens that individual animals under pressure would turn the same way and were described as either right or left-handed, and he wondered whether similar characteristics might emerge by studying Mulisi's movements. Would some pattern appear, some idiosyncrasy that would predict his next move? We all thought that the idea had merit and Inspector Donald said he would follow it up.

Amory then came up with an idea of his own. This was to take the form of a propaganda operation designed to counteract the Mulisi legend and show him up for what he really was, a murderer, outlaw and disturber of the peace. There was an old regulation which empowered the District Commissioner to compel the attendance of all men of taxpaying age. So far as he knew it had not been used for many years but it was still on the books and he felt that this was the time to invoke it. My job would be to address the assembled taxpayers, show them that we were in earnest and tell them to mend their ways. Amory's task would be to convince the Mukama of the necessity of the move and handle the criticism that could be expected from the government down-country when it reached their ears, as it certainly would. He thought that the Banyoro taxpayers would get fed up if they were called to the *gombolola* headquarters on a weekly basis and required to listen to me ranting at them. The month of June, he pointed out, was fairly quiet. If they hadn't already done so the people were preparing their fields for planting cotton and everyone knew the seed would be distributed by the Department of Agriculture during the last week of June and the first week of July.

We discussed the plan for over an hour. It seemed better to be doing something than to be doing nothing, to be taking the initiative and not just waiting for Mulisi to make a mistake. When we broke up I called Stephen to my office and discussed it with him. Next, I made out a touring plan and prepared the letters to the five *gombolola* chiefs saying when I would be at each headquarters and requiring them, quoting the specific regulation, to have every taxpayer present. The *muruka* chiefs were to check all names against the tax registers. Stephen translated it into Lunyoro and Amory signed it after which the office messengers took the letters by motorcycle to the *gombololas* and obtained receipts for them. Copies went to the Mukama and his government, so that all would know what we were doing and where our priorities lay. In no time there were people in Amory's office whining and bitching but his patience was at an end and he dealt with them in short order.

The first meeting was held at Kabwoya in the south of the District where the main road crosses the Nkussi river on its way to Fort Portal. I cannot deny I was nervous and when I met the *gombolola* chief realized that he was also. He had arranged for two meetings, one in the morning and one in the afternoon, because his area was so large than he felt this was the only way to be sure that all attended.

I liked the *gombolola* chief of Kabwoya and had got on well with him on my previous visits. He was trying to co-operate although he didn't seem to be a strong or resourceful man. He needed encouragement more than anything and that is what I attempted to give him as we drove to Kyangwali at the western end of his territory. It was near there in 1864 that Samuel Baker had been the first white man to see Lake Albert, the place where he stood being marked by a mound of stones. The view from that spot is magnificent in clear weather with a wonderful panorama of lake and mountains.

We arrived to find several hundred men waiting in a school yard and the three of us, the *gombolola* chief, Stephen and I were relieved that there seemed to be little resentment. They had, after all, been called from their homes by the *muruka* chiefs who had gone round the villages in person. For many it was a long walk or bicycle ride along village paths and yet they seemed unconcerned by the inconvenience. The *gombolola* chief introduced me as I had requested him to do, with the simple statement: 'The Assistant District Commissioner has come from Hoima with a message. We will listen carefully to his words.'

'As your *gombolola* chief has said,' I began, 'it is my duty to pass you a message from the District Commissioner. He says that this ancient kingdom of Bunyoro has, during these past two years, neglected its proud heritage and its history that goes back so long that no man can remember all of it. People are now ignoring His Highness the Mukama and the wise rule of his chiefs and have become infatuated with a man who leads them in the wrong way. They even forget the symbols that mean so much to the Banyoro, the white beards of the Bachwezi, the sacred white elephant tusk and the Mukama's white herd of cattle, and they are misled by the promises of a man whose symbols are foreign to the history of this people: venereal disease and a gun.'

I waited for that one to sink in.

'Bunyoro is like a strong man bitten by a tsetse fly. The poison goes all through his body and he becomes so ill that the doctor in Hoima is afraid he will die. Why, asks the doctor, were you not more alert and did you not drive off the tsetse fly before it did its evil?

'I will tell you more. Mulisi Alideki is like a snake that lives in the roof of a house. The snake has already killed and eaten one of the children and now threatens the remainder. With its poisonous bite it terrorizes the owner of the house but the eldest son is planning to abandon his father and go to work for the snake, acting as its eyes and ears. The snake promises a life of violence and cruelty but the father advises against it and says that hard work in the fields is the honourable way to live, not by terrorizing and killing people.'

I went on in a way that I knew the Banyoro would understand, all of it having been discussed with Stephen to make sure he could translate it without losing the meaning. There was even some applause when I finished but more discernable was a murmur, a sort of sigh, though whether it was of approval or disapproval I wasn't sure. A man stood up.

'How shall we catch him when he uses witchcraft? He can disappear and fly to another place. He is a magician; even the police *askaris* know that to be true.'

'When his hands and feet are tied with rope,' I replied, 'and his gun is taken from him, his witchcraft isn't going to work any more. And when he is in a prison cell he is not going to fly anywhere.'

The meeting broke up after little more than an hour. I had asked the people to return to their homes and think carefully about what I had said. We drove back fifteen miles to Kabwoya and had lunch in the chief's house. He apologized for not having prepared food but I kept a few cans in the Landrover and we managed well enough. During lunch I gained the impression from him that the morning's talk had been effective and decided to make no changes in the format that afternoon. In fact the afternoon passed off much as the morning had done and I was able to report to Amory that the people had listened attentively and seemed to have taken it in.

Next day the mood changed. We were at Kiziranfumbi, a mere twelve miles from Hoima, and when I arrived with Stephen we found the *gombolola* chief haranging a huge crowd. I parked the Landrover and walked across the grass toward him. Stephen whispered: 'He is saying very bad things.'

For a few minutes we stood at the edge of the crowd and watched. All except the *gombolola* chief were seated on chairs or on the grass so we could be seen by everyone present. The chief's voice was high-pitched and emotional, almost effeminate. I didn't understand all that he said but the few words I caught gave me an idea of the direction of his remarks. My eye travelled over those hundreds of men seated on the grass and I wondered what they really thought. Could all those people be afraid of Mulisi because if so they could be afraid of me. Suddenly the chief ended with the words: 'The Assistant District Commissioner has arrived.'

It was my turn to put on a performance. I didn't approach the chief or greet him but simply moved forward into the crowd.

'*Gombolola* chief,' I said, 'report to me whether or not your tax-payers are all present.'

He got to his feet again. 'The *muruka* chief says that only the sick and a few others whose business requires . . .'

'Very well,' I broke in, 'then listen to what I have to say.'

As I spoke I was acutely aware of two things. First that this was a hostile audience and that it was up to me to put on the performance of a lifetime. I was not afraid of these people, with luck and a good speech some of them might even be won over, but I had to act the part and speak well. Secondly, I had somehow to consider Stephen's position. He owed his allegiance to the District Commissioner and ultimately the Governor of Uganda but these were his people, his friends and relatives. I would one day leave the District and be sent elsewhere but he would live here for the remainder of his life. My language and thinking and everything about me was different from theirs, his the same. It was easy for me to tell them to be more courageous, to accuse them of disloyalty to their Mukama and of aiding and concealing a common murderer but it must have been desperately hard for him.

I said the same things I had said in Kabwoya but I spoke slowly and deliberately and spun it out for half an hour. My words were received in silence but it was a threatening silence, not a respectful one. If nothing else they realized that they were witnessing high drama. A young man from another country had the effrontery to stand there and challenge them, to walk amongst them and use biting sarcasm and outrageous insult against their popular hero. It must have seemed unreal, almost beyond comprehension. They looked back to their *gombolola* chief who was on his feet again. He said that his people did not want to capture Mulisi; it was a matter for the Acholi, meaning the police. No one in his *gombolola* was tempted to betray him in order to gain the reward the government offered. He turned to me and said that I was acting foolishly and should remember the fate of the game guard who attempted to arrest Mulisi.

With deliberate slowness I took my notebook from my pocket and pretended to be writing, then closed it and put it back. Amory had said that this had an unsettling effect on people.

'Are there any questions?' I asked.

No one spoke or moved so Stephen and I picked our way out through the seated figures. We stood and chatted for a minute before climbing into the Landrover, but it was gamesmanship designed to show them that I would take my time. I looked at my watch, laughed and got in the car.

I had no meeting planned for the following day and went to the office as usual. The place was buzzing and I soon discovered the reason. Mulisi Alideki had been at the meeting at Kiziranfumbi the day before and had heard every word that had been said. He had been sitting on the grass jammed in among hundreds of others and while no one was sure how many people recognized him or knew he was there it seemed almost certain that the *gombolola* chief knew. Roy Wyndham, the soldier, saw the point immediately and announced that it had been a victory for our side. Mulisi had hidden himself, cowered on the grass and had taken refuge in anonymity. 'What army commander does that?' Roy asked.

The three remaining meetings were held on three consecutive days and went off reasonably well. When they were finished the mood in Hoima was one of optimism. Inspector Donald thought he was getting closer and that it was only a matter of time before someone would come in with specific information about Mulisi's whereabouts.

At this point the unexpected happened. The District's allocation of cotton seed had not reached the Agricultural Department for distribution to cultivators and the rumour was spreading that this was the government's retaliation. According to Henry Berunga the cotton seed was a week or two late but he had been promised a full allocation and expected it any day. As usual it would be delivered to the two ginneries, one in Hoima and one in Masindi, and then distributed to the *gombololas*. It would have been unthinkable for the government to deprive the people of their annual income from cotton by refusing to release the seed, but word was flying around that until Mulisi was captured no seed would be allowed to enter the District.

Amory heard about it from the new Co-operative Officer who had replaced Warren Thorpe. He accused Amory of withholding cotton seed deliberately from the co-operative societies and when Amory denied doing any such thing he took the matter to his superiors in the co-operative movement. He was not the kind of person who would discuss it in a reasonable manner, nor would he listen to Henry Berunga's version of events. We heard later that the matter had reached the Governor and all sorts of high-priced people were drawn in: the Director of Agriculture, the manager of the research establishment which produced the seed cotton and the Director of Co-operative Societies.

Amory immediately realized that the cottonseed rumour, however wrong it may have been, was a godsend. Information about Mulisi began to pour into the police station and then, late one evening, one of his 'scouts' walked in and asked for Inspector Donald. Mulisi was near Kabwoya *gombolola* headquarters and had wanted a bottle of liquor which Donald proceeded to supply from the 'exhibits' room. The doctor added a sleeping potion to it and the man took it back to Mulisi while Donald mustered his team: himself, Amory, Roy Wyndham and the African sub-inspector. Unluckily for me I was in the north of the District that night on some other duty.

The rest was predictable. The informer led Donald and his team to where Mulisi was sleeping under a mosquito net in the bush, his loaded rifle beside him. They pounced on him, tied his hands and he was led to a waiting police vehicle. Mulisi's first comprehensible words were, 'I'm glad it's over.' The date was 4th July 1952, and a continent away in the United States people were celebrating Independence Day. For Mulisi Alideki it was quite the reverse of independence.

The best account of the incident came from Roy Wyndham. He said it was so dark he could see nothing until he caught sight of the mosquito net and made a dive at it with Amory, a very big man, on top of him. A black foot kicked him in the face so he got hold of the foot and twisted it, thinking it to be Mulisi's. A voice came from the pile of struggling humanity: 'Sir, would you have the kindness to release my foot.' It was the African sub-inspector who had taken his boots off so as to make less noise.

The day after his capture a very bedraggled Mulisi Alideki, one time game guard, was brought into court between two Acholi policemen and charged with the murder of Erinayo Muno. Stephen translated the charge and asked him if he understood it. He nodded. Amory thought at first that he might plead guilty but with a shrug he said: 'Aaaah' – no, not guilty. He was ordered to be kept in confinement until the day of his trial.

Meanwhile Inspector Donald was busy with his *askaris*. Mulisi's two sons were arrested plus a long list of others furnished by the informer. Some were already known to Donald as accomplices, others were new to him. A magistrate recently out from England was sent to Hoima to deal with the court work. One of those whom he sent to prison was the *gombolola* chief from Kiziranfumbi who had consorted with Mulisi on many occasions and, in the rather quaint wording of the criminal code, given him 'aid and comfort'.

Mulisi's lawyer was an African barrister from Kampala and Donald learned by way of beer-party gossip that he was planning a rather original defence. He was going to claim that Erinayo Muno came to his house drunk, challenged him and when he put up his hands Erinayo fired at him, the bullet striking him in the hand and taking off one of his fingers. It was a fact that Mulisi was missing an index finger. The story they would tell was that Mulisi, having just had his finger shot off, picked up his own rifle, which happened to be loaded, and killed Erinayo in self-defence.

In rebuttal, Donald not only had the two men who had been with Erinayo at the time and witnessed his murder but a small army of witnesses, Stephen being one of them, who had known Mulisi minus his finger many months before. In fact he had lost it when setting a trap for a leopard and the trap had sprung by accident. He had gone to the nearest medical dispensary to have the injury cleaned and bandaged and Donald had little difficulty getting the medical register which contained the details, including the date.

Anyway his case was heard by the High Court of Uganda sitting in Hoima. Mulisi was convicted of murder and sentenced to death. The governor-in-council did not exercise the royal prerogative of mercy and Mulisi was subsequently hanged.

When it was over Amory opened a session of the District Native Council. He wore his white uniform and entered the chamber with the Mukama. Inspector Donald commanded the guard which the Mukama and Amory inspected together. Amory's opening speech had a sting to it.

'We have lost two years of progress; thirty people are in prison for being accessories to a murder, many of them chiefs: we have made ourselves appear ridiculous in the eyes of other Districts.'

He glared at them over his paper.

'If you pass a resolution calling for any further steps toward self-government it may be difficult for me to recommend them to His Excellency the Governor. For two years, two full years, you have allowed a murderer to roam the District as though he were an honoured guest. You made him your hero, you believed what he told you and during that period the number of children in school declined. The amount of cotton sold remained the same but did not increase and there was a sharp rise in tax defaulters. It is now time to look to the future and repair the damage that has been done. Only hard work can accomplish this.'

Amory, I thought, had got it exactly right. Self-government, although we did not know it at the time, was only ten or a dozen years away. The Mulisi affair seemed to be a prediction of what self-government would be like. A man with a gun exploits fear and weakness and gains a foothold. The chiefs, native police and people as a whole are mesmerized and willing to give up everything for a bit of buffalo meat. Not even the ancient and respected kingship of the Mukama stood firm and it was not until Amory himself intervened that matters were set right.

A few years later another syphilitic murderer, Idi Amin, enslaved the country, but by that time there were no Amorys in Uganda.

Epilogue

The tragedy of that first year was, of course, the polio epidemic which claimed two young lives. I never discovered what my illness had been, whether polio, malaria or something different, but as the doctor said, during a polio epidemic your best guess is that you have polio. Nor of course could I know whether my absence at the Kafu bridge had saved my life by getting me out of Hoima or helped me to contract it by becoming exhausted. I can only ponder in sadness the fate of the two who died and wonder at my own recovery.

In the years that followed a referendum was held in the 'lost counties' of Buyaga and Bugangaizi which were then restored to the kingdom of Bunyoro. The Mukama, however, did not survive self-government and his ancient kingship was abolished.

Stephen, who had taught me so much, and whom I remember with such gratitude, retired from his position a year or two later. I had hoped that his knowledge and wisdom would be put to account in the office of *gombolola* or even *saza* chief, but unhappily he was bypassed.

Mr Amory was transferred to another District in Uganda's Eastern Province and subsequently retired to England.

My wife and I and our three young children continued serving in Uganda until independence in 1964.

* * * *

Since these words were written it has been decided in Uganda's highest councils that the ancient Mukamaship of Bunyoro is to be restored. Prince Soloman Iguru will be crowned as 27th Mukama of Bunyoro – Kitara.